SECOND COMING

Also by Sam Smith

The Jordan Rules

SECOND COMING

The Strange Odyssey of Michael Jordan— from Courtside to Home Plate and Back Again

Sam Smith

HarperCollins*Publishers*

For my best friends, Kathleen and Connor

Photographs follow page 138.

HarperCollins books may be purchased for educational, business, or sales promotional use. For information please write: Special Markets Department, HarperCollins Publishers, Inc., 10 East 53rd Street, New York, NY 10022.

FIRST EDITION

Designed by Nina Gaskin

Library of Congress Cataloging-in-Publication Data

Smith, Sam, 1948–
    Second coming : the strange odyssey of Michael Jordan—from courtside to home plate and back again / Sam Smith. — 1st ed.
        p.   cm.
    ISBN 0-06-017502-8
    1. Jordan, Michael, 1963–   . 2. Basketball players—United States—Biography.   3. National Basketball Association.   I. Title.
GV884.J67S54   1995
796.323'092—dc20
    [B]   95-37153

---

95 96 97 98 99 ❖/HC 10 9 8 7 6 5 4 3 2 1

ACKNOWLEDGMENTS

Did you ever notice that only nonfiction books feature acknowledgments? Ask Andy Rooney why . . . I don't know. Anyway, since I get to acknowledge both help and cooperation, here goes:

My thanks especially to the members of the Bulls organization and team. It's been a long, eventful, sometimes strange ride with them over the last decade. I wrote features about the team and covered games occasionally from 1984 through 1987, then in 1988 began traveling with the team extensively, covering virtually all the games through late 1991 and the release of *The Jordan Rules*.

I've been asked many times whether it was more than coincidence that, with the publication of that controversial book, I stepped aside as the team's regular beat reporter. Sounds like a good theory, but like many good theories, it collapses under the weight of the facts. With my son then two years old, I was pining to reduce my travel load. To an outsider, traveling with a pro basketball team, especially one led by Michael Jordan, appears glamorous. And it sure beats most, if not all, jobs. But flying out of Chicago's O'Hare Airport throughout the winter and being on the road three or four nights a week puts your life and family second and third. Covering a pro basketball team is not a healthy priority for a long period of time. And the growth of the NBA made it harder.

Plus, with astronomical salaries, the players have grown more remote. After all, why does someone with an $84 million contract—like Charlotte's Larry Johnson—have to talk to any-one, let alone be pleasant.

Fortunately, the *Chicago Tribune* was kind enough to accom-modate me and offer me a position writing about the NBA, but *without* traveling extensively with one team.

I jumped at the chance.

Jordan, of course, was not particularly happy with *The Jordan Rules*, but the rest of the team seemed to enjoy both the book and the controversy. At its height, former Bull Bill Cartwright called me at home to say he thought the book was great fun and if I was uncomfortable in the locker room, just to stay with him. Horace Grant, John Paxson, Will Perdue, and Scottie Pippen were likewise encouraging.

So the relationships built up with the team remained strong, which allowed me to write *Second Coming* when Jordan returned.

Pippen, who suffered through a frustrating season with management before Jordan returned, is as misunderstood an athlete as I've ever known. He's incredibly stubborn, which would get him into trouble; he could never accept being as politic as Jordan. But he's an unselfish player, reminiscent of Magic Johnson, and easily the most popular Bull, even after Jordan's return.

Among the remaining Bulls from the championship years, B. J. Armstrong had, during the second literary tour of duty, grown the most remote, mostly the victim of a basketball version of the seven-year itch. He simply tired of everything associated with the Bulls, as Grant did a year before, and wanted a divorce. It made him moodier than ever, but he was always cordial, and, at times, playful. I'd watched Perdue suffer for years in the shadow of Cartwright and mocking fans, so I was thrilled to see him have his best season though he continued to clash with coach Phil Jackson. Will could always be counted on for perspective and a humorous look at the wackiness around the Bulls.

Among the new group, Steve Kerr was a godsend for the media. Here was a modern-day athlete who actually liked reporters. He is smart, funny, and accessible—the rarest of triple threats these days. I give him the highest compliment I could give a pro athlete: You'd want to spend time with him even if he wasn't a pro athlete.

Bill Wennington, Jud Buechler, Pete Myers, and Larry Krystkowiak, all journeymen type players who'd bounced around, always remained in good spirits even with the Jordan madness, and also were always cooperative and friendly.

This past year, the Bulls may not have put together a championship team, but with the likes of Kerr, Wennington, Krystkowiak, Buechler, Myers, and Perdue, it was the first time I'd seen large groups of players going out together and having fun. Adding to the chemistry was the genial Luc Longley, who made up for his lack of dexterity on the court with a sharp wit and willing manner.

Toni Kukoc was usually difficult. He clearly didn't care much for American reporters, only showing animation around the media when European reporters were in town. Most in the media attributed that to Kukoc's having spent too much time with Bulls general manager Jerry Krause, an avowed media-basher, before coming to the NBA. But Kukoc had a boyish charm that would occasionally creep out.

Ron Harper was usually cordial, but a big contract and then a reduced role always made it somewhat embarrassing for him and he didn't talk to reporters much. Likewise, the youngsters, Dickey Simpkins and Corie Blount, whose focus remains resolutely on how to get more playing time.

I'm grateful to all for their cooperation.

Also, my thanks to Krause. He was angry at me over the publication of *The Jordan Rules*. And if he never strained to be informative afterward, he nevertheless always returned my calls. And I saw acts of great kindness of his that he kept quiet.

Thanks, also, to Bulls vice-president Steve Schanwald, whose marketing and public relations staff, especially Tim Hallam, Lori Flores, and Tom Smithburg, was always helpful. I argued with Schanwald about the role of marketing in the NBA, but he always listened and was one of the true innovators in the league.

Other team staff members, namely Drs. David Orth and John Hefferon, trainer Chip Schaefer, Joe O'Neal, Bob Love, Al Vermeil, Erik Helland, John Ligmanowski, Karen Stack, and Pam Lunsford were always cooperative.

And it was good to see Paxson still around. He personified the dream of the Everyman in athletics. As a kid he practiced that game-winning shot in his driveway with associated commentary, and even if his athletic skills gave him no reason to believe he'd reach the pro-level, he did—and he hit the shot— several times. Out of uniform, he was more relaxed, but it was easy to see he missed the game, and some team would be fortunate to make him their coach someday.

And I still consider owner Jerry Reinsdorf special. Of course, so does baseball negotiator Don Fehr, though in a different way. Like bosses everywhere, it's not easy to like owners, nor are they popular. But I always found Reinsdorf's perspective particularly refreshing and his interest in keeping his teams competitive serious. He was always approachable and more humble than one would expect. He usually knew the right thing to say, so he didn't come off as the lovable teddy bear, but he was a lot closer to that than the rabble in baseball would have you believe.

Again my favorite this time around was coach Phil Jackson. I was sorry to see assistant John Bach go, but his place was filled by the able Jimmy Rodgers. I enjoyed seeing Jim Cleamons grow into one of the best, if most overlooked, coaching candidates in the NBA, and venerable assistant Tex Winter always maintained a good humor as I fenced with him over his offense.

I always looked forward to the summers, which meant a long vacation between seasons, with some ambivalence because it meant I wouldn't talk with Jackson for three months. There are few people I've known who've opened up as many areas of thought that were previously unexplored. I found spending time with him more of a reward than a job. For his cooperation and consideration, I'll always be grateful.

My deepest thanks to my literary agent and friend, Shari

Wenk. In the midst of the Jordan comeback hoopla she always saw a book where I wasn't sure. And when there was a book to be written, she was always there for guidance and editing, all the while taking care of three kids.

Although I remained close to the Bulls, I couldn't have completed this project without the help of my successor on the Bulls beat, Melissa Isaacson. Her unerring eye and expanding knowledge helped shape the work and provide needed insight. Also, another *Tribune* colleague, Paul Sullivan, was invaluable for his knowledge of baseball and Jordan's role as a major league hopeful.

Thanks also to friends on the basketball beat for their help, Mark Heisler, Mike Imrem, Kent McDill, Lacy Banks, Corky Meinecke, Scott Cooper, David Moore, and Mike Kahn, and team officials, Dale Ratermann, David Benner, Alex Martins, Harold Kaufman, John Cirillo, Matt Dobek, Arthur Triche, Julie Marvel, and Chris Brienza.

Thanks to my editor at HarperCollins, Rick Horgan, who was a delight to work with. As much as any editor I've dealt with, he had a personal confidence that allowed him to treat writers as professionals. It made for a pleasant experience even with accelerated deadlines. Also, thanks to his assistant, Airié Dekidjiev.

Thanks, too, to my editors at the *Tribune*, particularly Howard Tyner. Almost 20 years ago, Tyner and I were general assignment reporters together working off the city desk and grousing about editors. *I* still do. He doesn't, since he's the editor of the *Tribune*. Of course, I haven't seen any need to complain about his fine stewardship.

And the biggest thanks and gratitude, as always, to Kathleen and Connor.

CONTENTS

MICHAEL AND ME: OUR BASKETBALL ADDICTION

Everyone has a favorite Michael Jordan highlight.

There was Jordan's 63-point playoff game, still a record, against the Celtics in 1986, when Larry Bird would say he had seen "God disguised as Michael Jordan." There was "The Shot," Jordan's buzzer beater that shocked and knocked the Cleveland Cavaliers out of the 1989 playoffs, followed by his 69-point scorching of those same Cavs the following season. There was the "here-it-is-no-here-it-is" switching hands layup against the Lakers during the 1991 Finals, "The Shrug" (Jordan's response to six 3-point field goals against Portland during the 1992 Finals, after it was suggested by some that Clyde Drexler might actually be his equal), and the 55-point game against Phoenix the following year in the Finals after Charles Barkley told his pal Jordan the Suns were destined to win the NBA title. "You're reading a different Bible than I am," Jordan shot back.

But I most recall this: a Thursday afternoon in October 1991, when Jordan, walking out of a Bulls practice, stopped, shot me a hard look in the eye, and said, "You're a fucking asshole."

That is my most memorable moment with Michael Jordan.

In retrospect, he hadn't had a very good day. Jordan had

just set off a national firestorm by refusing to go to the White
House with his teammates in honor of the Bulls' first NBA
championship. The visit had been scheduled before the start of
training camp, so technically, players had no obligation to perform any team functions. Not only was Jordan angry with the
Bulls for scheduling the White House event on his vacation
time, but unbeknownst to anyone at the time, Jordan had
planned a golf/gambling weekend with convicted drug dealer
James "Slim" Bouler, at whose money-laundering trial Jordan
would later have to testify. This was a high-stakes weekend of
$10,000-per-hole golf matches that actually required a
"banker," a bail bondsman named Eddie Dow, who was later
murdered by associates. When checks signed by Jordan
showed up in Dow's estate a few months later, the truth began
to be revealed. But Jordan didn't announce his golf trip as his
excuse for skipping lunch with the president; he stated instead
that he had planned a family vacation, that he owed it to his
family, that he'd already met George Bush when Bush was
vice-president, that family came first, and certainly George
Bush could understand that.

It seemed reasonable, the local conquering hero sacrificing
a trip to the White House to be with his family, and although
other players with prior commitments were forced to attend,
Jordan was not. The Bulls would not be invited back.

Then the media began suggesting that Jordan was intention-
ally distancing himself from the team, even though the Bulls
had finally managed to pull together to win the 1991 championship title. (Jordan might have agreed with former president
Richard Nixon, whose disdain for the media rivaled Jordan's: "I
don't mind being examined with a microscope," Nixon once
said, "but when they start using a proctoscope . . . ") I was one
of the writers who had questioned Jordan's actions, but I was
surprised when, during a preseason press conference, he specifically mentioned me by name several times, saying he didn't
need Sam Smith telling him what to do.

Two months later, the *Charlotte Observer* reported that federal officials had seized $57,000 from one James Bouler, money

he claimed to have won from Michael Jordan during a golf weekend the previous October. Jordan initially claimed the money had been a loan to Bouler for a golf driving range, but at Bouler's trial a year later he admitted the money had come from gambling. Jordan explained he was too embarrassed at the time to admit the truth.

Teammates Horace Grant and Scottie Pippen began calling him "Scarface" and "Five-Card Charlie." Jordan, nervous that other unsavory types might be attracted by all the negative publicity, began carrying a laser-sighted pistol, which he started practicing with and occasionally carried in his bag to the Chicago Stadium. Bulls coach Phil Jackson talked to Jordan about carrying the weapon and tried to engage him in a discussion on gun control. But security was a concern for someone in Jordan's position; he had even invested heavily in a security system at his son's school, just to be sure.

Over the four years during which I traveled with the Bulls, Jordan and I had always maintained a good relationship. That is, until 1991 and the publication of *The Jordan Rules,* a book that I truly believe was neither unfair nor unflattering. I had always found him to be charming although somewhat confrontational. Every conversation was like a game to him. He'd have to get the last quip, as if it were a win. In public, he hides his sharp tongue, but he's notorious around the league; he never misses an opportunity to make a remark or get the last word. But he was always fun to be around, a real "man's man." Even when talking seriously about basketball, he always tossed in a bit of whimsy, just to catch you off guard. Once when talking about being the player to take the game-winning shots, he said, "It's what separates the good players from the great players. The good players are there to pass the ball to the great players to take the last shot. And," he added, "it gets you on the highlight films."

Sometimes his wit was biting, like when he began calling Will Perdue "Will Vanderbilt" because he didn't think Perdue was good enough to be named after a Big Ten school. When he'd see former Bull Stacey King carrying a bag, he'd ask whether King had finally bought himself a game. One night on the flight home after a particularly tough playoff loss to the Pistons, Jordan walked past Grant on the plane, took away his dinner tray, and announced, "You didn't play well enough to deserve to eat." Even when he returned to the NBA in 1995, a more patient, less vitriolic Jordan couldn't control his sharp tongue while practicing alongside Pete Myers, generally a poor shooter: "You can't shoot," spat Jordan. "What you need to do is go to my basketball camp with the kids and learn how to shoot."

Yet there is a magnetism about Jordan that is gripping. Even those who know Jordan well enough not to be drawn in by his fame still find it hard to stay away, so infectious is his personality.

"You almost have to define the lines," said Bulls coach Phil Jackson, whom Jordan came to admire as much as his college coach, Dean Smith. "If you join the entourage you get sucked into the party, the whirlwind, and everything. There's so much adoration going on that it becomes dangerous."

I actually once played golf with Michael Jordan. It was a last-minute substitution, made when some Chicago Bears canceled. We were at a private club, Exmoor, in Chicago's north suburbs, where Jordan isn't a member and I haven't been invited to play since. Jordan is known around the nation's golf clubs as "America's Guest": Someone calls to say Michael Jordan wants to play and an accommodation is made. And when Jordan arrives, there's usually a pro happening by to offer a few tips (although on this day, Jordan was struggling with his driver, and after a few tips from the pro, he stopped and said, "Every time I show up, someone wants to give me a lesson and it's screwing me up.").

Jordan is generally regarded as a decent golfer, though not pro caliber. He has a long, looping swing, which sends the ball arcing wildly about every third swing. But he hits it long and has a deft touch around the greens despite his enormous hands. One of the disadvantages of being Michael Jordan.

One of the advantages, though, is that you do not wait. As

we moved to each tee box, the group ahead would invariably step aside to let us play through, partially out of homage, partially out of curiosity, and partially to collect a great story to retell for the next fifty years. We started calling him "Black Moses," as he parted sea after sea of heartland Protestants outfitted in their plaids.

He was as intense about golf as he was everything else. On one hole, he topped his drive, rolling it about thirty yards. He angrily stalked after it and didn't talk for the next two holes. But when he rolled in a twisting birdie putt a few holes later, he celebrated like a six-year-old with a new toy, asking everyone at least several times if they saw how the putt broke and how he had just the right speed.

Unfortunately, Jordan was clearly disappointed that no one in our group was in any position to wager with him, since we consisted of reporters and Bulls staff members, none of whom made anywhere close to a six-figure income. What good was gambling if only one side could afford to lose? In retrospect, we probably should have bet with him that day, since he didn't play particularly well and shot about 80.

By the time we arrived at the eighteenth green, word had spread of Jordan's presence, and about a hundred golfers and staff members had gathered to watch. Jordan hit a good drive and then lined an iron onto the green, about thirty-five feet away. As he approached the green, the group began cheering, as if he had just won the U.S. Open and was striding up the final fairway.

Jordan walked up to his ball, marked it, and began walking around looking at the line of the putt in a greatly exaggerated fashion. He looked from behind, from the front, from both sides. He plum-bobbed the putter, suspending it in the air to read the break of the green. Very theatrical. Clearly, he had virtually no chance of making the putt; it was just too long. Yet for nearly five minutes he continued to bait the crowd, analyzing this one putt. Finally, he stroked the ball, it twisted down the hill—and rolled miraculously into the cup for a birdie. The crowd, of course, went wild. The legend lives on.

Ever the competitor, Jordan was always looking for action. Even on team planes and buses, he was invariably involved in a card game, and even when he returned to the NBA from his venture into baseball, he was always seen tapping away on a portable laptop computer. Figuring out his bank statement? Hardly. He was playing video poker.

Jordan was not what you'd call "book smart," and he admitted to never reading any of the books that Phil Jackson handpicked for him for the long Western Conference road trips, something Jackson did for each player (although once Jackson jokingly handed Jordan a guide to gambling in Las Vegas). No, Jordan was decidedly not a reader and had little interest in books. But it was clear he had heard about *The Jordan Rules*.

I have always suspected *Sports Illustrated* of slipping an early draft of the book to Jordan. At the time, the book's publisher had shown the manuscript exclusively to *SI*, hoping the magazine would buy and print an excerpt. The decision was ultimately made not to run an excerpt, and I learned from friends on the staff that there was a spirited debate over some of the more controversial aspects of the book. *SI* was about to name Jordan its Man of the Year; how would it look if this provocative story ran just prior? Also, the gambling controversy was starting to percolate, and Jordan was starting to curtail his interviews. It was going to be tough for someone to get him to sit down and talk. I've always wondered whether someone at *Sports Illustrated* showed him the manuscript as sort of an unspoken quid pro quo: Here, we're your friends. Take a look, and remember us when we need that interview.

Whatever had happened, Jordan was awfully mad at me on that October day, as the rest of the media drilled him for missing the White House trip. Why me? I wondered. *The Jordan Rules* was still a month from being published, and as far as I knew, I was just one more writer covering the team, asking the usual questions. Why was he so mad at me, at a time when just a few months prior we'd played a convivial game of golf, and even more recently we'd run into each other on a public course and stopped to chat about the upcoming season?

I figured he had heard something about the upcoming book and believed what most people did who hadn't read it: that *The Jordan Rules* was a one-sided, nasty rip job. Of course, anyone who read it would tell you otherwise, but just the rumor of it was enough to turn Jordan against me.

Ironically, the writers who covered the Bulls over the years had gone out of their way to protect Michael and his carefully groomed image. He would constantly use the wrong words to describe something, and the writers would get together later in the locker room to decide what it was that he had actually meant to say. When his first child was born several years before he married the child's mother, he asked that the media not report it; no one, including me, ever violated that request. It wasn't so much that writers feared being shut out by Jordan; it just seemed to be the right thing to do, since it was so important to him. He had been so cooperative with the press, and we tried to cooperate with him.

Image was everything. Once, sitting with a group of reporters, everyone was talking about the worst jobs they'd had as kids. Jordan talked about being a maintenance worker and failing to make it through the first week because the work was so distasteful. Then he stopped. "Don't write that," he said. "I don't want maintenance men to think I'm putting them down."

Another time he was approached by U.S. Senate hopeful Harvey Gantt, a black politician who was running against Jesse Helms in North Carolina, Jordan's home state. Gantt had hoped that Jordan's name would help him defeat Helms, widely regarded as a virulent racist. But Jordan declined. He wasn't into politics, he explained, didn't really know the issues. And, as he later told a friend, "Republicans buy shoes, too."

If image was everything, *The Jordan Rules* was not going to make Michael Jordan's recommended reading list. He would never again speak with me in a one-on-one interview.

Ironically, most people came away from the book with the message that Michael Jordan was human and that humans make mistakes, something Jordan has always said himself.

"Be like Mike?" wrote *Philadelphia Inquirer* reviewer Bob Ford, referring to examples of Jordan's temper and selfishness. "Hell, we already are."

Jordan never approached me about the book, and because I still covered the team and the NBA, we were forced to have frequent contact. For a few weeks after the book's publication, he'd keep his head down when I asked him questions in group settings. Eventually, he'd look me in the eye and answer my questions as if I were just another reporter. No quips or jokes anymore. Professional, formal. The new relationship suited us both. He never made a scene, never spoke out against me. I continued to do my job, and he did his.

That 1992 season, the Bulls went on to win a record fourteen straight games and a franchise-best sixty-seven games on their way to a second straight title. It was the best Jordan had ever played within the "team" concept, and although I'm in no way taking any credit, I believe that as a result of the firestorm of gambling allegations and hype surrounding the book, he retreated into the comfort of the team game and the safety of the group. The result was an explosive 37–5 start.

Phil Jackson, who had long struggled to make Jordan play a team game, saw his opportunity. Jackson had always seen Jordan as the perfect player: "A coach's dream. His footwork, passing, ability to read defenses is amazing, and he's able to take criticism. If you tell him 'bad shot,' he says 'yes,' and he doesn't argue. He'll take a shot and say, 'I fucked up. I probably shouldn't have taken that shot.'" Quite a change from players like Will Perdue, who was perpetually explaining why his mistakes weren't really mistakes, or B. J. Armstrong, who would sulk and kick chairs when his errors were pointed out. Coaches hate that. Jackson hated that.

But Jordan was pulling away from the team, and his game was showing it. Jackson, a disciple of the fundamental game, is something of a basketball Buddhist: His is a system based on selflessness. Jordan, on the other hand, is perhaps the antithesis of that, a brilliant individual, celebrated and revered, trying to cope within a team game. In some respects, Jackson felt he also was losing control of Jordan after that first title season. Now Jordan's thoughts were drifting toward baseball, perhaps toward making a grand exit from basketball. Jordan's father, James, counseled his son to walk away after that first title, to leave on top and pursue a baseball career, something they'd both talked about for years.

"Michael's mother always told me that was James's dream, for Michael to be a pro baseball player," said Bulls chairman Jerry Reinsdorf.

So when Jackson watched all the controversy swirling dangerously close to his star player, and the star player pulling away from the team, he grabbed the chance to bring him back into the fold. Look to the team for your support, he counseled Jordan. Let this be your cocoon. And Jordan, seeking shelter from the storm, came back to the team game. Suddenly he was holding the ball and faking his defender before passing, and running down court without the ball, something the coaching staff had begged him to do for years. Jackson believed it was no coincidence that the 1991–92 team was the best ever, simply because Michael Jordan played as pure a game as anyone had ever played.

After that season, with his second championship behind him, Jordan went to the Olympics, and the controversies kept brewing: Did he keep Isiah Thomas off the team by saying he wouldn't play if Thomas did, a payback for Thomas's freeze-out of Jordan in Jordan's first All-Star game in 1985? There was the licensing dispute with the NBA that resulted in Jordan being the only All-Star left off the T-shirts at the Orlando All-Star game. And the endorsement flap caused when he refused to wear the logo of the Olympic-sponsored shoe company, Reebok, because he was a Nike man, solving the problem by draping an American flag over himself (and the Reebok logo) during the award ceremonies. "I hear Jordan wanted to take part in the opening ceremonies," quipped syndicated columnist Scott Ostler, "but backed out when the USOC denied him permission to wear a huge Nike shoe on his head."

But Jordan sailed through it all.

Phil was right, he told a friend. He didn't have to worry about being perfect anymore. The bubble had burst, and he was still the hero-god. Nothing could stick to him.

Early the following season, after the Bulls won their second title, I was in Phoenix talking with Charles Barkley, whom I find to be a delightful, warm character, once you get past the outrageous bluster. I've spent time with him and his family, and he's always quick to make jokes about my clothes or my balding head. And on this day, once he'd finished attacking my saddle shoes and glasses, he mentioned he had just played golf with Jordan a few days earlier. Then he smiled widely and paused.

"Man," Barkley said, "Michael hates your fuckin' guts."

And that's how it's been ever since. He does his job, I do mine, and if our paths cross, they cross. And in March 1995, when word swept Chicago that Jordan had decided to return to the NBA, and national hysteria reduced the city to what one columnist called "the biggest hick town in the world," Michael Jordan issued a two-word statement: "I'm back."

Well, so am I. Although I needed a few more words to explain.

Chapter 1

AND ON THE FIRST DAY, HE SHOT

It wasn't until just after dawn on March 19, 1995, stepping from the door of a private, nine-seat jet into the brisk morning air in Indianapolis, that Michael Jordan knew he was finally back, not only to the game he'd mastered but to his destiny.

Soon he'd be in Market Square Arena, accompanied by only his security force and a few Pacers employees who had arrived early for work, taking shooting practice for the big moment later that day on the national TV stage.

But for Jordan, the hardest time had been in the loneliness of that airplane.

"I couldn't get off that plane," said Jordan, who admitted to being in tears as he sat, nervous, anxious, and excited with his thoughts. He wished his father, James, were there to counsel and reassure him, but that was not to be.

"He had always been there when I'd be moving to another stage of life," Jordan said. "He was my biggest adviser. Now I would be moving to another state. I knew it. And I had a tough time trying to move forward without him."

His friend from NBC-TV, Ahmad Rashad, was there, along with Jordan's security guards. His emotions were raw. "It took me a while to get up the courage," he would later tell reporter Jim Gray, an old friend.

Jordan's kids had stayed home, preferring to see a live show of the Mighty Morphin Power Rangers.

Although it was just a minor part of his decision, Jordan was proud that his children now were starting to understand who he was and just *what* he was. He had been back at North Carolina in the winter, playing one-on-one after a practice with North Carolina guard Jerry Stackhouse, the supposed next Michael Jordan, and Jordan had spent much time talking about his kids. And as the time neared for his return, he privately gushed over the kids being able to see him play, not to just hear the stories and read about the legend.

"My kids understand now who I am as a basketball player," Jordan said, "even though they like B.J. and Shaq and some of those other guys better than me."

When the jet arrived in Indianapolis, Jordan asked the others to leave the plane. Then he sat for a while, thinking mostly about his father. James Jordan had always been there for the pivotal basketball moments of Jordan's life—the first championship, the disappointments in Detroit, the seventh game against the Knicks in 1992—offering advice and counsel. And Jordan did have doubts. Was he just on the rebound from baseball? Was it the right time? He'd gone through a similar period of uncertainty on a baseball road trip to Memphis while he was with the minor league Birmingham Barons.

"I felt at a point where things weren't going my way," Jordan said. "It was beating me mentally. The game is so mental that at some point you don't want to beat yourself to death. At one point, I felt like I was of no use to anything and I was making a big mistake. Normally, I talk to my father in those situations, when I'm really unsure of what I'm doing."

But Jordan had pressed on that summer, as he would again on this infamous Sunday in March, with memories of his father to guide him.

Jordan called him "Pops," a man who was more friend and guidance counselor than father. It's an irony that though so many view Jordan as a role model, Jordan could never accept a role model other than his father. He understood, even if he never expressed it: Believe in your parents, not sports figures.

Jordan sat for almost an hour, crying, thinking about his

father, the lessons about moving forward and turning negatives into positives, himself, the game, his life and the circle it had taken. He had come back to play basketball because he missed the competition and the game, as well as the success, achievement, and reward he couldn't gain anywhere else. He had been a lost soul since he left basketball in October 1993, angry and resentful not only at what he perceived as unfair treatment by the media and the public but by the inequity of having his father and best friend snatched from him when there was so much more for them to do, so much more for them to experience.

There was always a ritual he went through before a game. He'd slap some resin dust into the face of broadcaster Johnny Kerr, a friend, and then he'd peer up into the stands to catch a glimpse of his family or friends for support. But his wife and kids would be home, and his dad, well. . .

And now he was about to return, this time without his father watching from the stands.

Eventually, he summoned up the strength to leave the airplane.

"The toughest part was getting off the plane," Jordan would say afterward. "Once I got off the plane I knew I was back."

Michael Jordan, perhaps the game's greatest player, certainly one of the great athletes ever to retire in his prime, was going to play basketball again.

It was not only a sports headline but a cultural phenomenon.

And to fans worldwide, the reappearance of Jordan was something divine. Somehow, it seemed that while Jordan was playing, no matter what he did he was never fully appreciated. He just made it look so easy. But now people were about to get a second chance, and they weren't going to make the same mistake again.

Few great talents are appreciated in their times. Stories are legend of great contributors to history, particularly in the arts, starving during their prime earnings years. Would you like to read a new Shakespeare play? Debate with Plato or Aristotle?

Paint with Michelangelo or study the heavens with Copernicus? Can't be done. Society rarely stops to appreciate its great products, taking them for granted and then regretting it for decades.

But here was an opportunity to see maybe the greatest ever, still in his prime. A second chance to see Babe Ruth at the plate again, not to just hear or read about it. This time they'd appreciate what they were seeing and they would celebrate it every day, remembering every detail so they could tell their kids and their grandkids, recall every dunk and hanging tongue and reverse spinning layup.

Jordan didn't have to be as good as he was; he didn't even have to be better than everyone else. He just had to be back because no one knew if Shaquille O'Neal or Anfernee Hardaway or Glenn Robinson would be a legend. But everyone knows Michael Jordan is—and always will be—a legend, and here was a chance to see him again doing what he does best and at nearly the level he did it before.

No one was going to let the chance go by again. This time it would be recorded for history.

Yet even if there was a rationale for the reaction to Jordan's return, that reaction still defied belief.

After all, no disease was being conquered, no war being stopped, no fountain of youth being discovered, no particular contribution to society.

There would, however, be new shoes.

Hundreds of extra security were on duty that day in Indianapolis, as mobs stood outside the players' entrance just to gain a glimpse of Jordan, even an hour after the game. Tickets were being scalped at $1,000 each.

Hundreds of reporters descended on Market Square Arena, and no one was happier than Pacers public relations chief David Benner that Jordan had given just one day's notice of his return. "At least there wasn't more time for the foreign media to get involved," Benner said.

But the Pacers were nervous enough about the media crush to assign a police bodyguard to Benner. Why? He was assigned to allot seating for reporters and photographers, and everyone wanted to be there for history. And in the relatively small Market Square Arena, someone was going to have to sit in auxiliary areas to watch the great event on TV. The Pacers feared a media riot.

How valuable was it to know Benner that day? When Benner went back to the Bulls locker room before the game to find out what number Jordan would wear, the answer was still a mystery to everyone but the clothing manufacturers who already were pumping out those number 45 jerseys. One of Jordan's bodyguards offered a deal: He could tell Benner the number—if Benner could get him a seat behind the bench.

None of that mattered to Carmen Villafane.

Confined to a wheelchair since birth with a severe case of cerebral palsy, Villafane first met Jordan in 1988 when she gave him a Valentine's Day card during a rare trip to the Chicago Stadium to see a game. A few days later, she happened to be attending the Chicago Auto Show, and saw Jordan, who was making an appearance for one of his sponsors; he remembered her. Later that season, he noticed her at another game and demanded, "Where you been?" When she explained that tickets were hard to come by, Jordan promised to provide her with two tickets to every game.

After that, she became a friend and inspiration to the entire Bulls team. She often has violent spasms when she speaks, and her obvious courage has endeared her to everyone who meets her. Players and coaches stop by as she sits in her wheelchair, which is usually outside the Bulls locker room before games. And it was not uncommon to see Jordan stop by and joke, "How do you keep your shoes so clean?"

"Because I can't walk," she would respond with a grin.

"He teases me, I tease him," says Villafane. "He likes me, not because I'm disabled, but because I'm his friend. He's such a good person."

And there at Market Square Arena, in the midst of all the madness and commotion, sat Carmen Villafane, whose motorized wheelchair had been the magical carriage that whisked her that day to see her handsome prince.

It's that image, that hope, that attracts so many to Jordan, especially the kids. A fourth-grade teacher wrote to the *Chicago Tribune* after a critical article was directed at Jordan: "Don't dare tell my kids there's no Santa Claus." Jordan, she said, was crucial in getting them to read.

A fifteen-year-old high school student told the *Tribune* about Jordan, "If I try, I can't fail." Another teenager said Jordan "never thinks 'What if I go in and mess up?'" Another high school student explained: "Michael tried his best in baseball. It didn't quite work out for him, but if you try your best you can accomplish anything." To these kids, Jordan represents the spirit of achievement, of hope, of escape from the grinding poverty and danger that stalks their ghetto streets.

When Jordan finally left Market Square Arena that afternoon, after the Bulls had rallied from 16 behind in the fourth quarter to tie and then lose in overtime, after the world saw number 23 become number 45 (if only for a few weeks), after Jordan charmed the breathless media for almost an hour after the game with soliloquies about the ravages today's players have brought to the game, how his motives were pure and it was time the proper legacy of Julius Erving, Larry Bird, and Magic Johnson be enforced, Jordan saw Villafane.

"What are you doing here?" Jordan wondered, knowing he would be playing in Chicago that week and that she could have seen him there without traveling all the way to Indianapolis.

"I couldn't wait," said Villafane.

Chapter 2

PARTING SHOTS

On a flight home late in the 1993 regular season, Jordan told several of his teammates that he was quitting after the season.

"Sure," said Scottie Pippen.

"Right," added Horace Grant. "You're not going any-where."

"You'll see," Jordan assured them.

During that season, he'd told his college coach, Dean Smith, of his plans to retire, and Smith went so far as to attend one last Bulls game just to see Jordan play one more time. He knew Jordan was serious: The practices were now a burden, the fun was gone. And the media attention, which concentrated on everything but basketball, had angered Jordan beyond repair.

"I knew what I was doing," Jordan told the *Boston Globe* during his first baseball season with Birmingham in 1994. "They [the media] said it was a bunch of bull, that I was positioning myself for more money. But once I won the championships, people got bored examining my game. The expectations were so high, and if I didn't increase them, it was like I was being bypassed. What I accomplished was no longer viewed as excellence. So they started looking at my life, trying to find something there.

"Less than an hour after my father died, people started associating that with gambling. It was so horribly unfair. I took offense to that. Why couldn't they wait twenty-four hours to get the story right? Why did they have to make that kind of assumption? And then, once there was absolutely nothing to it, when it was clear it was senseless violence, where were the retractions? Why couldn't they at least give the credibility back to my father that never should have been taken away in the first place?"

For all Jordan's media savvy, his anger and resentment over his father's death colored his view of the media as a whole, the same media that had always fawned over Jordan and covered for him, even when the gambling issues arose. The two major newspapers in Chicago, the *Tribune* and the *Sun-Times,* never pursued the Slim Bouler story with the same vigor as the North Carolina dailies because of Jordan's fabulous popularity in Chicago. And when many criticized Jordan's venture into baseball as selfish, the *Chicago Tribune* congratulated Jordan editorially.

Yet Jordan couldn't forget what had been written and said about his father. Well, he would show them. It was one thing to drag him through the journalistic mud over his gambling, but not his father, not his memory. And to suggest Michael was the cause? That was enough. They might still have the ball, but Jordan was taking his game and going home.

The fire that had always burned in him for achievement and success now continued to smolder with anger. He told the *New York Post*'s Peter Vecsey, "The media came after me the last couple of years because they couldn't write anything bad about my play. They couldn't write any longer I was a poor shooter. They couldn't write anymore I didn't make my teammates better. They couldn't write I wasn't a winner. So they harped on my gambling. Meanwhile, I did nothing that others in basketball, the media, weren't doing."

He also cited the Bulls' game plan as a problem. "I like Phil," Jordan stressed. "He cares about the players, but also knows how to separate himself, which is very important." (Jordan always complained that Doug Collins's penchant for trying to befriend players and then cracking down on them in coaching them doomed Collins as a coach.) "But what I objected to was Phil's insistence on diversifying the offense. I didn't like it because it put more pressure on me to produce at crucial times. I would have stayed if Phil came up with something where I wouldn't have had to play a large portion of the regular season, like Bill Cartwright. But let's face it. If I was allowed to sit out until a month before the playoffs, the media would have been all over me. They would have said, 'Who does he think he is? He thinks he's above the game. He's not a team player. He's selfish.' I'll admit I was selfish my first few years, but not after that. I could have averaged thirty-two, thirty-three for the next four years, but the last thing I wanted to do was defend myself to the media every night."

Jordan even questioned the NBA's support for him, recalling the bizarre meeting with Commissioner David Stern that he had been forced to attend a few years back in New York, the same late-March day the Bulls were to play the Knicks. Allegations of gambling had caused Stern to summon Jordan, yet the meeting amounted to a slap on the wrist; there would be no stern warning about his gambling and associations. Jordan complained to Stern that the all-day session had robbed him of his nap time on a day when he had a tough game at night. He would not forget what he believed was Stern's unnecessary zeal in pursuing some league face-saving. And later he would depict Stern as the players' enemy when, as a player once again, he took an active role in NBA contract negotiations during the summer of 1995.

Bulls chariman Jerry Reinsdorf had perhaps been closer to Jordan than anyone in the Bulls organization.

The two even went into business once, investing in a company that made wastebaskets with sports logos. It turned out to be a symbolic product for their investment.

At the time, during Jordan's first career as a Bull, Reinsdorf had been trying to figure out a way to pay Jordan more under the constraints of the salary cap, but the league was keeping a careful eye on such investments. Any equity Jordan would have would count against the cap, unless Jordan made his own investment.

Jordan felt comfortable with Reinsdorf, who could be charming, smart, and genuine. Jordan respected men who made money, and Reinsdorf made lots. He made sense, too.

But Reinsdorf admitted he missed Jordan's retirement plan, the burnout, the inability to face the rest of his life after his father's death.

"I always thought he'd play until we moved out of the stadium," Reinsdorf said. "I thought one more year and then that would be it. He surprised me. I should have seen the signs, the strain that last championship year after the Olympics when he had no time off that summer, the gambling stuff. But I remember him on the plane coming back from Phoenix after the third championship, smoking a cigar and telling everyone we're going to win six or seven of these championships."

At the time, Reinsdorf had even toyed with a limited schedule for Jordan after the 1993 championship season, but he felt it was unworkable.

"Maybe we could have anticipated Michael's burnout and said, 'Okay, start playing just in February,' but the fact of the matter is that's not practical," Reinsdorf would say just after Jordan's stunning retirement announcement.

"We did have a conversation in the playoffs in 1993, and I said to him at the time that I appreciated that he had kept his word and never said anything about the contract. I said, 'Even I think you're underpaid. There's nothing we can do now, but someday I will figure something out.' And Michael said that was good enough for him.

"The fact was the time had come for Michael to stop playing. And I don't know how we could have anticipated it. But our hope is Michael would always in some way be a part of our organization.

"We know, with him trying to make trades for guys like Walter Davis, he wouldn't be a good general manager," Reinsdorf said with a laugh. "But whether it's playing golf with sponsors or just being around, I'm not sure what. But we'll know when the time comes."

It was just a few months after that third championship—over Phoenix in 1993—that it all came to an end. The story burst into public view, ironically, during the White Sox's first playoff game against the Toronto Blue Jays, at which Jordan had thrown out the first ball. What had started as a horrifying rumor in the early innings of the game had erupted into the news story of the year by the final out.

Just a few days before, Reinsdorf had been meeting with Jordan and his agent, David Falk, in Washington. Jordan had sat down and said immediately, "This is not about money." They talked about many things, but in the end, there would be no way to convince him otherwise. A few days later, he began to say his emotional good-byes.

Teammates Scott Williams and newcomer Toni Kukoc were among those who completely broke down, and Bill Cartwright warmly embraced Jordan after an uneasy relationship for many years. Jackson was reduced to tears. He had suggested that Jordan say what he wanted to the public but just take a sabbatical. No, Jordan had insisted, his mind was made up, it was time to move on and put this all behind. It was the right time.

And then Jordan went outside to conduct his worldwide press conference announcing his retirement.

"I don't need a farewell tour like Dr. J. or Kareem," Jordan had said. When it was time to leave, he'd know. He was not going to let his skills deteriorate, or his enthusiasm. He didn't want to be pitied, or pity himself. And so on October 6, 1993, Jordan said it was time.

October 6, 1993: a day that will live in American sports infamy. Tom Brokaw came in to anchor the evening news from Chicago. The sports daily *L'Equipe* in France devoted its first three pages to the story, as did Argentina's sports daily. It was the main story in Kenya and drew immediate reaction in the normally stoic dailies in China. Newspapers in Spain and Germany carried multiple stories.

When Jordan retired, former Boston Celtic great Kevin McHale tried to put the hysteria into perspective.

"You won't believe this," McHale told anxious reporters, "but I guarantee you in five years people will be saying, 'Michael Who?'"

*   *   *

Jordan's farewell to the game in 1993 had been bitter and elo-
quent. He referred to the media as "you guys" twenty-one
times, saying at one point that while the media was not driving
him from the game, "This is probably the first time I've met
this many people without a scandal around."

Jordan said he would miss the game, the opportunities to
win more titles. And, he added, "spending more time with
teammates for eight months—and some of the things men do
in basketball. The psychological warfare that Phil put us
through. I'm going to miss all that. One thing about my
father's death—and it wasn't like everyone speculated about
the different media pressures and the pressures I was feeling—
is that it can be taken away from you at any time. There's a lot
of family members and friends I haven't seen because I've been
very selfish in my career to try to get to this point and make
sure I achieved all the dreams I wanted to achieve. Now that
I'm here I want to be a little unselfish in terms of spending
more time with my family, my wife, my kids, and just get back
to a normal life, as close to it as I could. So you guys can go
somewhere else to get your stories and hopefully I won't see
too many of you guys in the future."

Chapter 3

TWO-SPORT TYCOON

Jerry Reinsdorf was not used to losing battles. He had new baseball and basketball stadiums for his teams in Chicago, something considered impossible in the politically sensitive city where politics and corruption were close teammates. His Bulls had become the most popular team in the NBA, and certainly one of the most successful. The White Sox, which he'd almost lost to increasing debts a few years after putting together a group of investors for the team, had become the second most profitable team in baseball, and was successful on the field as well. Baseball was without a commissioner, due largely to Reinsdorf's manipulations, and the baseball union was naming him the power behind the management-labor struggle that had brought the sport to a standstill.

Reinsdorf's ego didn't require any credit for his power; just exercising it was enough, although he would publicly deny that he was a power broker in either sport.

"Certainly in basketball I have no power," he says matter-of-factly. "David Stern runs the NBA," Reinsdorf says. "Nobody else has anything to say. But he's done a great job, so you can't quarrel.

"In baseball, I serve on a lot of committees, so I have an opportunity to give input on a variety of issues," Reinsdorf says. "I have above-average intelligence, and I've always had the ability to simplify things, to find that most obstacles are really holograms and you can really walk through them. So if I make a good point, there's a tendency for people to listen. But if I really had power, it wouldn't have taken three years to fire

Fay Vincent and ESPN would still be doing tractor pulls. [White Sox vice-chairman] Eddie Einhorn had a great idea about putting baseball in the cable business ten years ago, but I couldn't pull it off. And if it were up to me, there wouldn't have been a change in the playoff system."

Jerry Reinsdorf is a traditionalist, a guy who believes in a handshake deal, a good cigar, and a trip up and down the aisles in a supermarket.

"I just love to look at all the items," said Reinsdorf, somewhat thickly built these days, with mousy brown hair and usually a plump cigar in his mouth. "My wife will give me a list of a few items and I still have to go up and down every aisle. I find it relaxing."

Cross-country drives relax him, too; Reinsdorf often drives to or from his Arizona winter home, "just to think," he says.

"COULDN'T YOU HAVE AT LEAST WON ONE?"

Reinsdorf has had a lot to think about over the years. The very average son of an itinerant sewing machine salesman, he still remembers walking home in silence from graduation at Erasmus High School with his mother, who, after several hours of watching awards being handed out to more than half the class, though none to young Jerry, finally blurted, "Couldn't you have at least won one?"

Young Jerry remembers, instead, twisting a coat hanger into a fishing line and reaching down into the corner drain sewers to retrieve lost Spalding rubber balls for stickball. He still has a huge picture of himself as a kid pitching at the Brooklyn Parade Grounds baseball fields; it hangs on his office wall, surrounded mostly by Brooklyn Dodgers memorabilia.

His first business effort didn't bode well for the future. He'd go to Chinatown to buy firecrackers and then return to his neighborhood to sell them. But every time he'd go to stock up on his inventory, he'd spend virtually all the profit eating. "Jews," Reinsdorf likes to joke, "know suffering and Chinese food."

Eventually, his business acumen would improve, but he

maintained his middle-class values: A handshake means something. Legions of friends will attest that a handshake with
Reinsdorf is a deal.

A story from his youth is a good example: Reinsdorf
attended George Washington University in Washington, D.C.,
and helped put himself through school with a job running the
school auditorium. He wanted to attend law school there, and
applied for and won a scholarship. He was married with a
child on the way. Just before school started, though, he was
informed a student couldn't have a job and a scholarship, that
he'd have to forfeit one. Reinsdorf said he needed both, that a
deal was a deal, he'd won both the job and scholarship fairly.
Too bad, said the school.

Feeling he'd been betrayed, Reinsdorf simply packed up
the family and moved to Chicago to attend law school at
Northwestern, even though he didn't yet have a scholarship. A
deal was a deal. Horace Grant would find that out later.

Good fortune always smiled on him, and when it didn't, he
made his own luck. He developed a reputation for making
things happen at Northwestern when he and a friend hatched a
plan to offset the faculty's success in the annual faculty-student
softball game. The umpiring always seemed to favor the faculty, so Reinsdorf managed to get the baseball commissioner's
office (lots of ironies in that story) to send a letter commenting
that the unfair umpiring was besmirching the game. The story
drew local media attention, to the delight of the faculty.

After graduating from law school, Reinsdorf became an IRS
attorney (one of his first cases was to pursue back taxes from
White Sox owner Bill Veeck) and later went into private practice. He had listened to his clients complain endlessly about
bad real estate deals they were involved in, and he offered his
advice on how they could have done better.

"Well, if you're so smart," a client once retorted, "why
aren't you out there making these deals?" He did, and created
Balcor, using OPM: Other People's Money, as he liked to call it.
Balcor became a major player during the real estate boom of
the 1970s and 1980s.

Reinsdorf founded Balcor with Bob Judelson, his closest friend to this day, and it used OPM to invest in properties. Eventually, they sold the company to American Express for more than $100 million.

These days, Reinsdorf's hobby is cooking up small real estate and financial deals with Judelson in a small office in Chicago. "Really just a place to sit around and smoke cigars," Judelson says.

THE KID FROM BROOKLYN WINS ONE

In the midst of the Balcor run, Reinsdorf saw an ad in the *Wall Street Journal*, looking for people to invest in a baseball team. Sounded like fun, he thought. After all, he still fantasized about being the kid from Brooklyn, on the hill, peering down at the batter.

The group was trying to buy the San Francisco Giants and move them, but it was unsuccessful. Then a friend enlisted Reinsdorf in what would become a failed effort to buy the New York Mets. By now, Reinsdorf was hooked on the idea of owning a team, but he realized that being a minority owner with no real say in the operations wasn't going to be much fun.

Why just be a silent partner? he thought. He decided to be the one to put together the group and pursue a team.

"When the Mets deal cratered," he recalls, "I thought, 'Why should I invest in something I'm not going to have a say in?'"

He started thinking about Bill Veeck, whom he had pursued relentlessly as an IRS attorney. Veeck, he knew, would buy a team so that he could sell it. "He wasn't in the game because he loved baseball," accused Reinsdorf. "He was in the game because he liked to buy and sell." And so Reinsdorf approached Veeck about purchasing the Chicago White Sox. As it turned out, Veeck was already trying to sell the team to another group, headed by Ohio supermarket executive Edward DeBartolo. But Veeck's fellow American League owners, who'd grown tired of Veeck's iconoclastic ways, blocked the sale with various spurious excuses. Eventually, Veeck had to deal with Reinsdorf.

Reinsdorf won the battle, but established himself as one of the most hated men in Chicago history for daring to offend the beloved Veeck, who refused to return to Comiskey Park after claiming he had been slighted by the new owners.

And Reinsdorf was soon faced with one of the harsh realities of owning a sports franchise. The old park was costing him a fortune in maintenance, and almost immediately Reinsdorf began losing money on the team. But he wanted badly to remain in the sports business, so he put together a group of investors to purchase the unimpressive Chicago Bulls in 1985 (from an ownership group that included George Steinbrenner). The purchase came with only one appreciable asset: Michael Jordan.

Reinsdorf's thinking at the time was that if he was forced to sell the White Sox, he would still have one team, albeit the less attractive one. Instead, Reinsdorf managed to keep the Sox afloat, and the value of both teams increased almost tenfold.

Eight years later, the Bulls had won three consecutive titles and were worth untold millions. And in the process, Reinsdorf became the only owner to challenge the tightfisted control of NBA commissioner David Stern, taking the league and Stern to court over his deal with superstation WGN and squaring off against the other twenty-six owners.

"Every vote in the NBA is one to twenty-six," said Atlanta Hawks president Stan Kasten about the league's renegade owner.

Yet Reinsdorf has beaten the omnipotent Stern in every legal confrontation, thus earning the wrath of Stern. And the reality is that Reinsdorf's Bulls have raked in enormous fortunes for the entire league, not to mention Reinsdorf himself.

"I never dreamed about anything like this," Reinsdorf admits. "My greatest ambition was to be a lawyer and have a car."

But the owner of two prosperous sports franchises has never been anything but shrewd, and if his most important asset had chosen to walk out the door, then it made sense to open another door to make sure he didn't wander too far.

Chapter 4

MICKEY, WILLIE, THE DUKE, AND M.J.

It was the biggest event in sports, since, well, Michael Jordan announced his retirement from the NBA.

Michael Jordan had arrived in spring training to try to become a major league baseball player.

Jordan called it a dream of his and his late father, James. Critics called it a circus, a joke, and the natural extension of an ego so out of control and out of touch with reality that Jordan thought he could do anything. He was a grown man with a candy-store mentality toward life: If I want to try it, I will. If it feels good, I'll do it.

A few months after retiring in October 1993, Jordan had begun workouts in secret in Chicago. His coach was the athletic director at the Illinois Institute of Technology who had prepared Madonna for her role in the women's baseball movie *A League of Their Own*. He had talked for many years about playing pro baseball someday, a dream he said his father always had for him. After the Bulls won the championship in 1991, Jordan talked with Charlotte Hornets owner George Shinn, who also owned a minor league baseball team, about perhaps playing baseball for that team sometime. But it was all very vague. At the time, Jordan was still talking about being a professional golfer.

In his early years with the Bulls, Jordan used to talk of his proudest sporting moment: hitting a home run to win a Babe

Ruth League tournament. He also pitched and batted .500.

But that had been fifteen years before.

So when Jordan started showing up at Comiskey Park taking batting practice in mid-December 1993, just two months after saying he wanted a life out of the spotlight, Chicago was abuzz again.

At first, the White Sox were in denial. "It's just like a fantasy camp for him," said White Sox general manager Ron Schueler. "He's just having a blast. But he's been coming in for treatment on his wrist by our trainer. He wants to be ready for the golf season. That's his real love.

"We will not sign him," said Schueler. "He never once has mentioned it, that he'd like to play ball, and we haven't considered it. A guy laying off thirteen, fourteen years can't just start up again. It takes a long time to be able to play at this level."

But Reinsdorf had given Jordan the go-ahead, and Jordan was already entertaining thoughts of being on the White Sox opening-day roster. He believed he could hit enough; a few years back the major leagues had cut back to twenty-four-player rosters, after which Reinsdorf said almost anyone could fill out that last roster spot.

"I don't think there's anything Michael couldn't do," said Reinsdorf, "so I wouldn't be surprised if he did [play baseball]. I certainly wouldn't say no if he said he'd like to try it."

And Jordan was trying it, even though he played coy when the media finally caught up with him in December 1993. Home might be where Jordan's heart was, but his interests were elsewhere.

"I'm just having a good time," he said. "I'm trying to see how good I am. I'm hitting off the machine. I'm just going through the phases, trying to see how good I can get. I haven't seen live pitching, but I'm hitting the ball real well. I'm driving the ball against the machine.

"I'm not committing to anything," said Jordan, "but if I'm not adequate to play in the major leagues, I'd say, 'Thanks for the good time.'"

Jordan went skiing at Christmastime, but in early January

1994 he was back at Comiskey Park, hitting in two- and three-hour sessions against the batting machine with instructions that no information be given out to the media. Reports began to fly that Jordan had become serious about baseball only because so many in the media and in baseball were laughing at his Walter Mitty attempt and saying he stood no chance.

But the decision was made. Jordan would be in the big league camp with a shot at making the team.

When he arrived at the White Sox training camp as a rookie in the spring of 1994, he didn't exactly receive a hero's welcome. Then Sox pitcher Jack McDowell, battling with Reinsdorf over a contract extension, practically snarled at Jordan every time he saw him. Here it was, the beginning of the season, and who was on the cover of *Baseball Weekly*? Not Frank Thomas or Ken Griffey Jr. or Barry Bonds. It was Michael Jordan. Ozzie Guillen, the playful shortstop, harassed Jordan mercilessly. Just as Jordan had tormented weaker basketball players like Brad Sellers, Sam Vincent, Steve Colter, and Dennis Hopson for their lack of skill, Guillen constantly harped on Jordan's many deficiencies and never let Jordan forget that he had received a free pass to a place that many with far more talent had been unable to reach.

Then manager Gene Lamont bristled at the realization that keeping Jordan with the club meant losing more deserving—and more talented—prospects. But he was interested to find out just what kind of stuff his new player had.

"I'm curious to see if baseball is as hard as I think it is," Lamont said. Jordan appeared to prove that it was.

Clearly, the adoration and idolatry Jordan had become accustomed to stopped when he put down the basketball and picked up a glove. "Nobody thought he'd make it to the big leagues unless it was for show," said former major league executive Bing Devine to *Chicago Tribune* columnist Jerome Holtzman. "He didn't have the talent." Others in baseball, like former Cub Mike Krukow, said they were "insulted" that Jordan was even being given a try. The coach of the 1992 U.S. Olympic baseball team, Ron Fraser, offered this scouting report: "Great body, great car." And baseball great and fellow grambler, Pete Rose, offered this assessment: "He's got two chances. And Slim just left town."

"Just because I can shoot a free throw doesn't mean I'm a basketball player," said Yankees third baseman Wade Boggs.

But Jordan was serious, and motivated by the challenge; his ability to overcome adversity and critics had been the cornerstone of his basketball career. During his nine years with the Bulls, he'd created challenges, depicting himself and the team as underdogs, then daring others to beat them. He'd predict outrageous victories, and then deliver. Whenever the team was uncertain, Jordan would rise up with a promise or prediction, stare down a challenge or a deficit. This confidence was perhaps the biggest factor that later persuaded Bulls coach Phil Jackson that the Bulls did have a chance to win the NBA title when Jordan returned in March.

As Jackson recalled, "I'll never forget the night before the start of the Finals in 1993, and Michael had a big cigar in his mouth and was insisting we were going to win two in Phoenix. We were just talking about winning one game, but he said we'd beat them twice on their home court. He could always give us confidence when we felt the odds were against us."

That was the way Jordan worked, making the high school varsity team after being demoted to the junior varsity his sophomore year, becoming an all-American at North Carolina after being lightly recruited out of high school, becoming the NBA star for the ages after being only the third pick in the 1984 draft behind Hakeem Olajuwon and Sam Bowie, winning defensive titles when many said he was only a scorer, showing an awesome all-around game after averaging more than 37 points in his third season.

"I showed people I could pass," he said after that year. "I showed I could play defense. I showed I could shoot. They said, 'Let's see him do it a whole year.' I did it for more. My team won."

He felt the same way during spring training, always hearkening back to the advice his father would give him in such situations: Be aggressive, trust your instincts, trust your talent.

"I love to hear them say [they doubt me]," said Jordan before leaving for spring training. "That's something that's always driven me. You tell me I can't do something, and that's what I'm going to try to do."

And Jordan would have his moments, like the day in July 1994 when he was still fighting to get back to .200, the famed Mendoza Line of baseball, the mark under which a player is considered ineffective at best. Jordan had been hitting over .300 early in the season, but the pitchers soon figured out that although his quick reflexes allowed him to hit fastballs, curveballs made him look like a giant getting out of a Volkswagen, one body part going this way, another that way.

On this day, he had fallen to about .190 when he came up in the bottom of the eighth inning. Then the hometown organist in Birmingham began playing the Alan Parsons Project music that had become synonymous with the opening introductions at Chicago Bulls games.

"I got the chill bumps," Jordan admitted. "I thought back to my past and those circumstances on the basketball court when I heard the music and it would made me focus. I always got the chill bumps then. I get them just talking about it."

Jordan ripped a double down the left field line to drive in the tying run.

Unfortunately, they wouldn't let him play baseball with headphones.

What had worked so well in basketball wasn't working in baseball: He had no frame of reference for making miracles. "In basketball when I'd get in a tense situation, I could go back to a similar situation I'd been in and that would relax me. In baseball I couldn't do that."

It was with some satisfaction during the summer of 1994 that Will Perdue went to watch Jordan play baseball.

Jordan had become Will Perdue.

"Here's eighteen-, nineteen-, and twenty-year-olds and he's swinging and missing, swinging and missing," related Perdue. "It had to be humbling. The effort was there, you could see that, but not the skill. Where before you're up here at one level and you have the same expectations for players, now here's Michael at this other level down here and I think it helped him start accepting some of the limitations of other players."

Jordan had been an NBA star immediately. Sure, there's much in legend about Jordan's sensational rise to superstardom: the failures in high school, his determination to prove everyone wrong, and his lack of realization even when he was drafted of how good he was. But he was a huge college star, college player of the year twice in three years, winner of an NCAA championship game with the winning shot, and then the star far above the rest of the stars on the 1984 Olympic team, which was then made up of collegians.

And if the coaches and general managers didn't see it right away, the players did when the Olympic team played a scrimmage game against a team of NBA stars. Jordan would knock Magic Johnson flying, rip a ball away from Kevin McHale, be virtually unstoppable. McHale, who was in the midst of a Hall of Fame career with the Celtics and took over the Minnesota Timberwolves in 1995, saw this was the next big moneymaking star of the NBA.

"Hey," McHale yelled at one point, "somebody guard the guy with the wallet."

But if Jordan were left to baseball, he'd be bankrupt.

"He struck out almost every time," remembered Perdue. "He'd screw himself into the ground, those eighteen- and nineteen-year-olds throwing him curveball after curveball. Then the game goes into extra innings and he gets the key hit. That was just like him." But those moments, as commonplace as they had been in basketball, were rarities in baseball.

In basketball, he knew every team's game plan well enough that he could tune out the pregame talks. "He still goes into the john when we have team meetings before games," said Jackson, after Jordan's return to the NBA. "I'll go in there and say, 'You're sitting on the toilet and I'm making one of the best speeches I've ever made.' But he's so focused that he's always ready." Unfortunately, that uncanny ability failed to spill over into baseball.

Still, although Jordan didn't earn universal acclaim for his ability, he worked hard, coming to the field almost daily at dawn.

He admitted the experience was humbling and that it almost drove him to quit several times, especially when he fell under .200 and was striking out about one of every three times up.

He went to his manager, Terry Francona, and said he was afraid he was taking someone's place who was more deserving.

"Sometimes I'm a little down," Jordan told the *Chicago Tribune*. "But they told me I was making progress, that everybody in baseball goes through what I've been through. I didn't realize that. So it was encouraging. Nobody expected me to hit .300, except maybe myself.

"Baseball is a game you could fail today and tomorrow and then you can fail the next day," Jordan said. "And each time, mentally, you're taking a shot. I was getting to that point. I needed some Band-Aids to plug these holes and try to build myself up.

"I found I was pretty much in control on the basketball court, but not as much in control on the baseball diamond. It shouldn't be any different from a mental standpoint. As long as I worked hard and would believe in myself, I could put myself in a position where I was thinking positive. I missed fourteen years of baseball and was then trying to be successful at it. You don't have a measuring stick for that."

But even as Jordan suffered with baseball, he remained defiant about his refusal to ever return to the Bulls, as so many said he would do.

"I don't see myself being back in the game at any time in the near future," Jordan said in response to reports in late June 1994 that he was close to returning to the NBA. "Okay, the far future. Either way you put it, I just don't like to say never. I don't like to close doors. But if you want me to say it, okay, never. I will never play basketball again, except recreationally.

"There's no truth to the rumors," said Jordan. "It's nothing but rumors. I'm not going to throw a curveball at the fans. I told them I would be here, and I'm here."

So Jordan rode the buses and stayed in motels. "I didn't start out with the luxuries of life," Jordan explained, remembering his father's frequent comment that the family once had "nothing and no place to put it." Jordan could deal with the cow-milking contests and kids' games that were standard fare on the field between innings of minor league games. After all, several years with the Bulls' three-ring circus of activities had, at the very least, prepared him for the minor league schlock.

He also tried to defer to the major leaguers; he was often nervous and unsure around them, as NBA rookies had been around him. Jordan recalled meeting Isiah Thomas at his first All-Star game in 1985 and being embarrassed about talking with him, not wanting to seem like another fan asking for something. Ironically, it would be that same attitude that would split the Bulls on Jordan's return, casting him in the hero role apart from his teammates. But now he was the rookie again, uncertain how to act around successful major leaguers, paralyzed with embarrassment when fans applauded his routine catches and virtually ignored future MVP Frank Thomas.

It seemed he was really trying to fit in, trying to overcome the obvious favoritism. Once, a minor leaguer was supposed to be in the batting cage, but one of the coaches yelled for Jordan to get in.

"Is that okay?" Jordan asked the kid somewhat sheepishly.

"Sure," the kid replied. After all, Jordan did play golf in his spare time with the manager.

"Asshole," the kid spat as Jordan took his swings.

One teammate in Birmingham told NBC-TV he resented Jordan getting a chance because "this is all I've worked for and a guy can come right in and get the opportunity."

But in general, it was the youngsters who were most accepting of Jordan. The kid quoted by NBC told Jordan his remarks were taken out of context. Jordan could understand.

At times, Jordan seemed as if he was trying to become a father figure, even paying a teammate who didn't speak English $100 for every new word he'd learn.

One day a pitcher sought an autograph, and Jordan

obliged, even though Jordan thought the pitcher had thrown at him. And the night before he left in March 1995 after effectively quitting, he went out with a few of the young players, telling them he'd have the pilot of his private jet dip the wing in appreciation when he flew off the next morning.

That morning, most of the minor league players were staring at the sky, waving. "There goes Michael." Yes, he can fly.

Major leaguers like Deion Sanders and George Brett called to offer advice and counsel. Even Sox star Frank Thomas had befriended Jordan. "Mike's a nice guy," said Thomas. "He's strong-minded and that's why I like being around him. I like what comes out of his mouth. It's all competition. He lives for that and I love it."

He worked hard, and if his playing abilities didn't impress anyone, his work ethic did. Mike Huff, a Sox backup whose job was being threatened by Jordan, was initially resentful, but came to admire him.

"One of the things was his genuine sincerity to learn," said Huff, who has since moved on to the Toronto Blue Jays. "It makes it easier to help someone who is sincere and genuine. If he had come out and said, 'I'm the greatest basketball player and I think my athleticism is going to carry me,' I may not have been as willing to help him. But he was very hardworking. The questions he asked were intelligent. He was able to stick with it and learn."

But Jordan was confused at both the barrage of information and his inability to excel as quickly as he thought he would after that batting practice the winter before.

"People were telling me a lot of different things," Jordan said. "I didn't know what it all meant. It helps to relax, but I couldn't. When you do you produce a little bit better."

Still, it wasn't happening as Jordan had planned. When Jordan launched his baseball career in the summer of 1994, he was immediately promoted to Double A Birmingham, where he hit an unimpressive .202. But at age thirty-one, he had to be moved through the system if there was a slight chance that he'd ever make it to the major leagues. So the Sox sent him to the

Arizona Instructional League, where he batted a respectable .252. Maybe he could change a few minds. Finally, he was promoted to Triple A Nashville, where it seemed he was preparing to play the 1995 season, showing up at the park at dawn just about every day in February 1995 to work with White Sox hitting coach Walt Hriniak. He had joined a country club in Nashville for $17,500, rented a house near a local PGA golf course, and spent the afternoons in Florida playing golf, then card games at night with friends. It wasn't exactly staying home and cutting the grass, as Jordan said he would do when he made his famous retirement announcement, but it was a pretty relaxing life. The family would occasionally come down, and Jordan would hire someone to keep an eye on the kids, even though he did admit he was mistaken about the notion that he could remain a family man and play baseball.

"I did miscalculate," Jordan said. "With the smaller cities, it was tougher on the family."

He also seemed to be looking and feeling more comfortable in his new sport.

"I don't know what to say to 'Shoes,'" said former major leaguer and replacement player Dennis "Oil Can" Boyd of Jordan. "I don't want to crowd the man. Lord, he looks like a baseball player to me. I like the way he wears his ballcap, a little bit to the left on his head. It shows a beautiful flair."

ALL'S FEHR IN BASEBALL AND LABOR NEGOTIATIONS

For all the hard work and effort, though, Jordan was becoming distracted and upset by issues that would not go away. It bothered him that the White Sox had featured him on the cover of the program that was being used for games featuring replacement players.

"When I'm around, people tend to make a little more money," said Jordan, echoing a complaint his agent, David Falk, would often express.

Falk, in fact, went so far as to get a published author, Jim Patton, who was writing a book for Addison-Wesley Publishing called *Rookie* about Jordan's baseball season, barred from Birmingham's media facilities in the minor league stadium.

Patton, who would learn Jordan had never purchased that much publicized bus for his teammates in Birmingham, also wrote that Falk intimidated club officials and even manager Terry Francona into not cooperating.

Jordan was also annoyed by hints that general manager Ron Schueler kept dropping, suggesting that Jordan play in games with replacement players who were substituting for the striking major leaguers, saying that perhaps Jordan needed the practice if he were to even get to Triple A Nashville, as promised.

"If he's going to compete and win a Triple A job at Nashville," said Schueler, "he needs the at bats."

Which meant playing.

Baseball's labor mess had made it clear to Jordan that he would be used by both sides.

"I won't put myself in the middle of the players and owners," Jordan said. "I'm for the players. I will stand that way. If that means I don't play in games that charge money, then that means I have to do that. I think management understands."

There was a major league players' union meeting nearby in Tampa, but Jordan skipped it, saying, "It's just a media issue for me to go. I don't want to walk in there. Then that ties me to the whole situation. My issue is more media than anything. I'm a whole different scenario."

Jordan felt each side was looking to capitalize on what he might do.

"I was being drafted into a position in the middle," said Jordan later, "a position where I didn't have the credentials to be. I was being tugged by both sides. So I thought the best way in a predicament like that was to walk away and let things be settled the way they should be settled. I didn't want to be part of that."

Of course, Jordan didn't have to be if he was serious about going to Triple A Nashville. But there was still that question, and having Michael Jordan around was just too big a temptation for either side to resist.

Despite Jordan's attempt to stay out of it, he was dragged in anyway.

Don Fehr, the players' representative, issued a directive that became known as the "Jordan Rule": Anyone playing in an exhibition game in which admission was charged would be considered a strikebreaker. Essentially, it barred Jordan from exhibition games—a blow to the owners, since Jordan was the only attraction left in baseball with all the major leaguers on strike.

Jordan was growing uncomfortable. "I'm not here to break down what the striking players are trying to achieve," he said. "If minor league players play against minor league players, is that breaking the rules? I'd like to think I'm not doing anything that's wrong. If I'm doing something wrong, then I'll have to reevaluate it. The last thing I want is to get in the middle of this whole mess. I want to stay out if it and suddenly the focus is turning toward me."

Jordan was growing frustrated, and after he left, Schueler and Reinsdorf blamed Fehr.

"He's not only hurting baseball," said Schueler of Fehr. "Now he's hurting the industry by not letting it get players from other sports. It's disappointing that with all the effort Michael put in, he wasn't able to continue it. Especially hitting-wise, he made tremendous improvement. Just the hours of dedication. I hated to see him throw all that away."

But the Sox had assured Jordan that spring training didn't matter, that he was going to Nashville, and since the minor leaguers were about to leave major league camp for their own minor league spring training, he'd soon be away from the labor problems of the major leaguers. Yet Jordan had insisted to Reinsdorf that this was all costing him a chance at being on the roster in April, a ludicrous notion since Jordan was still playing at the lowest minor league level.

"Something happened," said Reinsdorf. "All of a sudden he just didn't want to go to Nashville anymore. We never could figure out why."

Suddenly, there was an angry Jordan, stalking away from

Sox general manager Ron Schueler in spring training with Schueler in hot pursuit. Schueler had told Jordan that players who refused to act as replacements for the striking major leaguers would be demoted to the minor league clubhouse.

But Reinsdorf wasn't convinced that that was the reason he quit. Reinsdorf told Schueler that if it came down to such an issue, an exception could be made in Jordan's case. "We would have let him stay in the major league clubhouse if that's what he wanted," said Reinsdorf. "All you ever have to say is, 'It's Michael Jordan.'"

Jordan's entire baseball career had been an exception, really. A guy in his thirties with no apparent hitting, running, or throwing skills, he was allowed to play simply because he was Michael Jordan. "Hey," said Phil Jackson, "the pretty girl always gets kissed. It's not fair, but that's the way it is."

When Jordan complained to Reinsdorf that the ongoing baseball strike would prevent him from playing against major leaguers in spring training, essentially barring him from making the White Sox opening-day roster, Reinsdorf thought Jordan was kidding. The opening-day roster? Reinsdorf told him that, at best, Jordan could possibly be added to the extended roster in September 1995, if—and only if—he played well. And even then, he'd only have a chance, just a chance, of making the team in 1996 as a fifth outfielder. And considering the unimpressive state of Jordan's baseball career, either possibility seemed like quite a long shot, although he had come a long way.

"He made a lot of improvement," admitted Schueler, who had been among the major doubters about Jordan. "When you think about it, it's not even been a year and he's picked up a lot of knowledge. He still makes some mistakes, but his bat speed is better and he's better at things like throwing to the right base."

But as some with the White Sox looked back on it later, they wondered just how serious Jordan was about baseball in 1995 when, just days after the rumors of a comeback began to swirl, Chicago stores began carrying number 45 jerseys. Jordan sponsors like McDonald's and Gatorade were suddenly producing basketball-related commercials, and the usually open and approachable Bill Smithburg, the top executive of Gatorade's parent company, Quaker Oats, said through an aide he couldn't discuss anything related to what Gatorade was doing regarding Jordan. Jordan's old friend and Pistons guard, Joe Dumars, said Jordan had called in February to discuss the current NBA season. And, just as curiously, friends in North Carolina, especially at the university, were saying they'd heard long before that Jordan was coming back to basketball, that he was just waiting for the right time.

But would he really come back with fewer than twenty games to go?

There were so many inconsistencies in Jordan's words and actions. Just after he started his first spring training, Jordan said he was as happy as he'd ever been, that had he stayed with the Bulls, he'd now just be going through the motions, that retirement was right, felt right.

"If I would have played," Jordan told the *Chicago Tribune*, "we probably would have won seventy games this year. But I don't believe in 'if.' I think there always has been a plan for my life and that I don't have any control over it. Everything that happens was determined in advance.

"I promised myself I wouldn't look back and I'm not," Jordan said as the 1994 playoffs got under way. "I'm happy with the decision I made. It took nine years, but I felt I got to the point where I accomplished everything I wanted to."

Yet if Jordan sounded sincere, many close to him felt him fighting against his own desires, trying to fulfill a promise to his deceased father, to win the battle by challenging the skeptics and proving wrong those who questioned his sincerity and commitment.

There were always signs that basketball remained his first passion.

One day, in the White Sox locker room, a reporter noticed Jordan looking at a newspaper story the reporter had written.

"I see you're reading my article," the writer said.

"Is that yours?" Jordan responded.

"What'd you think?" asked the reporter hopefully.

"It was horseshit," Jordan said.

Then he wadded up the paper and tossed it into a large trash can. "Still got the touch," Jordan exulted.

Indeed, Jordan did. Even in pickup games with other baseball players, he never let anyone get the best of him.

"There were times he'd press and make sure the other team couldn't even get the ball past half-court," recalled Paul Rappoli, who played with Jordan in the Instructional League in Scottsdale. "He'd just turn it on whenever he wanted to."

Steve Olsen, a pitcher who was with Jordan in Birmingham, joined Jordan in some recreational basketball games when the team was on the road. Jordan always competed against others in basketball games or card games or Yahtzee rather than solo games like crossword puzzles, though he eventually started to work on even those to pass the long minor league days, saying that his father loved them.

"At first, everyone would be kind of joking around," said Olsen about the basketball games. "Then whenever the game got tight, we'd give him the ball and no one could stop him. He usually let the other guys do all the shooting. He'd be the playmaker until the end, and then it was almost unfair."

It was the game, the only one he really excelled at, the life, the success. It was Ahab's whale, Hook's crocodile. Jordan couldn't keep from pursuing it.

No matter the level of success or the money, how many really ever walk away from what they do best? Many try. But failure is a sure way to send anyone scurrying back.

For Jordan, no matter what he said or did, no matter how many times he denied it, the game would never leave him alone.

It's what he was, not a golfer, not a baseball player, actor, politician, or ambassador. If someone loves gardening, no amount of money would be worth not being able to garden. Jordan could do anything he wanted now and for the rest of his life. So could his family, and their families in the future: Jordan was now bringing in perhaps $30 million per year. Once, Reinsdorf got a call from a media company: Would Jordan be interested in a deal that was worth $3 million? The Bulls fielded loads of such calls, but this one Reinsdorf thought might interest Jordan. He talked to Jordan's agent, David Falk. Falk said they'd look into it but Jordan normally doesn't get involved in any deal if its value is under $10 million. Jordan had all the money he'd ever want.

As Jordan sat in Birmingham one sultry day in the spring of 1994, he mused to some reporters about the NBA.

"Yes, once in a while I think, 'What if I was there?'" Jordan admitted. "But it's more in the context of the young guys. I've proved my point with the Barkleys and Drexlers. It would have to be a shot at the Hardaways and the Webbers. I'd like to teach those rookies a lesson."

Just before Michael returned to the NBA, Pippen was asked why Jordan would want to play.

"There's a void in his life without basketball," Pippen said.

Chapter 5

LIFE WITHOUT MIKE

Fireworks were always a part of a Bulls season, although they were usually interpersonal. There was Jordan punching out Will Perdue in practice a few years back, Cartwright threatening to cripple Jordan after Jordan had ordered teammates not to pass the ball to him, Jordan refusing to talk to the media (usually a weeklong annual occurrence in the playoffs when the heat turned up), Jackson berating Perdue or Horace Grant, Grant feuding with Jordan, Jordan mocking Stacey King, Scott Williams blasting management, Krause and players seemingly always at odds.

"I keep asking myself if we're doing it the right way," wondered Indiana's president Donnie Walsh. "They're always fighting up there, someone ripping management, the players ripping each other. We've never had a guy speak out against the team here. And they've won three championships. Maybe that's the right way."

The Bulls' first season without Michael Jordan, 1993–94, would be as harmonious as the Bulls had had in many years. Jordan was gone, and everyone expected a collapse. Many believed he would just be gone for a short time.

"You better win this year, because he'll be back in a year," promised the prescient Vern Fleming of the Pacers.

"All over America," said Orlando general manager Pat Williams, "NBA teams are sitting up and saying, 'Hey, we have a chance.'"

Bill Wennington, who would make the team as a free agent

along with Steve Kerr, another little-used veteran, remembers sitting on the bench as the Bulls opened the season without Jordan. Both had taken a chance on coming to the Bulls for the opportunity to play with Jordan. "Now, just why did we come here?" Wennington wondered.

They saw a team, if not a city, getting ready to mourn. An economist from the Chicagoland Chamber of Commerce estimated the loss to the city in business and service opportunities at more than $100 million with Jordan retiring. The *Chicago Tribune* printed advice from grief counselors after Jordan retired about how fans should deal with the loss, explaining the stages of being numb, yearning and searching for the lost loved one, being disorganized and in despair, and then finally reorganizing.

That reorganization for the Bulls took far less time than expected. Going into the 1993–94 season, the Bulls were a huge favorite for a fourth straight title, rated 5–2 by Las Vegas oddsmakers, a figure that went up to 25–1 the day Jordan retired. Jackson wrote 25–1 on the chalkboard in the team's film room, saying the season really represented a great opportunity, a life raft they could climb into and paddle as far as they could.

Teams with retiring superstars, Jackson said, from Bill Russell to Magic Johnson to Larry Bird, had a history of winning thirteen to fifteen fewer games compared to the previous season.

"The last season with Michael we won fifty-seven," noted Jackson, "so we felt anything above forty-five would be a magnificent season."

That 1993–94 season went beyond all expectations. The Bulls battled the Knicks and Hawks right to the last weekend for the best record in the Eastern Conference. They impressed teams around the league with their unselfish team play, which seemed right out of basketball textbooks, the ball always moving, players moving, the ball going to the open man, the extra pass made, everyone retreating on defense, helping out. It was a nightly clinic that sometimes amazed even Jackson.

"I keep holding my breath and throwing them out there

and wondering if it's a mirage," Jackson said about the play of Kerr, Wennington, Pete Myers, all unwanted free agents who were outplaying the stars of other teams within the construct of the Bulls' equal opportunity offense. Jackson and Pippen were getting the accolades they deserved. Armstrong was named to the All-Star team along with Grant and Pippen, who was named the All-Star game MVP. Suddenly, there weren't as many tears being shed for Jordan.

"When I came to Chicago, I had a role to play," Pippen explained. "I wanted to win so I sacrificed what I had to. I never tried to step on Michael's toes. But my time has come now. We realized we learned to walk with Michael. Now it was time to walk on our own. I am, to some degree, the Man.

"With Michael, a lot of us were really taken out of the picture. After the game, it was all Michael. But now, everything in the locker room is shared. There's no one person enjoying all the attention. It's fun because even if you see a headline, it's 'Bulls Lose,' not 'Bulls Lose but Jordan. . . . ' We're all accepting the losses and enjoying the victories. There's no headlines saying, 'Pippen does this and Bulls win.' We're all being able to celebrate what we're doing."

And Pippen was displaying a unique all-around game that elevated him to the ranks of the great players of the day. As the Bulls kept with the top teams, even without Jordan, Pippen expressed little surprise.

"I won three championships with basically the same group of guys," Pippen said. "This is a good team. It's not like we're the Bad News Bulls."

"The difference now is we're a twelve-man team," said Grant. "We pass the ball around now and everyone gets involved."

"We didn't win three championships just because of one guy," said Armstrong. "We had great efforts overshadowed because we happened to have one guy who was maybe the greatest ever. But the team answered the question of whether it could win without him."

Grant, who long feuded with Jordan, did admit once that

"without the guy who retired, we do have to concentrate on playing better defense."

It was the conundrum that made Jackson perhaps the best coach of his era: how to win with a superstar who plays an offensive game. The great superstars in history who have dominated the championships—Bill Russell, Magic Johnson, Larry Bird—weren't scorers first. Jordan was. And then to win without him? Jackson showed the delicate balancing act of taking Jordan and doing the best with him, then taking a team without him and doing the best with them. It was perhaps the most remarkable two-year coaching stretch in NBA history, as the Bulls came within one foul call of getting back to the Eastern Conference Finals and probably the NBA Finals in 1994, without Jordan.

Of course, it wouldn't have been the Bulls without some commotion. Pippen opened the season on the injured list, and Scott Williams would miss half the season with a knee injury. The team would eventually dump troubled Stacey King for Luc Longley, and Pippen would launch into a series of embarrassments—an arrest, later dismissed, for gun possession; charges that the fans in Chicago were racists; statements that the Bulls should reward Horace Grant with a new contract, not Toni Kukoc; all leading up to his infamous refusal to play the last 1.8 seconds of Game 3 of the Eastern Conference Finals because Jackson had called the potential game-winning play for Kukoc and not Pippen.

Grant, entering the final season on his contract, was accused by management of sitting out of games to save himself for free agency. Grant volleyed back that he would leave the Bulls no matter what their offer and announced on national TV that he would go to Orlando, which resulted in a tampering charge against the Magic from the Bulls. And this was a quiet season.

There also was the continuing rupture of the relationship between Jackson and Armstrong. Armstrong never liked the Bulls' offensive system, which made him mostly a spot-up shooting guard, not unlike John Paxson. Armstrong saw himself as so much more, a guard who could run the team, play screen/roll on defenders, and use his one-on-one skills; Jackson never believed Armstrong had such skills. He believed that Armstrong thought himself far better than he was, and he preferred Kerr's grasp and acceptance of the offense better than Armstrong's. Jackson would also say, somewhat defensively, that John Paxson was really the starting guard, but just replaced by Armstrong because of injury.

But with Jordan gone, Armstrong got a big fan boost after a quick-scoring start and was voted to the All-Star team by the fans.

"Must have been a lot of fourteen-year-olds voting," Jackson told reporters one day. "You see the ballots in those teen magazines."

Armstrong was weak on defense, and after he made the All-Star team, a series of guards including Mark Price, Eric Murdock, John Stockton, and Kevin Johnson took turns whipping him in personal one-on-one duels during games. When Armstrong would try to retaliate, Jackson would either pull him from the game or scream at him to run the offense. Armstrong would sulk, and in a game against Phoenix in February 1994 and a month later in a game against Philadelphia, Armstrong's temper got the better of him, as he cursed out Jackson on the bench and kicked over some chairs on the way to his seat.

Armstrong would always downplay the flare-ups in the media, but he told Grant that Jackson said things were going too well for him—the All-Star selection, the higher scoring average, the national attention with the Bulls doing well—that Armstrong needed a little adversity in his life.

"Phil's an asshole," Armstrong told Grant. Grant offered no rebuttal.

Armstrong asked to be traded after the season, but the Bulls said they could find no takers and eventually let Armstrong go to Toronto in expansion in the summer of 1995. Jerry Krause didn't care much one way or the other. He had long wanted Kukoc as the starting point guard; only inspired play by

Armstrong in the 1993 Finals kept the Bulls from letting him become a free agent then. Jackson, however, said Kukoc would never play that position for him, that Kukoc's defensive deficiencies were too great and he was best suited to be a sixth man off the bench.

More fireworks.

As the Bulls went into the All-Star break in 1994, with the trading deadline approaching, Jackson promised the team that a deal would be made for another scorer. Dallas veteran Derek Harper had been a possibility; he had said publicly that he wanted to join the Bulls. Harper could play either guard position, and in the Bulls system, since the point guard was mostly a shooter, the off guard and small forward (Pippen) did most of the ball handling and distribution. At the time, the Bulls were still using journeyman Pete Myers as Jordan's replacement at shooting guard.

But the Knicks had lost starting point guard Doc Rivers to a severe knee injury, and they quickly traded for Harper.

Heading into the All-Star break with a 37–16 record and a chance to pull away in the East, Jackson wanted Philadelphia's Jeff Hornacek, whom the 76ers were ready to deal. Pippen was lobbying for the Clippers' Ron Harper, and after the Knicks obtained Derek Harper in January, Pippen lashed out: "If people expect the Bulls to contend, we have to have something to go to war with. We have guys who have trade value. We have to do something."

Just days before the trading deadline, Jackson was at war with Krause over Hornacek. They were already dueling about strength coach Al Vermeil's weight training regimen, Jackson claiming that weight workouts caused injuries. The staff used to joke that Jackson preferred chanting and meditation as a way to build muscles; Jackson had once even tried to prevent Kukoc from having his tonsils removed because he believed the body shouldn't be disturbed and every part was there for a reason.

Jackson was serious about the Hornacek deal. But Krause wasn't about to relinquish the team's first-round draft pick, which is what the Sixers wanted. It was the philosophical chasm the two could never bridge. Once after Krause had raved about several young players, Jackson spat: "How many times have I told you, you win with men, not boys!" But it was Krause's contention that a team should never trade its top pick before the season was over in case of a major injury; if something should happen to a key player and the team had a terrible finish, that draft pick would suddenly be a lot higher and extremely valuable. Jackson insisted that the Bulls needed to go for a championship now.

"You only want to keep that pick to justify that scouting staff of yours," Jackson said.

Krause was furious. He loved the draft and had one of the largest full-time scouting staffs in the league, men he was bringing up just as Krause had been by his own heroes, scouts like Freddy Hasselman and Tony Lucadello.

"I'm your boss, I can fire you," Krause raged at Jackson, insisting that the Bulls were good enough as they were.

And had it not been for Hue Hollins, Krause might have been right.

SOMETHING FOUL

Hue Hollins is one of the veteran referees in the NBA, a member of the closed, remote group of gypsies who travel from city to city all winter, men of little reputation and visibility but immense power. Their ability to alter the outcomes of games is almost infinite. That's why the NBA works so hard to shelter them. They are not permitted to grant interviews, and their schedules are secret, so the temptation of gamblers to influence them is lessened.

Chief of officials Darell Garretson, a longtime top official, has worked hard to remove individuality and flamboyance from officiating, striving to create a roving group of automatons. But personality often breaks out. NBA games are extremely difficult to officiate, principally because of the large amount of contact that is permitted. Referees have to maintain order and flow, not always easy in a game of great emotion. So individuals are bound to emerge.

And with individuals come personal preferences and biases. Jake O'Donnell, long regarded as the most proficient and decisive referee on the court today, had long feuded with the Portland Trailblazers. O'Donnell, impatient with the Trailblazers' habit of whining about foul calls, usually found targets in Buck Williams and Clyde Drexler, and often sent a message by putting them in early foul trouble. When Drexler was traded to Houston during the 1994–95 season, he met up with O'Donnell in the playoffs, where O'Donnell ejected him early in one playoff game. Apparently the ejection was so egregious that Drexler's fine was rescinded, and O'Donnell's work in the Finals was over. Garretson had finally found the hammer with which to go after the iconoclastic O'Donnell.

Likewise, the Bulls have long maintained that Hollins would go out of his way to penalize them. In the 1991 playoffs, for instance, the Bulls lost only one game to the 76ers in the Eastern Conference Semifinals, a game in which Hollins was a referee and the 76ers won by two points after shooting forty free throws to the Bulls' nineteen. The Bulls frequently complained to the league, yet Hollins continued to officiate Bulls games as much or more than any other official.

The Bulls were convinced it was a combination of several things that had made the team less than beloved at league headquarters. First, there was the Bulls' lawsuit against the league to keep their games on WGN-TV, which they won. NBA commissioner David Stern refused several entreaties to settle the suit, upset that Reinsdorf had sued his partners, and was determined to win the case. On top of that, the Bulls constantly defied league directives about making players available to the media during their championship runs, and they flouted league authority, knowing that with the Michael Jordan card in their deck, they were immune from retribution. Backs stiffened at league headquarters when the Bulls were involved.

"Everyone is going to be gunning for them now," the

Pacers' Reggie Miller said after Jordan announced his retirement. The Bulls wondered if that included the league.

Hollins would make his most indelible mark on the Bulls in 1994, during the pivotal fifth game of the Eastern Conference Semifinals against the Knicks. After losing the first two in New York (despite Jackson's team field trip on the Staten Island Ferry to relax the team), the Bulls won two back in Chicago in spite of Pippen's 1.8-second sitdown strike in Game 3.

It was in Game 5, with time expiring and the Bulls ahead by one, that the Knicks' Hubert Davis shot and appeared to miss. But suddenly, inexplicably, Hollins called a late foul on Pippen for hitting Davis's arm. Pippen had indeed knocked Davis's arm, but it was well after Davis had shot the ball. Still, the damage was done. Davis converted the two free throws and the Knicks went on to win the bitter seven-game series.

Darell Garretson worked that game with Hollins in what would be Garretson's last season of work on the floor before moving into an administrative position. After the game, Garretson would defend the call, but later in the fall, after a training-camp session with Bulls players about the new rules on hand checking, defense, and three-point shooting, Garretson told *Chicago Tribune* Bulls writer Melissa Isaacson, "All I can say is that it was a terrible call. Those are the types we're paid not to miss."

A few weeks later, just after the opening of the 1994–95 regular season, there was Hollins again. And he was in a foul mood.

He had a Bulls staff member summon Isaacson to the referees' locker room, where he stepped outside and unleashed a string of profanities. Isaacson had tried to contact Hollins after Garretson's statements, but the NBA doesn't allow such contacts and refused to help. Hollins screamed at Isaacson that he would have been available to talk. Isaacson asked for comment right then.

"I don't have anything to say," Hollins screamed. "Get it fucking right."

That night, with Hollins officiating, the lowly Dallas

Mavericks would beat the Bulls in overtime in Chicago, with Scottie Pippen getting a technical foul called on him two minutes into the game after complaining that Jamal Mashburn ran into him. Jackson called Hollins's officiating irresponsible and brutish and said Hollins took an anti-Bulls attitude into the game. Jackson also noted Hollins's attack on Isaacson, saying, "It told me he had an attitude about the game before it even started."

Jackson would be fined $10,000 by the league for improper comments about the officiating, and the league would continue to send Hollins to officiate more Bulls games than any other referee.

Chapter 6

LAST BULL OUT PLEASE TURN OFF THE LIGHTS

Following the harsh playoff loss to the Knicks after the 1993–94 series, it was clear that some changes were going to be made. And no one knew it better than Horace Grant. By the end of June 1994, Grant knew he would be leaving the Bulls; he had been sentimental about leaving the team following the bitter seven-game playoff loss to the Knicks, but he knew he had to move on.

"I was ready to re-sign then even though it would have been the worst thing for me," he recalls.

A few weeks before, in the spring of 1994, Jerry Reinsdorf had invited him to a private meeting at the Berto Center, the Bulls' practice facility. No Krause, no agents, just one-on-one.

"Let's work out a deal," Reinsdorf said. He scribbled some figures on a piece of paper and asked Grant to do the same. Then they compared: Reinsdorf was proposing a five-year deal worth about $20 million, with $6 million the first year. Grant was suggesting $22.5 million.

Reinsdorf was not about to get into any crazy bidding wars; he refused to make an offer only to have a player shop it around and then come back for a better one. He had always bristled about the insanity of sports economics and the partnerships he was forced into, such as his uneasy alliance with the other NBA owners, whom he essentially had to sue to keep his television deal with superstation WGN. He couldn't believe

that Charlotte, for instance, had given Larry Johnson an extension to make $84 million over twelve years, even when he had
several years left on his current contract. And now such deals
were becoming, in effect, "market value." Reinsdorf wondered
why he should have to pay whatever his dumbest competitor
paid.

So he was ready to pay Grant and be done with it.
Reinsdorf said he'd make up the difference in easily obtainable
incentives.

What happened next depends upon who tells the story.
According to Reinsdorf, Grant was beaming, saying he'd never
been offered anything like that. Reinsdorf said, "We have a
deal then?" Grant agreed, according to Reinsdorf, but said he
had to talk to his agent. Grant later said his only thought was,
"I've got to get out of here." He didn't sign anything, which he
later pointed to as proof of his lack of interest. They shook
hands and left. Reinsdorf, a man who'd made hundreds of
deals over the years on handshakes, felt his handshake with
Grant was good enough.

When Grant left Reinsdorf's office, Phil Jackson was waiting. "It's the best offer I've ever gotten," Grant said.

It seemed Grant would remain a Bull.

But Grant had no intention of staying with the Bulls.

Horace Grant is a relatively simple man who built himself
up from a 207-pound weakling when he joined the Bulls to a
245-pound powerhouse who could outlift friends who played
for the Chicago Bears. He was always a favorite among his
teammates, innocent and brutally honest, outgoing and cheer-
ful. But he was always a follower. When he and Pippen were
close during their years with the Bulls, it was Pippen always
leading the way, buying the first car, the clothes, the big fighting dogs. Grant would follow, buying almost identical items
for years. In their early years as teammates, they would
exchange a dozen phone calls a day, asking anything from
what the other was wearing that day to what the other was
having for a pregame meal.

The friendship cooled in later years when Grant married

and divorced, and Pippen, who was previously divorced, began living with a woman. Grant had found religion, going off to a Christian camp one summer with several other athletes, including David Robinson and A. C. Green. He often read from a Bible in the locker room before games, the Bible becoming his window of hope as he viewed a better NBA world outside the Bulls' walls.

Grant had had a wild, untamed life when he and Pippen were rookies. He discovered that life in the NBA fast lane was supersonic, so much so that the NBA has a group insurance policy for players with children born out of wedlock. Quite a change of pace for a small-town kid from rural Sparta, Georgia, one of four children brought up by his mother, Grady, in what Grant called "southern projects." His twin, Harvey, who is minutes younger, went to Clemson with Horace but transferred to Oklahoma before making it in the NBA like his brother.

Grant had managed to keep a little of the small-town kid in him as he joined the adult world. He still watches cartoons—he particularly likes the X-Men—and revels in old reruns of *The Andy Griffith Show* and 1950s and 1960s rock-and-roll music. But he also studies Greek mythology and likens himself to Hercules for his inner strength and Apollo for his sunny good humor. And once, during the playoffs a few years back, Grant befriended a homeless man in Philadelphia, bringing the man a few meals and getting him a room for a few nights. The staggering division between this man's poverty and Grant's good fortune and wealth left Grant bewildered for some time to come.

But at the same time, he could grow angry and frustrated over what he perceived as the Bulls' mistreatment and lack of respect for him, despite making about $2 million per season. He could be hard to figure out: Teammates would rally behind him as he'd stand up to Jordan or Jackson and as he'd give himself up on the basketball court to set screens and get an offensive rebound so someone else could get a shot. Then they'd shake their heads as Grant would fume openly in the media about private team matters and battles he'd have with management.

Now Grant was leading the charge to get out of Chicago, away from Jerry Krause and Phil Jackson as soon as possible. He was tired of the mental games Jackson played with him, sick of Krause. He was ready for a change and virtually certain he would sign a free-agent contract with the Orlando Magic.

Pippen never believed Grant would go, despite all their talks to the contrary and Grant's almost daily promises that he would leave when he was a free agent. Pippen had heard it for years, and he'd laugh and say, "G., you're not going anywhere."

"You'll see, you'll see," Grant would counter.

And they would. Later that day following his meeting with Reinsdorf, Grant called his agent, Jimmy Sexton, to say that Reinsdorf had tried to sign him to a deal without Sexton present and that he didn't want to sign with the Bulls. Reinsdorf later received a call from Sexton. We're not making any deals, said Sexton, who was not pleased that Reinsdorf was negotiating directly with Grant. They had plenty of interest from other teams, and Grant was pursuing all his options. And, Sexton stressed, Grant had in no way accepted Reinsdorf's offer.

Reinsdorf knew it was over. The only way he'd even consider reopening talks, he said, was if Grant personally came to see him. Krause was still certain that Grant would return, but Jackson, like Reinsdorf, knew Grant was gone. Grant no longer could accept Jackson's verbal lashings as motivation, and Jackson felt Grant had lost the playful quality in his anger toward the Bulls. In particular, Grant had not appreciated Jackson's comments that since Grant missed so many games, "He should sign on a sixty-game basis rather than eighty-two."

As for Grant, this had gone way beyond the usual management-player feuds: He said that the Bulls had a slave-owner mentality toward their players and that he didn't even want the Bulls to make an offer.

But the Bulls had never lost a free agent they'd aimed to keep, and Krause believed Grant would return. The Bulls had examined the salary cap maneuverability of the teams Grant most liked and decided none could make a significant offer.

But many were prepared to. The Pistons and Clippers, two teams Grant was not particularly interested in, were offering $5-million-per-year deals. The Lakers couldn't offer as much, but Lakers owner Jerry Buss is regarded as one of the few trustworthy owners in sports, and Grant liked general manager Jerry West's honesty. The Mavericks were a possibility, as were the Hornets, but Grant backed off Charlotte when team president Spencer Stolpen said he wouldn't renegotiate a short-term deal, which was what Grant would have to sign with the top teams that had so many high-salaried players. Stolpen changed his mind the next day, but Grant refused to return for more talks, saying Stolpen reminded him too much of Krause. Grant already had been to the Michigan estate of Magic owner Rich DeVos and had been treated royally on a visit to Orlando.

The Bulls, even with Grant threatening to leave, refused to court him as he wanted. He said he knew it was sophomoric, but he still liked it.

Grant had decided on Orlando when the Knicks made one last pitch. They had a plan to sign Grant and trade Charles Oakley to Seattle for Kendall Gill and put a younger team around Patrick Ewing for the next several years.

"You owe us one for signing Harvey Grant to an offer sheet," Knicks president Dave Checketts told Grant's agent Sexton.

Sexton also represents Pippen and Horace's twin, Harvey, who got an offer from the Knicks when he was a free agent in Washington, which resulted in the Bullets giving Harvey a long-term deal. Checketts wanted one shot at Horace as a payback.

Why not? Sexton thought. What a great way to get back at Krause—to sign with the hated Knicks, he told Grant. The Bulls felt nothing but hatred for the Knicks, fueled by countless incidents, including a playoff series when the Knicks arranged for renowned heckler Robin Ficker (a Washington attorney famous for taunting at Bullets games) to sit behind the Bulls bench. Krause was furious and cursed out Checketts and deputy Ernie Grunfeld and threatened to file a protest with the league. Then there was Jackson, constantly taunting Knicks coach Pat Riley from afar, questioning Riley's highly militaristic, controlling ways, and complaining how Riley had refused to let the Knicks' coaches shake the hands of the Bulls' coaches after games. Even after the 1993–94 season, with the Bulls out of the playoffs and the Knicks facing the Pacers trailing three games to two, Jackson condemned the Riley-induced Knicks style of basketball that was uglying the game. He also said Riley whined too much and played to the media too much, that he was more image than substance. Riley seethed, Checketts grimaced.

"He knows how to get to Pat," Checketts admitted.

Grant met with Checketts at Sexton's Tennessee office, but in the end, there would be no deal. Orlando and a young core built around Shaquille O'Neal and Anfernee Hardaway was a lot more inviting than New York and an aging Patrick Ewing.

Just as Grant was about to sign with the Magic, Reinsdorf held an unexpected press conference. Reinsdorf, who was taking considerable heat from Bulls fans for not doing everything possible to keep Grant, told his side of the story. Grant reneged on their deal, he said, and they could do no more in their efforts to sign him. Furthermore, Grant, who had missed a career-high twelve games that season, was malingering, and his absences had probably cost the Bulls a shot at a championship, since absences translate into losses, which translate into loss of home-court advantage in the playoffs, Reinsdorf said.

"I've always known that sports morality is different than most businesses," said Reinsdorf. "But there comes a time when you have to draw the line. So I've decided to say goodbye to Horace Grant."

Grant's buttons were there for the pushing, and he would never be able to get past Reinsdorf's comments. For months after he'd gone to the Magic, he was still ripping into Krause and Reinsdorf.

"They had a big press conference when Michael retired, they had one for Paxson, I guess I should feel honored," Grant said, trying to humor himself.

Months later, when the Magic would defeat the Bulls and Jordan in the Eastern Conference Semifinals, Grant would be the star. When he was criticized for taunting the Bulls after the last game by waving a towel, he explained he wasn't insulting the fans: "I had a jelly doughnut in there and I was showing it to Krause." He put a dartboard in his house with a likeness of Krause in the center. Asked about bad taste, he shot back: "Ask Jerry Reinsdorf."

The worst for the Bulls was that Grant backed it up on the court.

"He really stuck it up our asses, I'll say that," Reinsdorf admitted after the playoffs.

THE MOST FAMOUS MAN FROM ARKANSAS—WHO CAN DUNK

It was in the midst of the Horace Grant ordeal that the Bulls made headlines again.

They traded Pippen to the Seattle Supersonics.

Or at least they thought they had.

Pippen had committed two unforgivable crimes. One, he sat down on the bench in a playoff game with 1.8 seconds left. And two, he refused to admit he'd made a mistake.

In Game 3 of that wild playoff series against the Knicks, with the Bulls trailing the Knicks two games to none, the game was tied with less than two seconds to play. With time for only one play, Jackson called for a time-out and then called the play that would redefine Scottie Pippen's career: Kukoc would get the ball. Pippen refused to go in.

It seemed as though Pippen might actually go back into the game after Jackson called a second time-out amid the chaos on the bench, Bill Cartwright yelling at Pippen that the team needed him, Pippen stone-faced and determined, but weakening, assistant Johnny Bach pleading, the crowd in a frenzy about what certainly seemed to be the end of the season. The fans in the old Chicago Stadium were close enough to hear the commotion on the bench.

Then Jackson said, "Fuck him, we'll do it without him."

Pippen sat. And in an amazing twist of luck and irony, Kukoc scored at the buzzer.

After the game, Pippen was confronted boldly by Bill Cartwright who, in tears, said he had no intention of ending his career (Cartwright was planning to retire) with a fellow starter sitting on the bench in defiance, a desertion he couldn't accept, like his wife cheating on him or his kids abandoning him, something he could never have even imagined from someone he trusted.

"When Michael was here, we put up with a lot of his bullshit," Cartwright said as he chastised Pippen in the locker room. "I can't believe you would let us come so far and then be so selfish."

Pippen apologized to the team in a players-only meeting immediately afterward. But he went on to explain why he wasn't wrong and why he'd acted the way he did, that Jackson owed him the chance to win the game, that the bumbling Toni Kukoc had prevented him from doing so on the previous play, and that now, of all humiliations, Jackson was asking Pippen to pass the ball to Kukoc, who would take the game-winning shot—to Kukoc, whom Pippen had routinely brutalized in practice all year.

"Toni would pick up the ball, and Scottie would knock it out of his hands all the way down to the other end of the gym and make Toni get it," recalled Grant. "He was tough on him."

Even Jordan, who occasionally dropped in to watch practices that season and who had tormented more than his share of underachievers, noticed how tough Scottie was on Kukoc.

"Scottie was too impatient with him," said Jordan.

Johnny Bach, the Bulls assistant who was fired after that 1993–94 season and went to the Charlotte Hornets, says he remembers Kukoc, perplexed, coming up to him and asking him about Pippen.

"'He teammate,' Kukoc would say," recalled Bach. "'Why?'"

And Bach would tell him the obvious. "You're a pussy. He's trying to toughen you up."

It was the same way Jordan treated players whom he considered weak. Show me, Pippen was saying, you're strong enough to stand up. If you can stand up to me, you'll stand up to anyone.

Kukoc would shrug.

Unfortunately for Kukoc, he was viewed as a favorite of Krause, thus making him an enemy of the rest of the team. Bill Cartwright, the veteran center, would always shake his head watching the players torment Kukoc.

"They'd try to kill him, embarrass him," said Cartwright. "Some saw him as a threat."

It was more of a test, though, not unlike what virtually all foreign NBA players have gone through in the United States. Even the late Drazen Petrovic, who was on the verge of being an All-Star when he was killed in an auto accident after the 1992–93 season, was often rejected by his Nets teammates, reviled for his personal habits, and left virtually alone on the road, just as Kukoc was when he first came to the Bulls.

It was one thing to harass and bully a teammate in practice. But Pippen's actions in that crucial playoff game represented the ultimate sin in a team sport, an outright defiance of the coach, personal mutiny.

Yet Pippen never wavered when asked about the circumstances again.

"I'd do the same thing," he said, which didn't surprise friends and those who knew Pippen well, like former Bulls coach Doug Collins.

"He is very stubborn," says Collins, "which can be a blessing and a curse. It's very difficult for him to stand up and admit a mistake, like he never quite said he was sorry about that 1.8 seconds or some of the other things that have happened to him [like calling Bulls fans racists when they cheered Kukoc and booed other players, and being arrested for weapons possession]. He's like Charles Barkley in that way, like when he supposedly made a comment about whites. They go on the attack, they go in all different directions. They won't back off."

Pippen wears a tough shell, designed to cushion him from

the endless blows of negative publicity. There was the migraine headache in the seventh game of the 1990 Eastern Conference Finals that led Jordan to tell Reinsdorf he should trade Pippen because Pippen had no heart, the humiliating taunting by Xavier McDaniel during the 1992 playoffs about Pippen's lack of toughness, the arrests for weapons possession and alleged battery on his girlfriend, the walkout in the playoff game, the battles with fans and management, the trade rumors. Yet never has Pippen withdrawn on the basketball court, his game seeming almost to improve with every incident, his mental state undeterred.

"I think people understand me, [but] maybe not the Bulls," said Pippen, whose long face is dominated by a broad nose and wide-set, sleepy eyes. He carries the demeanor of someone who is suspicious and wary, someone who has endured much and survived.

"They understand why I didn't take that ball out. They understand my feelings about Krause. Krause is in love with Kukoc. He'd send him gifts when he was still in Europe," said Pippen. Krause had once sent Kukoc luggage when he played in Italy, which the coaches found amusing, since much of the luggage was made there in the first place.

"He thinks he's going to be Michael. He's no Michael. It's totally ridiculous the way they praised this guy and paid him and treated the rest of us like they did. The fans understand why I want out of here. Hey, I'm the highest qualified person and you should be rewarded that way. You're not going to tell Phil Jackson that Jimmy Rodgers is coming in here and going to make more money than him. I'm the highest qualified person, I should receive the highest benefit.

"With that 1.8 seconds, that's the moment of the game you live for," said Pippen. "And I felt it was an injustice the way Phil treated me. Do you think teams are saying, 'We've got to stop Kukoc?, Or, 'We've got to stop Pippen?' I had to say something, whether it was the wrong time or the wrong thing. Maybe the opportunity would never come again. It was the right thing to do for me.

"When it comes down to speaking and voicing your opinion, if you don't say what you feel you're cheating yourself," said Pippen. "You're allowing people to run over you. I'm not going to be a phony like some guys, afraid to voice my opinion.

"The Bulls want somebody to go out and be quiet and they get guys like that," says Pippen. "But I'm no slave to anyone. This is my job; I'm not their slave. You do the work and say nothing and they'll be thinking they're your master. Krause is always telling me, 'Be quiet.' No more. He doesn't want to face me anymore. They know they can't control me."

But they could trade him, and in June 1994, as Horace Grant was preparing to make his own exit, and just before the collegiate draft, the Bulls thought they had. It would be Pippen for Shawn Kemp with an exchange of draft picks; the Bulls would then use that Seattle pick (from Charlotte) to move up in the draft and take shooting guard Eddie Jones. The plan seemed brilliant, an All-Star power forward in Kemp to replace Grant, the draft pick for Jones, who projected out as an athletic guard in the mold of Jordan, and then the big salary slots from Jordan and Cartwright to go after free agents now that the Bulls wouldn't need Ron Harper.

But Seattle owner Barry Ackerly got cold feet just minutes before the deal was to be agreed upon. Kemp was wildly popular in Seattle, Pippen had the reputation of a bad guy surrounded by controversy, and the now famous 1.8-second walk-out hadn't exactly endeared him to the national audience. As rumors of the trade swept through Seattle, swarms of Sonics fans called a local radio station owned by Ackerly to protest. Coach George Karl was urging Ackerly to make the deal; Karl had conferred with none other than Michael Jordan, who said that Seattle was getting the better of the deal. Jackson, too, had his doubts about Kemp, about whether Kemp, who never even played college basketball, could adjust to the system and give up his offense to rebound and block shots.

"We'd have ruined him, too," Jackson joked later.

But it was a tremendous opportunity to put the pieces of a potential championship team in place for years, one without

Jordan and created by Krause. But when Ackerly pulled out, it looked like Scottie would remain a Bull, at least for now.

When Pippen heard about the trade, he was at home in Arkansas, and he was stunned. But Pippen was in the right place to accept what could only be seen as the Bulls' rejection of him.

Yvette DeLeon, his then girlfriend and mother of his child, with whom Pippen split after DeLeon filed battery changes that she later dropped, urged Pippen to embrace the deal when word began to leak out.

"Scottie was the star, and then to focus that play around Kukoc was a joke, almost like belittling Scottie," she said. "I took it as an insult, like he did. He always said if you believe in something you have to speak out for yourself. And he did the right thing as far as he was concerned. So why should he have to take it back? He had nothing to apologize for."

Pippen's personal story is one of the most remarkable never-thought-he'd-make-it tales in sports literature. The youngest from a family of twelve, with a brother crippled and his father disabled, Pippen wasn't even a particularly noteworthy athlete in high school in Hamburg, Arkansas. He wasn't offered any college scholarships, even to the smaller colleges in Arkansas. As the youngest in the family, he sought to graduate from college, perhaps get a job in recreation at a park, and went to the University of Central Arkansas on a work-study grant after a recommendation from his high school coach.

Arch Jones, then the assistant coach, thought Pippen had potential enough to make the team, so they gave him a job as equipment manager, picking up towels, cleaning the locker room. "He was kind of shy," recalls Jones. "He seemed to have some potential as a basketball player, so we said we'd take care of him with a work-study grant. We let him be our manager and then he could work out with the team some.

"You could see he had some ability," Jones recalled. "He had those long arms, but as far as becoming a great player, no one could have any idea. He was the manager. He'd sweep the locker room floor, wash the clothes, put the equipment out for the players, bring the balls out. He never complained about it.

He seemed to like what he was doing, liked hanging around
with the guys. Because once you get to know him on a personal
basis, you find he's a super person, congenial, gets along well,
has that smile that radiates that certain warmth you can feel.
But that he'd become one of the best players in the NBA? No
way anyone thought that."

At about six one and 150 pounds out of high school—"like
a stick," Jones recalled—Pippen sprouted to almost six seven,
and suddenly was a graceful gazelle, his long arms extending
toward the basket, but with the instincts of a guard, which he
was as he first learned the game.

He went on to become the best player on the UCA team,
which was like being the biggest guy in a midget's club. But
word started to circulate about this player from Central
Arkansas, and Krause, always looking for a "find," sent then
scout Billy McKinney down to look at him. McKinney, however, reported back that the competition was so poor that it was
hard to tell if Pippen was any good. He looked to be a second-
round pick, McKinney said.

The rest, though, is history. Brilliant performances in the
postseason predraft NBA camps rocketed Pippen to the number five pick in the draft. Grant was grabbed tenth by the Bulls,
and Krause earned the 1987–88 Executive of the Year award for
his efforts. The foundation that would lead to three Bulls championships was in place.

But that was all in the past, and the future was looking
uncertain at best. Pippen took comfort in the safety of his home
in Hamburg, with his family and friends around him. After his
father died in 1990, his mother hadn't wanted to move, so
Scottie purchased most of the surrounding properties and combined them into one parklike area where friends frequently
gathered for games and picnics. It was also back in Arkansas
that Pippen ran a basketball camp in the summer with his mentor, Jones, now the UCA head coach, and spent considerable
time with Jones's handicapped daughter.

"He always calls to ask about her, comes over to swim with
her," says Jones.

But that's not the Pippen people see.

"I know people say I'm arrogant," Pippen acknowledges, "and I guess that's due to some of the incidents that have happened. But I don't get caught up in image, just trying to be myself and enjoy myself. I'm Scottie. I'm human. I say what I want and if people view that is the right thing, fine. If not, fine. My friends who have known me awhile, if you asked them, they'll say, 'He's the same person,' that they can't tell any difference in our relationship.

"I watch TV and videos, I like to play board games and hang around with my family, my brothers and cousins. I don't go around saying I have all these celebrity friends. Like Michael and Charles [Barkley]. To me that's one of the phoniest relationships I've ever seen. Karl Malone is a friend of mine, but I won't say he's this great friend like you hear Michael and Barkley are these great friends. Guys like Barkley, he's one of those players who only gives respect to the superstars, Michael, Larry [Bird]. But it's all a front. He kisses their butts. Not me. I'm satisfied to be at my house in Chicago, on my boat, or back home in Arkansas with the people I know."

So although Pippen was angry about the trade, particularly upset that the Bulls never told him they were trying to trade him and disgusted that Krause kept denying it, he tried to view it as yet another challenge, something else to overcome.

"The thing about life is things come at you and it's a question of how you handle it," says Pippen, his stony expression belying a puckish streak that reveals itself only to his closest friends. "Like even making it to the NBA, having that migraine and coming back, the press never forgetting, the 1.8-second thing, X [McDaniel] talking and running his mouth in the playoffs. It's always a test of your manhood.

"I wasn't one of the guys the league promoted, like Michael and Charles and David Robinson and Karl. I was a player who had to work his way up, and I'm proud of that. I'm also proud of what we did last year without Michael, and if they had kept Horace I know we would have won sixty games [in 1994–95].

"Winning those championships," recalled Pippen, "guarding Magic, a guy I used to idolize, playing with Michael and learning from him, that team we had, a team we felt could turn it on and off whenever we wanted, almost like having a switch—those were the greatest times in my life. But they broke it up, so why should I want to stay?"

In the end, though, Pippen would stay. And Grant would go.

It was Pippen's greatest fear, the recognition that things can change so suddenly, that you can lose all control. The way his father lost the ability to support his family. The way his brother lost the use of his legs. The way Grant was leaving, as Michael did before him.

Everything had changed, and there was nothing Pippen could do about it.

Chapter 7

THE STORM BEFORE THE STORM: THE 1994–95 SEASON BEGINS

As the Bulls prepared to open the 1994–95 season, the best thing that could be said was that they had somehow managed to pull a team together. Jackson told a friend before the season that he thought he might be facing his first losing season as a coach. "This team could win thirty-five games, it could win fifty games," he admitted.

He decided at the last minute, just before camp started, to allow Pippen to remain a co-captain, hoping that Pippen's anger over Grant's departure had subsided and that Pippen was more contrite about his behavior in the playoffs the previous year. Jackson also feared that the players' salaries might become an issue with Pippen, since Kukoc had become the team's highest paid player, signing a six-year deal for more than $4 million per year, a contract about which Jackson jokingly said, "He'd have to go to the black market in Serbia to get himself a deal like that." Ron Harper, a free agent from the Clippers, was second, making just under $4 million per year. Armstrong was the third highest paid player. And finally, there was Pippen, the team's fourth highest paid player, even though Jackson was telling Pippen that he would have to lead the team in scoring, rebounding, and assists for the Bulls to have any reasonable chance at success. Pippen also would go on to lead the team in blocks and steals, matching a one-season all-around effort only previously achieved by former-Celtic MVP Dave Cowens. Much of Pippen's accomplishment, however, would be forgotten and overlooked with Jordan's celebrated return.

But despite the disparity in paychecks, Pippen would remain confident for a while, bolstered by a preseason talk with Jordan, who knew firsthand what it was like to have less talented players making lots more money.

"Scottie now understands the business of the game," said Jordan, who had told Pippen to block out his personal feelings about management.

"I told Phil he won't have a problem with me," Pippen said as the season opened. "I want to show some leadership and hope this team can make a turnaround."

Though privately expressing his desire to be traded, Pippen would remain quiet and cooperative until late December, when he would blast Krause and accuse him of being incompetent and a liar.

The Bulls had been busy during the off-season. They had picked up veteran power forward Larry Krystkowiak from the Magic as a free agent, re-signed Kerr and Wennington, and eventually brought back Pete Myers. But Grant was gone, and so was Scott Williams, whom the Bulls decided to release. Jackson, who felt he'd supported Williams by working him into the rotation during the title seasons, felt betrayed by Williams's demand for a trade during the 1991–92 season. Williams, likewise, hated Jackson's nickname for him, "Psycho."

Williams's parents had died in a murder-suicide while he was in college, and Williams, usually cordial and friendly, could be prone to violent outbursts of temper and anger. Once on a team trip, he had supposedly broken up a hotel room in a fight with his brother. And Jackson considered him just a part-time player because of his fragile body, something Philadelphia would discover after signing him as a free agent in 1994. But, again, as with Grant and later Armstrong, the Bulls would lose a valuable player without any compensation, a process that was debilitating the team.

Now the Bulls had players like the injury-prone Krystkowiak, rookie Dickey Simpkins (whom Pippen called Dickey Simpson for a few weeks before he finally learned his name), second-year man Corie Blount at power forward, and Luc Longley (who would miss most of the first half of the season with a leg injury).

And Ron Harper. With Jordan gone for good, or so it seemed, the Bulls figured they could slide into that shooting guard position a veteran who'd averaged 20.1 points per game in the 1993–94 season, who had a career scoring average of 19.3, and was perennially among the league leaders in steals.

But Ron Harper was no Michael Jordan.

Heck, he was no Pete Myers.

The much ballyhooed signing of Harper was proving a huge mistake just weeks into training camp. Jackson was stunned at Harper's inability to move side-to-side, a necessary ingredient to play defense, and Harper's habit of always trying to poke the ball away after his opponent had passed him. Harper had never been known as a good shooter, but the Bulls thought his quickness and open-court play would enable them to score more in transition. But Harper was such a liability on defense that Jackson grew uncertain about even playing him.

Harper's signing looked like a mistake that might haunt the team for years with talk already of a "hard" salary cap like the NFL's in the future. The Bulls would be stuck with Harper's approximately $4 million annual salary through 1999.

One of six children of a divorced factory worker from a poor neighborhood in Dayton, Ohio, Harper had a severe stuttering problem as a child, one that still remains obvious, although under control. But Harper blossomed as a basketball player at Miami of Ohio and became a number one draft choice of the Cleveland Cavaliers in 1986 when the Cavaliers were putting together the foundation of the most disappointing team of the era, a group that included Harper, John "Hot Rod"

Williams, Brad Daugherty, and Mark Price but that eventually fell victim to injuries and change.

Harper was the first to go, traded in November 1989 for Danny Ferry, then a highly touted first-round draft pick of the Clippers who refused to play in Los Angeles and had gone to Italy. Although an inconsistent shooter, Harper was a brilliantly athletic scorer not unlike Michael Jordan in many ways. In fact, when the teams played in those days, Harper and Jordan engaged in some legendary dunking duels, and Harper averaged almost 20 points per game during his nearly four years in Cleveland.

But Harper was always the wanna-be. Back in the 1988 playoffs, Harper was enjoying offensive success while he watched Jordan scorch teammate Craig Ehlo, Jordan's legendary victim. It was over Ehlo that Jordan hit his famous shot in the fifth game of the 1989 playoff opener, and against whom he had scored 50 points in the opening game of the 1988 playoffs.

"Michael would never get fifty on me," Harper had said afterward.

So coach Lenny Wilkens put Harper on Jordan in the next game. And Jordan passed 50 midway through the fourth quarter on the way to 55.

Yet it wasn't Harper's mouth that the Cavaliers were most concerned about. A conservative franchise, the Cavaliers were primarily worried about Harper's friends. Although Harper had escaped the streets, his friends hadn't; some were in trouble with drugs, and although Harper wasn't, word kept circulating that his "associations" were a problem. And Harper had that hard, mean look of a guy who, if he hadn't already committed a crime, was about to.

"A certain general manager [Wayne Embry] thought it would be a very smart move to trade me," said Harper. "They thought what I was doing off the court made me a bad player on the court. I was just living my own life, my own way."

But when Ferry came along, a six-ten white player who was a good shooter and passer and considered to be the next Larry Bird, the Cavaliers made the trade, in part believing that Harper's childhood friends might bring him down.

They wouldn't, but a severe knee injury in 1990 would, robbing the six-six 200-pounder of that edge that separates good players from great players. Harper just played out his contract with the Clippers, scoring and not caring about much else.

By that time, Harper had befriended Scottie Pippen, and Pippen was urging the Bulls to sign him.

It had, of course, been a horrible summer of 1994 for the team. Horace Grant left for Orlando as a free agent, Scott Williams signed with the 76ers, Bill Cartwright signed with Seattle, and John Paxson retired. Wennington and Kerr were awaiting better offers from the Bulls while talking with other teams.

The Bulls began to panic. Jackson urged Krause to sign someone, lest the team end up replacing their stars with castoffs. And Harper was one of that group of players around the NBA whom Krause had always eyed, stopping to chat whenever he'd seen him, wondering how he might pull off a deal someday and perhaps steal him away. But there would be no heist this time.

The Bulls had eyes for Harper, but so had the Knicks. And the Knicks were now pressing. They would sign Harper for the $1.2 million one-year salary slot they had open. The Bulls were interested, and Harper took a tough stance.

The Bulls had two salary slots open, the slots being the major way for teams to add players despite being over the salary cap. One was Cartwright's $2.4 million slot expiring in July 1995; the other was Jordan's $2 million slot expiring in November. But Harper's agent, Mark Termini, who had gone through two unhappy experiences with the Bulls with clients Brad Sellers and Dennis Hopson, was going to make the Bulls blink first.

If the Bulls didn't come up with the larger slot, and for five years, Harper would sign immediately with the Knicks. At the same time Pippen was having difficulty accepting that Grant really was gone. Most of the top free agents had already signed elsewhere, and he was threatening to hold out from training camp if the Bulls did not sign Harper.

Jackson interceded. "I thought it would help Scottie, show the organization was doing something for him," Jackson said.

Harper did not take a physical exam, although it was routine in the NBA in player transactions, especially with a large-dollar signing. But Harper had averaged 20 points the year before with the Clippers, and at age thirty said he was fully recovered from his knee problems.

The Bulls flinched a little and accepted. It would be the tying of the team's hands behind its back before the blindfold was put on.

It wasn't long afterward, when it was clear that Harper had little left in his career and Krause was being criticized in the media, that Krause started saying it was Pippen's fault, that the Bulls wouldn't have signed Harper if Pippen hadn't been so adamant.

"Yeah, I wanted Ron," Pippen agreed. "But the one I told them to sign was Horace. That's who I wanted most. And where is he?"

Players joked that the Bulls, notorious for their hard-bargaining ways, had given Harper a pension. Jordan, in a conversation with *New York Post* writer Peter Vecsey when Harper was talking with the Knicks, said the signing would be a mistake, that Harper was too undisciplined, fundamentally weak, an old player. Jordan didn't give Harper much thought—until he discovered Harper would be earning more than him.

"Four million for that," Jordan muttered to reporters.

It was becoming obvious that the Bulls would be powerless to challenge the best teams in the league. The Bulls had dismantled like no championship team in sports history: Jordan, Grant, Williams, Paxson, Cartwright—all gone, and Pippen would have joined the pack had the Seattle trade gone through.

Bill Cartwright had apparently retired with chronically bad knees but was then offered a deal by Seattle; he would play one more season before being bought out of his contract in the summer of 1995. Krause would try to bring back Cartwright as a coach for the 1995–96 season, but Cartwright was determined to remain on the West Coast. Unlike the other veteran Bulls, he got along reasonably well with Krause, and Krause virtually idolized Cartwright.

Cartwright, admittedly from the so-called "old school" of basketball, watched mostly in amazement from the bench in his one season in Seattle. He remembers telling coach George Karl that the team's offense was too scattered, too disorganized. Karl explained that the team was organized because of its disorganization, that if the team was disorganized, opponents couldn't figure their patterns and defend them well, and hence, they were organized by virtue of their disorganization.

Cartwright would just roll his eyes. The Sonics never did make it beyond the first round of the playoffs, contrary to everyone's expectations, and Cartwright moved his family back to Sacramento, presumably for the final time, although he agreed to do some scouting for Seattle.

Another missing piece of the championship puzzle was John Paxson, the only one among the championship starting five never to be an All-Star, the shooter who was a true hero in the 1991 and 1993 Finals. He had joined the broadcasting team and was doing color commentary on the radio for sixty games.

It had been toughest on Paxson, who had fallen out of the starting lineup for the 1992–93 season, even though it was his symbolic 3-pointer against Phoenix in Game 6 that season that wrapped up the Bulls' third straight title. The following year, he dragged himself through one final season before retiring.

Paxson's retirement in early 1994 received far less attention than his world-famous teammate's. Asked the night of Jordan's nationally televised retirement celebration when his own retirement ceremony would be, Paxson said, "I think that was it."

He missed the game, but more than anything he missed the team, the guys, and he had decided he wanted to coach someday, to join Jackson's staff, something he would do starting in the 1995–96 season.

If Jordan embodied near perfection and effortless grace and beauty on the basketball court, Paxson symbolized the struggle of lesser players. A kid who had to be held back in eighth grade to even be good enough to compete in high school, Paxson went on to excel at Notre Dame and become a low first-round draft pick of the San Antonio Spurs in 1983. It was a two-year deal, $85,000 the first year and $95,000 the second, and Paxson stayed in the NBA only because of that guaranteed second year. Paxson had innocently chosen Larry Fleisher, then head of the players association, as his agent, not knowing of Spurs' owner Angelo Drossos's dislike for Fleisher. Paxson got caught in the middle and became an unwanted holdout, the irony being that after Paxson's 1991 starring role in the Finals, it would be the Spurs who would bid for him as a free agent, pushing the Bulls' $800,000 one-year offer to $1.25 million for three years. "I'm paying you more than I should," Reinsdorf reluctantly told Paxson when he signed.

This time, Paxson had the last laugh, since the year before, Paxson had asked for only $750,000, comparable to Craig Hodges. The Bulls had said no. In fact, had Paxson not hit those five jumpers in the final game of the 1991 Finals against the Lakers, shooting better than 60 percent in the series, the Bulls probably would have let him go.

Which wouldn't have been a big surprise, since the Bulls always seemed to be looking for a replacement for Paxson. Back in 1985, the Bulls had bought his contract from the Spurs, and then brought in a half dozen other guards to replace him. Yet he held on, and Jordan loved having him on the court. Even when Jordan returned to the Bulls in March, he would often come up to Paxson and ask, more seriously than not, "Bring your sneakers today?"

Ironically, Paxson had signed with the Bulls when Jordan broke his foot during the 1985–86 season and missed most of the year. But Jordan always remembered the two playing together on an international team when they were in college and Paxson hitting a winning shot. He had also soured on the long succession of point guards who couldn't, such as Steve Colter, Sam Vincent, Rory Sparrow. The Bulls needed a point guard to play with Jordan. Jordan said he was the point guard, too; he just needed a guy to bail him out.

"I felt like I had that niche as the guy to play alongside

Michael," said Paxson. But more than that, he had established himself as a guy who would win in the clutch, as his dramatic shot that won the final game of the 1993 Finals in Phoenix proved. "I had more than one person tell me I should have quit after that," recalled Paxson.

It had been a battle for Paxson after that first championship in 1991. B. J. Armstrong was pushing hard for his job, frustrated at remaining on the bench while Jackson preferred Paxson, demanding to be traded if he couldn't start. Armstrong would take his aggression out on Paxson, beating him during scrimmages, taking him one-on-one and scoring regularly. For his part, Armstrong struggled mightily trying to adapt to Jordan as Paxson had done, while some of the coaches told him he had too much talent to try to replicate Paxson. It confused Armstrong even more. He took books out of the library about genius to try to understand Jordan, someone who was so good that things came too easily for him. It was a struggle: Jordan couldn't adapt to the play of mere mortals like Armstrong, and waved him off time and again in games, as though Armstrong were a kid being sent to his room. Armstrong, with boyish good looks and fleshy cheeks just right for pinching, had to learn to drift off into the corner to take Jordan's bailout passes.

But Armstrong could never do it as well as Paxson, and he knew that Jordan was fighting to keep Paxson in the starting lineup over him, even as Paxson was being eased out during the 1992–93 season. So he tried everything possible to outdo Paxson. But it would never make him acceptable to Jackson.

"I understood where B.J. was coming from," Paxson said. "He didn't have to prove he was better than me at getting to the basket. I knew that. He was a young guy who was talented and wanted to make his mark."

But Jackson felt strongly that Armstrong would never be right to be the lead guard in his system. Only when Paxson was hurt in the third championship season did Armstrong become the starter, and even then Jordan and Pippen privately complained that they'd rather have Paxson in there.

"Phil had confidence in me," said Paxson.

But finally, during the Western Conference swing in February 1994, Paxson got the dreaded DNP–CD: Did Not Play–Coach's Decision. Meaning he could have played, but the coach chose otherwise.

"It was my first in like eight years, and mentally, that's when it clicked that it was over," related Paxson. "It happened several more times that season and I hated it. I'd go home and tell [wife] Carolyn, 'Don't let me forget how I'm feeling now. I don't want to be paid for that anymore.'" John Paxson was never one to walk away from a battle. But when he couldn't run the next season, his knees finally giving way, he was eased out of the regular rotation and toward retirement.

"You're always told in the NBA, superstars are the key to the game," said Paxson. "And you hear it so much you start to buy into it. I always came from team backgrounds, and when you're in the NBA you start hearing all that and get to stop thinking of yourself as important, you're not an All-Star, you're not scoring in double figures. But I was able to play a role and do the right things and the team benefited. That was special."

It was Jackson's hope entering the 1994–95 season that his current players would feel the way Paxson had. Although Pippen was a star, he was still the ultimate team player, and Jackson was optimistic that if the right players performed their roles and worked within his system, the team could have some success, despite the loss of Paxson, Cartwright, Williams, Grant, and Jordan from the title teams. It was a long shot.

There was a certain calm about Jackson going into this season, a little more reflection from an unusually reflective man. He would stand aside as Pippen and Krause clashed, and he rarely challenged Krause as he had in the past. It had taken a tragedy to enervate and energize him and renew his passion for life.

A few weeks before the 1994–95 season started, Jackson got a surprise call from an old teammate and roommate from the Knicks, Eddie Mast.

"He just wanted to talk about family, about his kid going to college and playing middle linebacker. I felt it was a special kind of message being sent," Jackson would decide later, "a plan to contact folks he loved before he passed away."

A few weeks later, just after his forty-seventh birthday, Mast died playing pickup basketball.

Jackson had just turned fifty, an age at which many people consider their lives, their mortality. Jackson described his friend: "This knucklehead, a roommate, a companion, a guy I shared philosophically a lot of stuff with, who turned me on to Bob Marley before anyone was into him, a guy who wore green, black, and yellow of the third world, who sang the praises of Rastafarian, a free spirit. He was a lovable guy." Jackson left Bulls camp to attend the funeral and talked with Mast's four school-aged kids.

"It does show the fragility of life," Jackson agreed. "I don't usually look for harbingers and things like that, but I was happy to have known him and to have had our friendship and I came to think about what I do, and while I know it's not something you do forever, I feel I have a feel for it and a passion. And I found as the year went on I renewed my passion for the game and this team and what we could accomplish."

Jackson did hold out some hope, though, saying on the eve of Jordan's retirement ceremony in October: "When Michael crosses the age of thirty-six, I will feel at that point he won't have the abilities to come back. Until that time, he can come back and play basketball at any time. And I wouldn't put it past him. We buried Michael Jordan, number 23 of the Bulls' three-peat championship team. If he came back, it would be a whole new deal. He'd need a week of pregame work and a week of playing, but after a couple of weeks, Michael would be right back into it."

The next night Jordan said he'd never, ever return to basketball.

The Bulls opened their season amid clichés aplenty; they had their ups and downs, peaks and valleys, ins and outs. Win one or two, lose one or two, they went 6–6 for the first month,

3–3 on their western trip in November. They were buried by Houston and then lost by 30 in Utah. With Karl Malone still in the game late, Jackson yelled at Malone, "Still getting your average." Malone laughed and yelled to Jackson, "At least I go in the game when the coach tells me to." Pippen was taking it all well and even had Thanksgiving dinner with Malone and his family when the team was in Salt Lake City.

But injuries were wreaking havoc, and Jackson found himself starting Simpkins, Blount, and free agent Greg Foster, who would not make it through the season. Perdue suffered a broken nose but continued to start and would for the rest of the regular season with Longley out until January with a stress fracture.

But if they weren't artistic to watch, at least they were something to look at. Everyone was making the newest NBA fashion statement: a tattoo.

Foster had the word "Bowie" spelled out on his left arm; people always told him he looked like journeyman center Sam Bowie, now with the Lakers, "So I decided to get a tattoo in tribute to him." Whatever. Toni Kukoc and Ron Harper had sharks, with Harper also adding a Batman symbol. Larry Krystkowiak had a grizzly paw with his number in the middle, and Dickey Simpkins had Wiley E. Coyote dribbling a basketball and holding a bag of money: "It's me getting away with the money after playing basketball," he said. Simpkins had planned to get another with an eight ball (his uniform number), but he said the first one hurt too much. Blount was preparing to have a tarantula engraved on his chest, but he'd have to do it in Los Angeles, as the Bulls would trade him after the season. Even Jordan would fit in later, with his horseshoe brand above his left breast, long a source of some embarrassment and one reason why Jordan always liked to be dressed before talking to reporters after a game.

Fashionable, yes, but Jackson wondered if they were dressed for success.

"My coaches let me know we're going to battle shorthanded," Jackson said.

And it didn't seem Jordan was getting any closer.

He finished the Instructional League season hitting well, finally getting some power into his swing.

"I feel I'm going to come back to spring training a totally different player," an optimistic Jordan told reporters as he left Arizona at the end of November 1994.

"We're just not a good team," Pippen said.

The Bulls hung around the .500 mark and continued a pattern of losing close games, such as their December loss at home to the Nets after leading by 19. There was the loss to Charlotte after leading by 19, and a loss to the Knicks after leading by 22.

Incredibly, Jackson found cause to be optimistic. He felt the Bulls were just one good player short of competing effectively, and he wondered about the players who might have made a difference: Grant and Williams gone, Jeff Hornacek and Derek Harper ineffectively pursued. After an embarrassing 77–63 beating by Cleveland, Jackson said, "Maybe you should ask Jerry [Krause]. I'm just working with what I've got here," Jackson said.

It finally started to become too much for Pippen, who, right after Christmas, earned an ejection for questioning the referees, and the Bulls lost to the Clippers, a team with a 3–23 record and the potential to become the worst team in NBA history.

A few nights later before a game in Boston, sitting calmly and answering questions from Boston writers, Pippen matter-of-factly said Krause had lied to him about the Seattle trade. In fact, he said, "He lies about everything. You don't even bother yourself in dealing with him. He's one of those guys who can look you in the eye and lie."

Pippen also said Krause had mismanaged the team in letting Grant escape without any compensation in return and he wished he could join Grant by getting out of Chicago.

Krause, after being asked by reporters to comment, stalked into the Bulls locker room and started glaring at Pippen.

"What's he looking at," Pippen demanded. "What the hell does he want?"

But Krause kept his distance and wouldn't talk with Pippen.

That Krause was even in the locker room and in Boston was a distraction for the coaching staff and players. Rarely do NBA general managers travel with their teams, believing that a boss-looking-over-your-shoulder feeling isn't conducive to relaxed play and coaching. But Krause traveled more than half the season with the team, far more than any league executive. He simply had little to do and was a basketball junkie anyway.

Krause's travels would ultimately cost Will Perdue dearly. While most players just grimaced and put up with the GM's presence, Perdue took the team's feelings public in a newspaper column he had been writing for a local suburban paper: "For the most part, our entourage consists of twelve players, four coaches, one trainer, one scout, a couple of public relations people—and general manager Jerry Krause, of course. Believe me, I'm not alone in my inability to understand why Jerry accompanies the team on trips so often. It seems that most general managers stay away from the spotlight and work behind the scenes. Not Jerry. When the players know that 'Big Brother' is watching, it just puts more pressure on them. Even when we win the guy is never in a good mood. He's the only real distraction on the trip."

Krause was livid about the column and ordered Perdue to stop.

"He hates the media," Perdue said, "and now he said I was a part of it. He said I'd crossed the line and I was one of those guys instead of us. It's us and them with him. There's no in-between."

Pippen, meanwhile, had plenty of fight in him. He'd decided he'd had enough: He was going to try to force a deal now. Grant was gone, Jordan was gone—there wasn't even anyone around to talk to. Okay, Pippen could socialize with Harper, but Harper seemed so indifferent about the team's success. He seemed to have a losing attitude and didn't even seem to care whether he played, since he never complained of being benched. Pippen had never been on a losing team in the NBA. In fact, only once had a Bulls team of his won fewer than fifty games, and that season, 1988–89, they had gone to the Eastern Conference Finals.

The day after Pippen's explosive comments in Boston, the team was back in Chicago at practice, where two dozen reporters and camera crews were waiting to take their shots. When Pippen walked in he was surprised.

"What are they here for?" he asked Jackson. "For you," Jackson replied. Pippen was stunned; he had no idea his remarks about Krause were big news.

The seething and feuding was growing nastier and more public by the day, but the Bulls still had some basketball to play. They would get a little boost by thumping the Orlando Magic and Horace Grant by an overwhelming 109–77. (Amazingly, they had been successful in beating good teams, such as San Antonio and New York, and, later in the month, Houston.) Pippen arose for a triple double with 26 points, 11 assists, and 10 rebounds, and the Bulls exposed the Magic's ultimate weakness, their inability to cover in transition defense and when teams move the ball. It would come to hurt the Bulls more against the Magic with Jordan back, actually, because Orlando was a team that would lose focus when teams made an extra pass, something that didn't happen much with Jordan on the floor.

"When you work together against them, you can have success," said B. J. Armstrong.

Pippen was feeling so good, he even offered some perspective on Shaquille O'Neal. "If he doesn't get the block [inside post position], he can't do anything," said Pippen. "He won't turn and hit a shot on you. And I don't like his decisions with the ball."

Pippen's composure didn't last long, though. The next night the Bulls went to Philadelphia, where Pippen blasted Krause again.

"The relationship between Krause and me is hate. Trade me or Krause," Pippen demanded. "They could send me anywhere. Nowhere would be as bad as here."

Would the 76ers be interested? "That's Jerry Krause we're talking about," said Sixers coach and general manager John

Lucas, referring to Krause's reputation for demanding exces-
sive prices for his players, one reason the Bulls end up making
so few deals. "He'd want the 'P' in Philadelphia for him."

Jackson summed it up: "I'm going around with a fire extin-
guisher and there's a forest fire."

And then an earthquake. Enraged about a foul call in a
home game against the Spurs on January 24, Pippen had to be
restrained from going after referee Joey Crawford, one of the
best in the game, and then tossed a chair onto the floor in dis-
gust.

The next day he said he had only one regret: "I wish the
chair had been the referee instead."

Kent McDill, the Bulls writer for the suburban *Daily Herald,*
said Pippen told him before the game, "I might have to do
something to make them get rid of me."

Grant had been watching the replays in disbelief that night
on TV and was concerned for his friend. "He wants to be
traded," said Grant. "He's at the end of his rope."

Out west with the team in early February, Pippen averaged
nearly a triple double in six games, as the Bulls went 2–4 and
Pippen said he was showcasing himself for teams in California
and Arizona, where he wanted to play. He even spread a rumor
about himself just before the All-Star game in Phoenix, saying
the Bulls were talking about sending him to Phoenix for Dan
Majerle and draft picks, a tale that became so widely dissemi-
nated that Majerle went into a funk during the All-Star weekend and Suns executives had to scramble to deny everything.
Pippen was especially pleased about upsetting Majerle, since
Majerle had been a player that Krause desperately coveted,
once trying to talk him into skipping the predraft camps so
Krause could get him with a third-round pick. Krause would
often tell Jordan and Pippen their defense was nothing compared with that of Majerle, whom Krause likened to Jerry
Sloan. Jordan had loved humiliating Majerle in the 1993 Finals,
and Pippen loved his private joke now. Pippen then said after
the All-Star game that he liked the purple Eastern Conference
All-Star uniform because it reminded him of the Suns, with
whom he wanted to play.

Pippen's comments even produced a rare response from Reinsdorf, who said that he had no intention of redrafting Pippen's contract, which extended through 1998, and that the more Pippen talked, the less likely he was to go anywhere. Still, Reinsdorf was growing angry at Pippen's continued disloyalty and began making plans to trade Pippen to an expansion team. If Pippen had trouble with this Bulls team, Reinsdorf said privately, he could go to Toronto, or maybe Minnesota, and see how he liked that. Reinsdorf reveled in the thought, but he knew he would never favor cruelty over good business. And good business said to deal Pippen after the season for the best offer and start rebuilding.

Reinsdorf had met with Jackson in Phoenix when the Bulls were on a road trip through the Western Conference just before the All-Star break. Jackson would be going into the last year of his contract in the 1995–96 season and starting to think about a jump to the rich Knicks, where he might earn up to $3 million per year. Reinsdorf wanted to know if Jackson would stay around for another run with a new group.

"There was a lot of reflection, a lot of thinking ahead to what was going to be," said Jackson. "Jerry Krause had always said ten years was what he'd hoped I'd stay with the club. Yet, I always felt seven years was a good run, that after that time they would get tired of hearing what you had to say and you would get tired of them. You saw that in Cleveland with Lenny Wilkens, in Golden State with Don Nelson, in Los Angeles with Pat Riley. One of the guys I watched more than anybody else was Mike Fratello, who coached six, seven [actually eight] years in Atlanta and left looking kind of haggard and went over to television and came back looking refreshed and rejuvenated. Then you watch the change in a guy going through a coaching season. My friends call and tell me the same thing: 'Wow, it looks like you're under a lot of stress.'

"I'd had an interesting conversation with Jack Ramsay about that time," Jackson related. "He said there's a tendency when things are going good to stay too long. He said he'd found that out in his coaching career and that he'd coached perhaps a year too long in Portland.

"But it wasn't just the personnel. He said sometimes you just need to freshen up, go to a new gym, with new talent, to take your system to another level, to get out from all the power struggles in the organization, the political struggles, the pettiness. All those things can freshen up a coach.

"And I reflected on my father's pastoral message that you can only stay in one place five years and then your message starts falling on deaf ears," related Jackson, whose father was a Pentecostal minister.

Jackson was earning about $850,000, exceedingly low for a coach of his talent and reputation. Larry Brown had just signed a new deal for about $2 million per year, and the Knicks were holding a renewal for Pat Riley, eventually to go unsigned, for $3 million per year. They would instead sign Don Nelson for $2 million per year. Jackson doubted he could get into that neighborhood with the Bulls, and there had been interest from other teams. Golden State, before the forced resignation of Nelson, had put out some feelers, as had San Antonio before settling for Bob Hill. Jackson wanted eventually to move west to finish up his coaching career, but his wife, June, dreamed of a return to New York. And the Knicks were secretly hoping Riley would just complete the final year of his contract so they could lure Jackson to New York in the summer of 1996.

Jackson thought, too, of his family. A first marriage, producing one child, had been short. His marriage with June had endured the tough times as he worked his way as a player in the NBA, as a coach in the Continental Basketball Association, and as the coach of the Bulls. The girls, Chelsea and Brooke, were now out of the house in college. They had begged Phil not to move them out of high school. Jackson thought of his boys, twins Ben and Charley. They had become involved with teams at school, and Jackson would even postpone his annually awaited return to Montana for the summer for a few weeks so the boys could finish off their basketball seasons.

"The fact that I like Chicago and want my kids to grow up in the same neighborhood, to go to the same school and finish high school, the stability, that's just as important," said Jackson. "I'm not one of these guys married to a winning percentage. That's not who I am or who I want to be."

Jackson later broached the idea of moving with the boys, that perhaps he might have to change jobs and they wouldn't be able to finish high school in the Chicago area. No problem, they informed him, they'd love to move.

"That took the wind out of my sails," Jackson admitted.

But Jackson told Reinsdorf he wanted to sign a new contract, probably for two seasons, that he could embrace a new team, a chance to get back to the top. Jackson had shown in the 1993–94 season that he was not just a coach who rolled the ball out to Jordan.

"Everyone always believed that anyone could coach Michael Jordan," agreed John Paxson, who asked Bulls management after he retired in 1994 if he could eventually join the coaching staff, but only to work under Jackson. "Phil opens up parts of your mind you would never have used. He makes you consider things you never would consider. I'd always hear people say they could win fifty games with Michael Jordan, that Michael would make anything work. But that season showed Phil's ability as a coach, that his system would work without even Michael. The season also was Scottie Pippen's coming out and showed his greatness as a player without Michael there. But it mostly proved Phil's ability as a coach."

Still, Jackson wanted a whole new group, no one left from the championship era if Jordan was not to return. And while Jackson believed Jordan was not yet set on remaining a baseball player, he had stopped believing Jordan's return to basketball would be imminent.

The Bulls had long soured on B. J. Armstrong and were trying to trade him already. Jackson wanted Will Perdue traded, too.

And, Jackson admitted, Scottie Pippen had to go.

SCOTTIE AND THE (OTHER) DONALD

Having lost Horace Grant to free agency the previous summer, Scottie Pippen was the last remaining piece of the championship team who could bring the Bulls any value and building blocks in return, and the Bulls knew it, trying, as was mentioned, to trade him in June 1994 for Seattle All-Star Shawn Kemp.

Jackson had not forgotten Pippen's boycott of the last 1.8 seconds of that playoff game against the Knicks the previous spring. "You forgive, you don't forget," Jackson said. "It's excusable, but there's no excuse."

And Jackson knew the Bulls, especially Krause, harbored the quiet hope of winning a title without Jordan, of the avalanche of praise that would smother management as well as the players.

Jordan was the only player Krause did not obtain for the Bulls' three championship teams, and Jordan used to love to tease Krause about that. Yet Jordan would also grow exasperated over stories he'd hear from management about Krause saying how certain players he'd brought in had made Jordan a great practice player.

"Pretty soon, he'll be taking credit for drafting me," Jordan once said. "But it was Rod Thorn. And I'll never let anyone forget that. And Kevin Loughery was the coach who gave me the chance to become the player I did."

Krause remained privately resentful of the notion that winning those titles was no big deal if you inherit a team that already has Michael Jordan. Krause would take great pains to point out that no team had ever won a title being built around a shooting guard, which Jordan was, and that it took years to get the right players in place. And when asked after the Bulls won in 1991 if Krause would ever get the credit he deserved, Reinsdorf said only if the Bulls win after Jordan. It became something of an internal mantra: to win without Jordan, to show perhaps not who was responsible for the Bulls' success but to show who was just as responsible.

Jordan knew all about the internal resentments toward him, Krause even once outlining his all-time NBA team without Jordan as a member. "He chose Oscar Robertson, Bill Russell, Jerry West, at small forward he had Dr. J. [Julius Erving], the

power forward was Gus Johnson," Jordan told *Playboy* magazine in 1992.

"He was excluding me. He put West at two guard," Jordan
said in disbelief.

So with Jordan gone and the team unable to win in the first
season without him, and then Grant, Bill Cartwright, and John
Paxson gone, too, the Bulls were not about to try to rebuild
around a twenty-nine-year-old Pippen, whom they viewed as
somewhat unstable anyway.

"He [Reinsdorf] said he wanted to do the rebuilding process
as quickly as possible," said Jackson, "to make it a team that
could win a championship without Michael Jordan, something
that would be a terrific feather for the organization and the
coaching staff. It was not an inspirational speech to stay the
course or whether I could take the losing, but that it was a unique
opportunity and would I be interested, not take it or leave it."

Jackson decided he could take it as long as none of the
players from the championship group remained.

"I'm not the kind of person who wants to jump ship just
because it's sinking," said Jackson. "I like to think I can survive
those things, and I feel I was doing a good job in handling
what was a roller-coaster season [in 1994–95]."

Yet Jackson also couldn't envision the bottom in the NBA.
He'd steeled himself for change during his five-year tenure in
the CBA, accepting almost daily turnover and putting in place
competitive teams every season, maintaining hope for the
group through his confidence and determination.

Jimmy Rodgers, who'd joined the Bulls' coaching staff in
1994 when John Bach was not rehired, had suffered through
losing seasons and firings as head coach in Boston and
Minnesota. He marveled at Jackson's resilience as the Bulls
bobbed up and down at the .500 mark for much of the season
before Jordan's return.

"Jimmy said he was impressed about the positive attitude
for a team that everyone said was a .500 team, kept playing
like a .500 team," related Jackson. "But I told him that's the
way I felt about those guys, the fact that they could grow and

make improvements and that's what made coaching enjoyable."

Yet when Jackson's assistant, Jim Cleamons, was offered the
head coaching job of the expansion Toronto Raptors in the
spring of 1995, Jackson had misgivings. "It's not happenstance
that coaches win. Take a great coach like Larry Brown and put
him with the Clippers and he's going to have trouble winning,
same with Pat Riley or Phil Jackson, who is going to have a lot
of trouble winning. If you have talented players you can win. If
you know what to do as a coach, you can bring out the best in
talented players. To go off and coach a team that's going to win
fifteen games," Jackson mused, "I can't imagine how you'd do
that after becoming attached to winning, you could become so
despondent."

However, Jackson had no such fears about the Bulls. He
was persuaded Reinsdorf was serious about a speedy rebuilding and that the team had enough pieces in place and plans for
Pippen to begin contending again within just a season or two.

So the plan was put in place: Pippen would be dealt in
February at the trading deadline, and the holdovers,
Armstrong and Perdue, after the season.

This time it was the Clippers who were interested in
Pippen. Donald Sterling, the unpredictable owner of the hap-
less Clippers, wanted a star.

Although Sterling was born in Chicago and moved the
Clippers to Los Angeles from San Diego, Sterling considered
himself Hollywood. And Hollywood was the place for stars. A
brilliant real estate investor and businessman who owned
acres of prime Beverly Hills property, Sterling was never quite
sure how to run a franchise, perpetually seeking advice from
friends and neighbors and moving with exasperation through
a series of coaches. He knew he wanted to have a winner,
although he could never quite figure out how to produce one.
The Clippers were unlucky, too, losing Danny Manning and
Ron Harper to serious knee injuries not long after they joined
the team, and ending up with the top draft picks when the talent pools coming out of college were at their worst, as in 1989

when Pervis Ellison was the number one pick and the Clippers had number two, and a year before when Manning was the top player. Manning, who would always be troubled by knee problems, was potentially a solid player, but never a star of the magnitude of a Shaquille O'Neal or Charles Barkley or Jordan.

Pippen was now a star and Sterling wanted him.

Back in the late 1980s, Sterling had tried to make a different deal with the Bulls, offering any five Clippers, which then included the likes of Danny Manning, Charles Smith, Ron Harper, and Ken Norman, plus draft choices, for Michael Jordan.

At the time, when the Bulls couldn't get past the Detroit Pistons in the playoffs, it was an interesting idea to Reinsdorf. The commonly held theory at the time was that Jordan was too selfish and that a team with him could never win a title.

But Reinsdorf, recognizing the wrath he'd incur by trading Chicago's most famous landmark, concluded that Jordan was untradeable. And now, in 1995, Sterling was still looking for his star. Jordan still wasn't available, but Pippen was.

With the trading deadline imminent, the deal was put in place: The Bulls would get the Clippers' next two number one picks, including the 1995 number one pick, which turned out to be the number two pick in the 1995 draft, along with the right to flip-flop draft picks two other seasons. In effect, the Bulls would be obtaining the Clippers' next four number one draft picks, assuming, as the Bulls expected, the Clippers would continue to have a poorer record than the Bulls every season, even with Pippen.

The Bulls were willing to give it a try. They had Toni Kukoc on board, and he was best suited to play small forward, Pippen's position. They had hopes for Luc Longley at center and felt a combination of Jackson's and Tex Winter's share-the-wealth offensive system and one or two star players from the draft would put them back in championship contention within three years. Which was about the same time Reinsdorf would need to begin obtaining renewals on more than two hundred costly corporate suites in the new United Center.

But Pippen had been spending too much time with Ron Harper. The former Clippers guard had departed the Clippers an angry free agent after earning $4 million in the 1993–94 season. Harper counseled Pippen that it would be a mistake to go to the Clippers, that management was erratic, the fan base was fickle, the team was on a treadmill to oblivion.

The deal had been agreed to, but the Clippers wanted assurances from Pippen that he was willing to come to the team. Since almost the beginning of training camp in 1994, Pippen had demanded to be traded, and by January he was calling Krause a liar and saying he couldn't remain with the team if Krause did. And Reinsdorf was angry, not only at Pippen's disloyalty, in his view, but for going back on what he felt was an agreement with Pippen.

In the fall of 1994 Reinsdorf paid Pippen $3 million in deferred money that was due years later. Reinsdorf felt what came with it was a promise by Pippen to remain quiet about his contract. Pippen said there was no promise to remain quiet about his feelings about Krause and management in general.

And Pippen felt the Bulls showed their lack of respect with an offer of a balloon payment back in November 1994. This was just before the deadline for altering contracts before the no strike/no lockout agreement went in place to make sure the 1994–95 NBA season was not disrupted even though the collective bargaining agreement between the players and the league had expired. The Bulls offered Pippen an $8 million extension for two years, for 1998–99 and 1999–2000. And Pippen actually thought about taking it.

One of his friends, Eric Murdock of the Milwaukee Bucks, had suffered an eye injury that appeared serious at the time. There was even talk Murdock might not play again. Pippen, having seen his father disabled early in life and a brother crippled, has a recurring dream about sudden injury or illness ending his career. So he thought about taking the money. That was until the Knicks gave Charles Oakley a $10 million balloon payment extension for one year, $2 million more than the Bulls were offering Pippen.

"And he hasn't won shit," Pippen spat when hearing the reports and Oakley's confirmation. It angered Pippen even more, and he now wished the Bulls had not made any offer.

But now Pippen was wavering about leaving. He told his agent, Jimmy Sexton, he wouldn't report to the Clippers if he were traded there.

Sexton asked Pippen to decide what he wanted to do, noting that just days before, Pippen said he wanted to play in Los Angeles, anywhere on the West Coast, or in Phoenix. No, Pippen insisted now, he wasn't going to the Clippers.

Clippers general manager Elgin Baylor and team executive Andy Roeser kept calling. They must talk to Pippen. Pippen reiterated, "No."

Pippen had a few drinks in his room late that afternoon. The team was in Miami for a game the day after the trading deadline, and the players liked to gather at the Hooters bar and restaurant across from their swanky Mayfair House hotel. Pippen and Harper headed over there and even invited Kukoc, whom Pippen often derided. Kukoc was only too happy for the invite, as he sought acceptance from the team's stars like a sad puppy, particularly from Pippen. An unlikely trio, laughing and joking about where Pippen would be playing the next day.

Just minutes before the trading deadline, Pippen called Sexton. His speech was just slightly slurred after an afternoon of cocktails and sun. The clatter of glasses and the hum of conversation at Hooters rose as Sexton's voice crackled through the line. The deal was off. The Clippers wouldn't go through without a promise from Pippen about his intentions.

"Good," Pippen said.

The next day in practice, Pippen was quiet. At one point, in reference to rumors of a deal with Minnesota, Steve Kerr yelled: "Hey, Scottie, look who just walked in. It's Christian Laettner and Doug West."

A few days later, Pippen said he had changed his mind about going to the Clippers. But it was too late. The trading deadline had passed.

Soon after, Pippen stopped speaking to the media. A week later, Jordan left the White Sox training camp. Pippen's contractual problems would not be an issue again for the rest of the season.

Chapter 8

FORGET THE CHICAGO FIRE, THIS IS REALLY BIG

On March 2, 1995, the Bulls came into the locker room at half-time in New York leading by 16 points.

Recalling the team's recent penchant for blowing leads, coach Phil Jackson said, "Well guys, they have us where they want us."

A few minutes into the second half, the Bulls moved that lead up to 22 points. And then went on to let it all slip away as they lost still another big lead and a game they seemed certain to win.

The Bulls seemed unable to do anything about it as they were trying to get back to .500 for the twentieth different time in the 1994–95 season.

The next day, March 3, Michael Jordan quit baseball.

Not long after Jordan returned home, he contacted Jackson. Was Jackson going to stay around after this season? Jordan wanted to know. Was Pippen going to be kept? Jordan came into the Berto Center the following Tuesday, March 7, and worked out with the team. No one thought it was unusual, since Jordan occasionally scrimmaged with the Bulls when he was in Chicago.

But unbeknownst to anyone, Jordan was more serious this time. He ran the offense, went to watch films, ran postpractice sprints. "No one runs lines [sprints] if they don't have to," thought reserve Larry Krystkowiak. "It was then I knew he was coming back."

The frenzy that ensued was embarrassing. Chicago TV stations broke in with breathless reports daily about Jordan's imminent return, the three network affiliate stations in Chicago and the NBC network taking turns breaking bogus exclusives of the date.

The week before Jordan actually announced his intentions, every local newscast was devoted primarily to the Jordan "story," everyone looking for an "exclusive." One night a station reported "exclusively" that Jordan had gone to a movie. Reporters went to the theater, and for a full five minutes interviewed people about whether they'd actually seen Jordan. One woman said she'd seen a "bald black man" but admitted she was behind him and couldn't tell whether it was Jordan. The reporter sought her reaction anyway.

A *Sun-Times* columnist said Jordan might be buying the Bulls.

A TV report stated that Jordan would play Friday, March 10, against Cleveland, and someone else reported that NBA commissioner David Stern would be in Chicago for that Bulls game. He wasn't.

When Friday arrived, the local CBS affiliate ran exclusive reports all day that Jordan was at a downtown office building. The station showed shots of the outside of the building— though not of Jordan—and more than five hundred people standing around blocking traffic.

Another station reported Jordan was in Phoenix getting counsel from Charles Barkley.

Then another exclusive: that Jordan would attend the March 11 game against the Lakers as a spectator. He didn't.

"As good a win as we could have gotten in Chicago against Michael Jordan," Lakers coach Del Harris joked about the reports after the Lakers won that March 11 game.

NBC out of New York reported on Sunday, March 12, that Jordan would be holding a press conference Monday, March 13, to make an announcement.

He didn't.

On that Monday morning, there were a hundred reporters and camera operators at the Bulls' Berto Center practice facility. There would be no story that day, except perhaps that Jordan, who endorses Chevy Blazers, was driving a Range Rover.

A local TV station reported that day that, contrary to what NBC said, there would be an announcement at a press conference on Wednesday, March 15.

A radio station sent someone to the downtown streets holding up a sign asking people to honk once if Jordan was coming back, twice if he wasn't. Almost 60 percent of about three thousand honkers signaled their belief Jordan was returning.

The Bulls were now canceling routine game-day shootaround practices because there were too many media types at their practice facility. Jackson decided to stay home and watch the game films there.

President Clinton acknowledged reports of Jordan's return in an announcement on employment, saying, "As of today, the economy has produced 6.1 million new jobs since I became president. If Michael Jordan goes back to the Bulls, it will be 6,100,001 new jobs."

The newspapers ran daily editorials and devoted valuable front-page space to the story; the *Chicago Tribune* one day headlined the front page with a story and graphics about which muscles Jordan would have to strengthen in his arm to improve his shooting, while somewhere below was a story about terrorism in the Tokyo subway system. The *Chicago Sun-Times* began printing separate pullout sections almost daily, seeking out the most unlikely reactions, like this from boxing impresario Don King: "Tell him I'll represent him. That man has been ripped off like no man on the face of the planet earth. Three million a year for Michael Jordan? That's highway robbery." Actually, it was four million, but who was counting?

At the United Center, fans gathered before the huge statue erected in honor of Jordan's retirement, leaving coins and other mementos at the base of the icon as if it were a weeping Madonna.

On Tuesday, March 14, while the Bulls were in Washington to play the Bullets, someone reported that the team had just been told at a meeting that Jordan would play Friday.

"Meeting?" Ron Harper wondered. "We had a meeting?"

"Nobody told me anything," said Pete Myers.

"We never did know anything," said reserve center Bill Wennington. "Reporters would stop me every day on the way into practice and I'd ask them if they'd heard anything."

Camera crews staking out the Berto Center put adhesive tape over the card reader for the players' private parking lot so Jordan would have to stop his car and get out. Jordan got word and called ahead for the gate to be raised as he drove through.

One night Reinsdorf got a call from a local CBS reporter.

"A press conference is planned for Thursday, March 16, to make the announcement, and Jordan will play Friday," the reporter said, looking for confirmation.

"No," Reinsdorf said. "That's not true."

"But I have reliable sources," the reporter insisted.

"So why are you asking me?" Reinsdorf shot back.

Chicago TV stations and newspapers printed up "Jordan Watch" logos and ran a half dozen stories and items every day. Reporters flew in from around the nation for the games of March 10 and March 11 at home, but there was no Jordan.

"Pack your bags and go back to your hometowns, or wherever you're from," Jackson told the reporters at the Bulls' morning shootaround before the Friday, March 10, game. "Wait a week and a half and come back and see us again at that time."

Even Jackson, who over the years had witnessed stampedes and riots in Jordan's presence—fans throwing themselves under team buses, mob scenes in hotel lobbies, and every other possible scene—was amazed by the fervor over rumors of Jordan's return to the NBA.

What a strange society we live in, thought the socially conscious Jackson, whose family supported a homeless shelter in Chicago and who was actively urging his friend U.S. senator Bill Bradley to challenge Bill Clinton in the Democratic primary. How strange to live in a world where a basketball player could actually lead the evening news over homelessness, violence, and other national crises.

There are many explanations for the astonishing popularity of a man who is, at most and at best, a basketball player. Jordan found it difficult to articulate his incredible popularity. "It's probably you guys [the media]," he told ESPN. "The exposure I get, my connections in the business corporate world, my personality, I guess. You never really know, and you can't create it. The Olympics, a major market city—I played basketball like nobody played before. The public attached themselves to me. How did I maintain it? I don't know. I've formed associations with corporations that have marketed me in the same light. Somehow it's blended. I can't give an explanation for it, really."

If he couldn't explain it, others would try. "He's someone of extraordinary genius in a particular endeavor, even if that endeavor is of relatively minor importance," offered the much quoted University of California sociologist, Harry Edwards, about the Jordan return. "He represents the best of the species, a Gandhi, an Einstein, a Michelangelo."

The *Chicago Tribune* quoted a University of Illinois sociologist, Leonard Newman, who said: "His second coming probably made people feel even better than his first."

Maybe Jordan would wait and come back on Easter Sunday.

Heck, by the summer he would advance to faith healing. The *San Jose Mercury News* related in July 1995 a story of Jordan visiting Mariann Sjotun, a Fresno State University basketball player who was seriously injured in an auto accident in June. Jordan was involved in a basketball workshop that Sjotun was to attend. But her doctors advised against it, so Jordan saw Sjotun back in the locker room. He signed some balls and books for her. After Jordan left, Sjotun was said to be so excited that she got out of her wheelchair and walked for the first time since the accident.

Being likened to the Son of God, reputed to have miraculous powers. That's a little too much. Even for Jordan.

"I was shocked with the level of intensity my coming back to the game created," Jordan admitted. "It was embarrassing. It's great to be respected, but not great to be praised. People were praising me like I was a religious cult or something. That was very embarrassing. I'm a human being like everyone else, but I was being treated like I'm superhuman."

The attention had become overwhelming and even a little frightening, even to Jordan. He had been positive that he would return to basketball. He missed the fame, the acclaim, the attention that drove him, and while the torpid life of baseball was a nice change after those three championship seasons, he missed the action, the stage for his talents. Jordan liked and needed the attention. It was almost like a drug to him by now. The lazy afternoons in the outfield just weren't enough anymore. But now he was confused and uncertain. Suddenly his basketball comeback was being heralded as a twentieth-century version of the Second Coming—"Jesus, can you look this way? Just one more picture." Reinsdorf and Falk were suggesting he wait perhaps until next season ("I felt like he was on the rebound from a divorce," said Falk. "I didn't think he should make a decision like that"), fans were swarming him like a modern-day Moses returning with the Ten Commandments, hordes of reporters were chasing him around, one even trying to interview his son on the way to school. Suddenly he was flustered as to what lay ahead.

Around the Bulls' offices, Jordan had long been referred to as "Jesus Christ Superstar" because of his celebrity and refusal to attend many team functions because of his outside-sponsor-related activities. But this time it was the media who were full of divine references: Michael the Almighty, the transcendent one, immutable and omnipotent, the first and last, preserver and destroyer.

Yet at the same time, Jackson also understood what Jordan represented, at least symbolically if not always in fact.

"The perception is that this is a person who deals from the right intentions," said Bulls philosopher-coach Jackson. "Because of those intentions, the love of the game, he was coming back to help a team that was foundering, with a happy ending to a story, which is what it was supposed to be. To many, Michael is the prototype of a hero, the Sir Galahad riding to the rescue, and it's elevated him to such high proportions, a Prince Charming, a storybook character, one of those things people carry in their hearts and their hopes.

"When I was a boy," recalled Jackson, "I would check the box scores every day to see how Mickey Mantle had done. If he was one for four, I was disappointed. But if he was three for four, it was going to be a good day. Michael has these same best wishes from people because that's what they perceive he is.

"You can peck away at the idol with small chips," added Jackson, "but this is not an idol made of wood, this one is born out of the imagination of people, an image too sturdy for mere events and actions to change."

But at the same time Jackson was getting worried about his own organization. Did the Bulls want Jordan back or not? Reinsdorf was in Florida dealing with the baseball negotiations and hadn't talked with Jordan since March 9. "Anytime you want to talk, let me know," Reinsdorf had told Jordan.

Jackson asked Krause what was going on.

"He knows where to find us," Krause said.

After Jordan practiced with the team on Thursday, March 9, Jackson told anxious reporters: "It's a reality, but it's not a reality."

Krause, who prides himself on maintaining total secrecy at all times, was furious at Jackson's openness. No one else was talking, he told Jackson, and he shouldn't be either. But Jackson was concerned; the team was letting an opportunity slip. The Bulls were starting to win now after concluding the toughest part of their schedule, and Jackson was energized by the possibility of Jordan's return. With Jordan on the team, they might be good enough to have a shot at a title.

The Bulls had lost so many close games, given away so many leads, faded down the stretch. And what was Jordan, if not the best closer in the history of the game? Teams would no longer be able to cluster around Pippen and Toni Kukoc down the stretch and rob the Bulls of their principal options. Even with Jordan, Jackson told his coaching staff, he didn't think the team could overcome its rebounding frailties, but Jordan gave them hope, a chance, which would become the message for the playoffs.

"About ninety percent of the games in the NBA are decided by six points or the last six minutes of the game," Jackson noted. "And it's an advantage to have a closer like Michael Jordan while other players are exhausted or at the end of their rope. This season is a marathon, a fifteen-round fight. We had players doing a lot of good things for two and a half, three quarters. And then they'd fall flat on their faces. That old comment by Patton that fatigue makes cowards of us all is a very true comment. We had seventeen-, twenty-point leads dissolving in front of our faces and we realized with one other player with some kind of ability we'd be winning those games. And Michael could bring that, as well as the confidence he exudes as a player.

"I remember that last team meeting the day of his retirement announcement. It was kind of an emotional time as all the players spoke. Bill Cartwright said he'd never seen a player with the kind of confidence Michael had for the team and himself, that even walking off the floor one night after losing he'd say we were going to beat them the next night. It's what we needed."

When there was still no communication between the team and Jordan the weekend of March 11 and 12, Jackson finally decided he had to act.

At practice on Monday, March 13, after Krause again had warned him not even to address the media, Jackson went out after practice to the growing legions of reporters and said he thought Reinsdorf held Jordan's fate in his hands.

"Most of it is in Jerry Reinsdorf's hands as to whether Michael comes back or not," Jackson told reporters. "That's just my own intuition. The impediment that might happen is in that area and not on the court, how well he plays, or maybe not even how well this team can do. . . . "

Jackson's garbled comments sounded like one of his *New*

York Times crossword puzzles, where he tries out words that sound good to him even if he's not sure of the meaning. "I do have a fractured sense of language," Jackson admitted. But he was clear enough to say the league ought to pay Jordan $100 million and get on with its other business.

Jordan did want a monster payday, about a $20 million one-year payment that he based on Patrick Ewing's $19 million for the 1995–96 season in a balloon payment that would equalize his contract from the previous "lower" salaries he earned. Jordan simply wanted to be the highest-paid player in the league, although he agreed he could never be paid the value he believed he was worth to the NBA.

But Reinsdorf told Jordan's agent, David Falk, that there was no way to make a deal now, even if one were allowed, which it wasn't under a moratorium on new contracts to prevent a lockout or strike until a new collective bargaining agreement was in place. It would be no coincidence that Jordan would take an active role in labor negotiations when the proposed new deal of late June 1995 effectively prevented large one-year payments, although Jordan insisted he was merely standing up for what was equitable for everyone.

Talk of Jordan's comeback was especially thrilling to the team player representatives who were participating in the ongoing labor negotiations. Many believed that Jordan's return would mean more licensing revenues and thus a bigger payout for the players, and less of a likelihood of any labor action now.

"Once they see him play again," said Bulls player representative Steve Kerr, "they're going to think nothing's wrong with the game. It certainly puts the owners under more pressure not to lock us out."

But Kerr would never hear from Jordan about labor matters, even as Jordan became a spokesman for dissident players. "I'm more involved in this situation than with baseball," said Jordan, who skipped the NBA's main players' meeting in late June when the tentative agreement was in question. "I played in this league. I understand certain things players should demand or request, so my voice is a little louder in this situation than in baseball."

Jordan just wanted one thing clear: No labor issue was going to stand in the way of a big payday for him now and a victory over his friend Reinsdorf.

Despite protestations that he was only returning for the love of the game (even those who enjoy their work like to get paid), Jordan had become virtually obsessed with getting a new contract and big payoff from Reinsdorf. It was almost like a competition for him. He had a grudging respect for Reinsdorf in an athletic sense for having won the deal, and he never publicly complained about his $25 million eight-year deal that would run through 1996.

"If anybody stepped up and wanted to give me a raise, I'd accept it," Jordan said. "But I'm not going to complain and ask for more money. Everyone knows I'm underpaid, that I deserve more money, but I signed the contract. If my boss decides not to give me a raise, I'll just be underpaid."

But Falk was embarrassed about having tied up the greatest athlete of his time for eight years, as Jordan would earn a fraction of what the new stars of the game—Hardaway, Webber, Glenn Robinson—were earning.

The thought of the huge salaries being paid to mere rookies was the genesis of Jordan's remarks upon his return that it was time the younger players learned to respect the game and those like himself, Bird, and Erving, "who paved the road for a lot of young guys." And while Jordan genuinely missed basketball, he still deeply resented the disparity between his godly status and relatively secular paycheck.

"He kept saying when he came back these kids wanted to be paid on potential instead of production," related Jackson. "He felt these kids didn't want to learn the game. They just wanted to step in and play and they didn't have good enough background skills. I always was amazed how fundamentally good he was even though he was known for the dunks and spectacular things. He always felt he respected the game by learning the game, and he said that when he came into the game he was a third pick with a less than outrageous salary, but that these guys were asking for $100 million and hadn't proved anything."

After Jackson addressed the media that Monday afternoon, the Bulls headed for Washington. The next morning, Reinsdorf called. What the heck was Jackson up to? Reinsdorf wanted to know. Was he crazy, saying this Jordan decision was in Reinsdorf's hands? He was to keep quiet from now on.

But the die was cast, and Reinsdorf called Jordan that day.

ZEN AND THE ART OF GETTING JORDAN BACK

Jackson, meanwhile, was positively exuberant about the possibility of Jordan's imminent return; not only did Jackson believe that Jordan could help the Bulls pull off a championship miracle, but he also believed he had been instrumental in persuading Jordan that basketball still held more thrills.

Jackson had called Jordan in late September 1994 to ask whether Jordan would mind if he missed the retirement gala. The Bulls had planned a gala tribute to retire Jordan's number 23 jersey in November. There would be stars from Hollywood, former teammates, a statue unveiled outside the new United Center, where the Bulls were moving, and a final good-bye. (Later, after the ceremony had been condemned by media and fans alike as a tawdry floor show not worthy of Jordan's image, the Bulls' vice-president of marketing Steve Schanwald would tell the *Sun-Times* that the Bulls had wanted "a Larry Bird night, an evening of basketball with entertainment thrown in," but NBA Entertainment had taken control and created "something like the Friars' Club roasts Shecky Greene with some basketball thrown in.")

"It was my twentieth wedding anniversary and I asked him if he minded if I wasn't there," said Jackson. Then he asked Jordan to come over to the Berto Center practice facility. It was late September, the players weren't in yet, and there were no media around. They could talk about the retirement party and maybe Jackson could figure something out about getting there. But Jackson had something else in mind. He always felt there was a chance to get Jordan back. He felt Jordan's search for challenges might eventually lead him back to basketball.

"I always thought he might think that no one had ever returned from retirement before and that he could lead a team to a championship again, win another scoring title after retiring. That's something he could want to do.

"He came in to talk and I said, 'Why did you ever agree to let them retire your uniform at such a young age? You could play five more years. Who knows what's going to happen with baseball, with the strike, the season may never get under way and you may miss your opportunity in baseball and what will you have?'

"He said that they'll probably get it straightened out," Jackson recalled. "But he said, 'I do miss basketball.'

"'Would you like to play again?' I asked him," Jackson said. "'How did it go in the Pippen [charity] game down at the Stadium [earlier in September]?' I asked. He said it was fun, but that he got tired because he had to play the whole damn time.

"I said, 'If we get in a situation this year where we look like we have a chance to win and baseball is not going anywhere, would you be interested in playing? Coming back in March and April? You start baseball in February. You'll know sometime then what's going to happen. Then you can come back and play the last six weeks of the season.' He said, 'That's too long.' I said, 'Would you be interested?' He said there were too many cities, too much traveling.

"But as soon as he said that," recalled Jackson, "I realized it wasn't an outlandish thought. I saw him four or five more times over the course of the next few months and always kidded him about it, and I could see basketball was still alive in him. He had come to the Berto Center a few times before, just to get ready, and you could see he was having a great time, laughing, kidding, joking, dunking, scoring, hootin' and hollerin'. He was challenging people. It was like a stage for him, a forum he couldn't get anywhere else.

"The guys like him, Magic, he travels the world now just to play," noted Jackson. "Julius Erving, Larry Bird, they'd love to be able to still play. Here was a guy who could. But he felt he could do so many other things.

"I told him, 'You're the Michelangelo of basketball, a genius, and we'll miss the heck out of you if you stay retired.' It's hard to tell a genius what he brings to the game. But it was also what the game brought to him."

Jackson knew then that Jordan's mourning period for his father was coming to an end. It was just over a year since James Jordan was robbed and murdered on a North Carolina highway. Michael, the son and companion, had gone ahead and done what his father had wished for: He had become a professional baseball player. He could do it. Had he started sooner, like his father always said, baseball would have been his career. It was probably too late. And basketball called him back. It would always keep calling.

Back in Jackson's NBA days, when he smoked marijuana, wore a beard, and listened to the rhythms of his generation, Jackson and several of his fellow free-spirit players had a plan.

"It was Bill Walton, Neal Walk, and a few others," Jackson said. "The NBA season is such a grind, and we felt that we could put together a group of twelve guys and buy a franchise, and then each guy would take one month off during the season so we wouldn't burn out. It would be a cooperative effort and we'd share the revenue. It was great sounding, but it was not workable. We couldn't do it. Michael was able to. He had to go out and try other things and step back and refresh his feel for the game. It was a great thing for him to retire. He needed the time away."

A few days after Jordan bolted from the White Sox camp on March 3, Jackson was ecstatic to see him at the Berto Center, enjoying himself, running around with Pippen, whispering and plotting like two little kids. They would get Krause fired, they'd get a new deal for Pippen, Jordan would get a new deal.

None of it would ever materialize, of course. When Jordan finally met with Reinsdorf to discuss a return, Jordan merely asked Reinsdorf about his plans for Pippen.

"I told him Scottie would be a member of the Bulls for the duration of his contract unless we could better ourselves by trading him," said Reinsdorf. "Michael seemed satisfied."

Pippen would tell friends for weeks afterward that Jordan had assured him that he would be getting a new deal. But as the weeks went by after Jordan's return, Jordan never raised the matter again with Pippen. Pippen wouldn't, either. But he had gotten the message. He eventually told his agent, Jimmy Sexton, that he wanted to be traded and even told reporters after the Bulls' final playoff game loss to Orlando that he believed he had played his last game as a Bull. He told Horace Grant he wished Jordan had just kept quiet and let the team trade him.

By the time the Bulls returned from Washington with another win that put them above .500 at 32–31, Jordan was ready to return.

Reinsdorf and Jordan finally spoke on Thursday, March 16, more than a week after the media circus began. Jordan was ready; his first game would be Sunday, March 19, in Indiana.

The league was notified Friday. Falk had talked with league officials about some sort of special remuneration for Jordan, considering the enormous flood of popularity the league was suddenly enjoying, but since virtually all the available tickets and advertising time had already been sold out for the season, the league insisted that Jordan wouldn't actually mean much in terms of additional profits, at least for now.

And on Saturday, March 18, the most famous two-word statement in the history of professional sports was issued by David Falk on behalf of his client Michael Jordan:

"I'm back."

Chapter 9

A LEAGUE OF HIS OWN

While Jordan's simple statement put an end to the avalanche of rumors, one nagging question still lingered: Had Jordan been banned from the league for one year for gambling?

It was the hottest and longest running rumor after Jordan retired. It went this way: The NBA had found something to link Jordan to serious gambling and organized crime, something so embarrassing that it would be undeniably damaging to both Jordan and the league. Supposedly, Jordan had been told to get lost for a year or so and all would be excused.

Actually, Jordan had done plenty of serious gambling, although there had been nothing felonious about it. Friends close to Jordan verified the particulars of Richard Esquinas's book *Michael & Me*, in which Esquinas said Jordan lost more than $1 million to him in golf bets and then failed to pay. It was not uncommon for Jordan to walk away from bets, although they were usually small, such as the one with the stadium usher with whom he had been betting free throws one day. Jordan missed several and then left. "Catch you later," Jordan yelled back to the usher.

Maybe it was because pro athletes rarely pay for anything. A surprising number of high-salaried NBA players don't even tip, having become accustomed to getting gratis treatment wherever they go. Jordan, who could be exceptionally generous on many occasions, was no exception, according to several golfing partners from around the Chicago area. He usually offered an autograph instead of a tip, although in many cases the autograph could be worth a lot more. Sports celebrities become accustomed to adoring fans giving them anything; rarely did the top Bulls players pay for a meal anywhere, and auto dealers were begging to give them automobiles. Some of the Bulls had jokingly taken to calling Scottie Pippen "No Tippin' Pippen."

Esquinas had allegedly won more than $1 million from Jordan, then he wrote a book to try to reclaim some of his winnings. But the book was generally viewed by the media as a way to recoup some of Equinas's unpaid winnings, even though Jordan was already enmeshed in a gambling controversy at the time, brought about by a late-night trip to Atlantic City when the Bulls were in New York to play the Knicks in the playoffs. No, said Jordan's loyal fans, certainly Jordan did not do what Esquinas alleged. The book was mostly dismissed.

But it was clear Jordan continued to gamble actively, and the league was coming under pressure to investigate. Jordan supporters pointed out that he had done nothing illegal, broken no rules, but between the allegations of a gambling addiction, the connections to drug dealer Slim Bouler, the high-stakes accusations of Esquinas, and the ill-fated trip to Atlantic City, the NBA was under pressure to look into Jordan's activities. After all, baseball had suspended Pete Rose for betting and had disciplined other players for transgressions similar to Jordan's. The problem was that the NBA wanted no part of punishing its hottest and most popular property.

It's not like Jordan's gambling was unusual in sports. One reason the Bulls started using a charter plane back in 1989 was that several players, Jordan and Pippen among them, would be playing cards in the airport gate areas waiting for commercial flights, with several thousand dollars in $100 bills lying on the seats between them. Wilt Chamberlain, the NBA great of the 1960s, was also known as a daring gambler, willing to bet teammates thousands of dollars as they flew over cities on airplanes, wagering on the population of those cities. He was also an aggressive card player, much like Jordan; the drive that made him a great basketball player emerged in whatever competition he was involved in. Former teammates said Chamberlain's strong personality would take over the card games much as Jordan's did in his games, trash talking as if it were a major battle, daring others to bluff or challenge him. No bet was too big to ignore for men like that; it's part of the makeup that made them the dominant players of their eras.

No, Jordan insisted, he didn't have a problem; the only problem, he told reporters, was that he got caught. In fact, it was only when Jordan's association with Bouler became public in a criminal case that the NBA took notice.

Meanwhile, the theory went that despite the league's bumbling efforts to avoid finding anything, the NBA, in an Inspector Clousseau–like probe, stumbled onto some incriminating evidence and told Jordan to walk away from the game for a year.

NBA commissioner David Stern was waiting for the call when it became clear that Jordan was returning to the NBA.

Jordan had been retired for more than a year, so under league rules he was eligible to return, no matter how many games he wanted to play. He was still on the Bulls' payroll, making almost $4 million per year, which was something of a thank-you payment from Reinsdorf. Jordan had received his salary in the 1993–94 season and wasn't supposed to in the 1994–95 season. That changed when he returned. He eventually earned $4 million for twenty-seven games, making him the highest paid player in the league for the lowest number of games played.

A TV reporter called Stern. "We've heard you've subpoenaed Jordan's phone records."

Stern had to laugh, at least after his initial outrage.

"The suggestions of grand plots, entanglements, webs of intrigue—it became a media riot," said Stern. "No matter how inaccurate or how silly a particular observation is, it's easily repeated and makes for a good story. Someone wants to write about his father and render an opinion that's crazy, and it gets interwoven with fact and picked up and repeated and from that perspective it's irresponsible.

"Our investigation? It's finished. I always looked at it that we were fortunate to have Michael for the nine years he played," said Stern, "for the three championships during which time we enjoyed extraordinary growth. And if for personal or other reasons he had to do something else for the peace of mind or equanimity, I didn't view that as the tragedy some others did. Illness, injury, or death takes players from us. Larry Bird, Drazen Petrovic, those were different tragedies or sad or unfortunate circumstances. For someone to have the ability to take from the game what he has and then leave, that's terrific."

And then on Friday, March 17, Stern got the call telling him Jordan was back.

"I knew there was going to be a real public outpouring," said Stern. "But I never could have gauged the size of the impact.

"People were looking for something to be happy about," he said. "He was walking into a starved sports populace, starved for good news. To the banning of postgame handshakes in high school games to the O.J. trial to labor problems, people are looking for something good in the area of sports. And as I've always said on behalf of the NBA, it's better to be lucky than good."

However, it wouldn't be long before Stern would find Jordan—with his league-defying change of uniform numbers in the playoffs, his role as agent-sponsored point man in overturning the NBA's labor deal with the Players Association in late June, and his attempts all summer to face a union decertification vote to block Stern—at least as much of a nuisance as a boon to the NBA.

HOW BLACK IS BLACK?

Bulls coach Phil Jackson always marveled at the way Jordan could step through controversies virtually unscathed. Jackson knew that his friend and former Knicks roommate, U.S. senator Bill Bradley of New Jersey, could never take the hits Jordan did and survive in his business.

Jackson watched carefully; he quietly harbored dreams of running for public office one day, even though he knew it was mostly fantasy, an exercise that made him consider what he'd do if he had a chance to change things.

Jackson still worked with the Native American tribes in the

upper Midwest, and he had recruited John Paxson to help him run some basketball camps there in the summer of 1995. Jackson and his family were involved in several charities for the homeless, and Jackson's wife, June, was a committed social activist.

They sometimes imagined what they might do with a combination of Jordan's popularity and charisma and their social conscience. Jackson marveled at the way Jordan juggled and charmed even the most cynical sportswriters, his warm eyes and brilliant smile melting the venom out of so many as they would sit transfixed around him like front-row fans at a rock concert.

"I always tell the guy he should be a politician," says Jackson.

Of course, politics is anathema to Jordan, who markets to all races, creeds, and colors. In the first week after his return, he managed to mention McDonald's when there was talk about team dietary needs and Gatorade when someone wondered how he kept from losing energy on the court.

And by being apolitical, and perhaps somewhat colorblind, Jordan has been condemned by some for not being black enough.

Harry Edwards, the radical sociologist, once complained that there was a statue of Jordan in Chicago, but not one of Muhammad Ali, because Ali spoke out for his people and Jordan never has.

It's been an oft-repeated charge that Jordan has been unable to counter, although it has never hindered his success.

Craig Hodges, who played for the Bulls' first two championship teams, pointed to Jordan during the 1992 Finals as an example of a high-profile athlete who doesn't do enough for the black community.

"To whom much is given, much is required," said Hodges, who was active in black economic concerns, trying to organize black athletes and entertainers and, in 1994, taking the head coaching job in basketball at predominantly black Chicago State University.

"While it's laudable to donate money to charity," said

Hodges, "we have to take more of a leadership role where it's not so much what we give in monetary terms but what we do in the trenches. Kids need to see us. We can make a difference in gang violence, drug abuse, homelessness, lack of jobs. A lot of us don't look at the responsibility end of it as much as we do the right to ask for as much as we can get.

"Nike, L.A. Gear, Reebok, the shoe companies have robbed our community of riches," said Hodges, who unsuccessfully tried to get Jordan to switch from Nike to a minority-owned sneaker company when both were with the Bulls. "If the kids in the housing projects across America didn't buy these products, they would not flourish. It's time for Michael, myself, all the fellas who represent these companies to hold them accountable."

Shortly thereafter, Hodges was released by the Bulls and out of basketball.

That summer, after the 1992 Finals, former NFL star and black activist Jim Brown came to Chicago and condemned Jordan's indifference toward the black community at a time when Brown said gestures by Jordan could mean so much.

"His main concerns are corporate America and he is not being a role model for his people," Brown charged.

The issue would not go away for Jordan.

In his bestselling book *Days of Grace*, the late Arthur Ashe acknowledged the dilemma for someone like Jordan, but said Jordan owed more.

"I do not think that every black athlete or entertainer has an obligation to thrust himself or herself into positions of leadership," Ashe wrote. "However, our situation is increasingly desperate, and I admire those athletes and entertainers who conspicuously try to give something back to the people, if only by exemplary behavior. I admire former stars such as Julius Erving in basketball, or Lynn Swann in football for what they have made of themselves. I am less happy with the demureness of someone like Michael Jordan, who is as popular as he is rich. While I would defend Jordan's right to stay out of politics in general, I think that he made a mistake in declining to give

any open support to Harvey Gantt, the respected black politician who ran for the U.S. Senate in 1990 from Jordan's home
state of North Carolina. For me, the main point is not that
Gantt and Jordan are both black; rather, it is that Gantt's opponent, Jesse Helms, has a long history of supporting segregation,
and the contest was close. For blacks across America, that
Senate contest was the most important in decades. Instead,
Jordan stuck to his apolitical position.

"'I don't really know Gantt,' he said, in response to criticism of his silence. 'Well, Michael,' I would have told him, 'pick
up the telephone and call him!' A few appearances with Gantt
might well have made the difference. Instead, Helms returned
to the Senate."

Even as he was dedicating a new Boys and Girls Club in
late July 1995 on Chicago's west side near the new United
Center, Jordan couldn't escape the pressure to do more, be
more, even though the club was funded by Jordan and the
Bulls and dedicated to his father's memory. Just a few days
later, at the Pro Football Hall of Fame induction ceremonies in
Canton, Ohio, inductee Kellen Winslow named Jordan as one
of the prominent black athletes who could do more to help in
the battle for more opportunities for African Americans.

Jordan is rarely seen in public in Chicago, particularly in
the low-income areas, and in *Washington Post* writer Jim
Naughton's 1991 book on Jordan, *Taking to the Air,* Naughton
quoted a black Chicago actor, Aaron Freeman, saying of Jordan
and Chicago: "We are a town of limited celebrity and there is
always one 'Model' Negro," mentioning Ernie Banks, Gale
Sayers, and Walter Payton.

"[Jordan] is clean-cut, wholesome, utterly nonthreatening
to white people," said Freeman. "When they [activists for black
causes] are trying to get the mayor to do something, maybe on
affordable housing, no one calls Michael Jordan to be part of
the movement. There are no illusions about him. He's not
going to fight for your rights or your job or anything. He's not
a hero. He plays one on TV."

Jordan, who has caused near riots by just attempting to

make appearances, has been stung by the criticism, as he fought hard during his life to come to terms with just what his beliefs were. Jordan doesn't engage in issues, he admits, because he's mostly ignorant of politics. He admits he doesn't read much or follow current issues, and teammates say they don't see him reading daily newspapers much. Not that many of Jordan's teammates have subscriptions to the *New York Times*, either.

Jordan operates mostly on gut instincts, and even if they betray him at times, he usually knows how to say the right thing. And he has feelings about issues of racism.

He once was actually a racist, he said, an impressionable kid growing up in racially divided North Carolina watching *Roots* on TV and having his eyes opened over how black people were treated for hundreds of years.

A girl in school called him a "nigger," so he hit her and was suspended from class. His parents counseled him, and Jordan said he outgrew his adolescent hatreds.

And then, ironically, he found himself years later having to defend not doing enough to strike down white gains.

"I've done a lot of things for the black community," Jordan told the *Sun-Times*'s Lacy Banks. "If I'm guilty of anything it's of not seeking publicity or keeping a record of everybody I've ever helped. I don't want any publicity for it anyway. As long as I know somebody is benefiting from my actions and contributions that's all I've ever wanted.

"People for years," Jordan continued, "have been asking for black role models to stand up and give our kids something positive to follow. I'm on a pedestal I didn't ask for, although I've accepted it. While I'm on the stage I am now, people are attacking me. What do kids want? Do they want me to be in position just for black kids and negative for everybody else?"

The role-model debate again. Should athletes be role models? Are they? How can they not be? What if they don't want to be? Edwards said athletes are not: "They are not intellectually, analytically, or politically prepared to deal with complex problems," Edwards says.

Yet Richard Lapchick, director of the respected Center for the Study of Sport and Society, has helped develop a program with universities that enables former athletes to return to complete their degrees without cost, but then the athletes must work in community service programs.

And the paradox remains that he who is singled out as a role model is not the one who is best prepared but the one who is most successful. Such is evident in the case of San Antonio center David Robinson, who truly works at what he feels is his responsibility as a sports role model.

"A lot of guys say they don't want to be role models," says Robinson. "I don't really think you have a choice. In this situation, you've got everybody's eye on you. So I take it not as a burden but an honor. I can say, 'Hey, look, I'm able to love my wife.' I don't care if seventy-five percent of the people in the country get a divorce. It's not impossible to have a good marriage and to be a good father.

"How do I perceive myself?" asks Robinson. "Father, husband, and I feel I have an unbelievable responsibility on the [basketball] floor to honor God's gift. It's far more than what I feel toward the fans. It's far more than what I feel toward the people paying me or even to my teammates. I have a responsibility to come out and work and make myself better, not for my own glory, but for his."

But one doesn't see many kids wearing David Robinson jerseys. They wear Jordan's, Charles Barkley's, even Dennis Rodman's. They used to wear Magic Johnson's and Isiah Thomas's. The difference is that Robinson has never been an ultimate winner on the basketball court, thus he hasn't been the one to be celebrated and emulated. What America really wants is winners, not role models, and Jordan continues to be caught in between.

"I read in a *Sports Illustrated* article where Hank Aaron and others said I should be more outspoken on different issues, political or whatever. I've always been an opinionated person," Jordan claimed. "But I've always kept my opinions positive and private. Nobody is going to make me say my piece in public if I don't want to. I have an obligation to all people. All people support me and make me the success I am. So regardless of what others say or ask, I have a responsibility to help and inspire all kids to fulfill their dreams. And that's what I'll continue to do. Because I don't publicize the good that I do, I get attacked and accused of not doing anything."

His mother, Deloris, is the impetus and driving force behind the Michael Jordan Foundation. Jordan, with the foundation and his work with Special Olympics and Make-a-Wish, has done more than many professional basketball players to funnel money to worthy causes.

"We still have racism," Jordan acknowledged. "But sometimes the more publicity you give it helps increase racism rather than decrease it."

Although he's generally uninformed about world issues, Jordan always becomes the team spokesman when something critical happens. After the terrorist bombing in Oklahoma City in the spring of 1995, reporters clustered around Jordan to ask him for his reaction. At the time, there was some suspicion that the bombing could have been the work of foreign terrorists, and Steve Kerr, who lost his father to a terrorist in Beirut, had strong feelings not only about the issue but about Arab Americans and their place in American society. No one talked to him. It was Jordan's opinion that a dozen reporters sought, as they gathered around him and then scribbled furiously, the general message being that it was a bad thing and shouldn't happen again.

"I'm not running for president," Jordan said at the time. "I'm not running for Congress, so I don't have to publicize what I do, as long as I do it out of the kindness of my heart. I have controversial thoughts, but the media might not understand and take it the wrong way if I say them."

MIKE AND THE BAD BOYS

Despite the usual controversies, the widespread consensus was that Jordan would be a lifesaver to the NBA. The league had just endured a slow-paced, rugged, TV-switching-off Finals between the Houston Rockets and New York Knicks in 1994, which in part resulted in rule changes to speed up the game and produce more scoring after the lowest scoring season in three decades.

And there was the embarrassing summer of Dream Team II, which had disintegrated into an absolute car wreck: too ugly to look at, too irresistible to ignore. There was Derrick Coleman and Larry Johnson, All-Stars, slam-dunking and taunting in the faces of tiny Asians and baffled Australians, the American team up by dozens of points.

Players like the noxious Johnson were out of control. Paid a staggering $84 million over twelve years, Johnson saw no rules or regulations as barriers, no social niceties as necessary. He had come to symbolize the ugly young stars of the NBA, greedy and not overly talented. Veterans chafed under the disregard for unspoken rules. In days past, rookies were shown around by the veterans and just hoped for playing time. Now, they were the highest paid players on the team, expected to play. When rookie Glenn Robinson from Purdue wanted more than $100 million to sign with the Milwaukee Bucks, team owner Herb Kohl finally offered to trade the entire franchise for Robinson's first contract to bring some sensibility to the negotiations, claiming that Robinson's contract would be worth more than the entire team. The veterans were determined to stick it to the rookies in the next collective bargaining agreement and enforce a cap on their salaries.

More than ever, the NBA was desperately in need of Michael Jordan and his charismatic image to boost the league. Problems and scandals were everywhere. Chris Webber, who would just be a senior in college had he not left for a $74.5 million contract, forced a trade and the eventual resignation of veteran coach Don Nelson in a feud born of Webber's dislike for being yelled at. Webber's Golden State teammates, particularly All-Star Latrell Sprewell, skipped practices out of sympathy for Webber's departure. San Antonio's Dennis Rodman, coloring his hair regularly and adding tattoos like makeup, missed part of the season due to suspensions over various team rules. Coleman, with a new $30 million four-year contract, and teammate Kenny Anderson openly criticized and baited management all year. Another teammate, Chris Morris, refused to tie his shoes despite his coach's request. Minnesota's Isaiah Rider shouted obscenities at coach Bill Blair in a game and then held a press conference to criticize the coach for criticizing him.

Portland's Clyde Drexler demanded a trade, the Bulls' Scottie Pippen demanded a trade and called general manager Krause a liar, Detroit's Oliver Miller and Washington's Don MacLean broke bones in bar fights, the Lakers' Nick Van Exel refused to enter a game after a spat with coach Del Harris, Portland's Cliff Robinson held out because of his paltry $2.6 million salary, Kevin Willis left camp also upset about money, as did Sedale Threatt, the backup guard upset with his $2.4 million annual contract.

Hello, Michael Jordan. His gambling issues long forgotten, now he was just a man returning to a spurned love, a man seeking a return to his youth for all the right reasons.

"I love the game," Jordan explained upon his return. "That's the only reason I'm here, believe me. It's not about the money or commercial things. At the time I walked away, I needed to get away, but I couldn't separate myself from the things I love. I began to realize over time I really, truly missed the game. And I felt I wanted to instill some positive things back in the game. There have been a lot of negative things happening—and in terms of the young guys, they shouldn't let it get to where the integrity of the game is at stake. I'm not making astronomical dollars playing the game itself. I just think you should respect the game. Be positive people. Certainly, you can act like gentlemen and professionals. You look at the great players and what they want to pass on as a legacy. They don't take this game for granted. You don't treat it like dirt. We're being treated like lawyers and doctors because of the salaries we receive. So let's act like sensible people."

Of course, by the end of the season Jordan would stage his own infantile media boycott, a defiant snit over his jersey number, and his own foray into what several Hall of Fame legends called a greedy grab for dollars—Jordan's efforts to break the players union. Once again he was back in the throes of a labor dispute, although unlike the baseball situation, this time Jordan was the public point man, appearing on the national Larry King cable-TV interview show to talk about the poor deal the NBA Players Association had negotiated with the owners.

Although many agents and players were working behind the scenes to strike down the deal, Jordan had become the front man, in part because of his obvious visibility and in part because his agent, David Falk, was heavily involved.

The resulting move to decertify the union produced a rare outburst from players who were the true union pioneers of the NBA: Bob Cousy, Oscar Robertson, Dave DeBusschere, and Tom Heinsohn.

"I would tell Michael Jordan that he is selfish, greedy, that his agent is selfish and greedy," Heinsohn told the *Boston Globe*. "They have abandoned the people who tried to preserve the game. Michael Jordan and his ilk think they are the be-all and end-all. He's never bothered to find out what the union is about. Well, he should. Because a lot of ex-players who paved the way for the game he is trying to rape are concerned."

Players Association founder Bob Cousy said, "If you can't get by on $2.8 million playing a child's game for eight months, you need serious counseling."

The legends were upset with the attempts to decertify the union, as well as losing a promised contribution to the pension fund for pre-1965 players. They focused on Jordan, in part, because they knew he had never been active in labor issues but had become so since he wanted to assure a large one- or two-year payment, perhaps up to $20 million per year, after his contract expired in 1996.

WHAT HAVE THEY DONE TO MY GAME, MA?

Another issue growing irksome in the NBA was the battle between basketball and marketing.

Years ago, there was just the game, which is preserved in its original unflashy form only by the Boston Celtics. Teams are required to list their promotional activities planned for that night for the benefit of TV: clowns, mascots, million-dollar shots, dancers, go-cart races, baby races, contests, whatever. In Boston, the sheet remains blank except for the notation "ball boy rolls ball cart to half-court at halftime."

The Orlando Magic, in its early days, was responsible for one of the louder and more expansive entertainment circuses. It developed an animated scoreboard, a dance team, the cheer-leading public address announcer, and rock music show, offered as an alternative to the game.

"With the players we had, we didn't want to attract much attention to them," admitted Magic personnel director John Gabriel.

And so around the NBA, the entertainment division of the league endorsed rap music, roaring automobile sounds in Indianapolis, hornet buzzing in Charlotte, dancers, video displays, laser shows, and fireworks, all of which came with speakers turned up loud enough to signal other universes.

The Bulls' much copied marketing department, headed by Steve Schanwald, was among the innovators of many of the concepts. The Bulls' thrilling, unique introductions had been copied throughout the league; now everyone was looking to come up with something new and different.

The basketball purists howled in protest: Let's see if people actually want to watch the game, they pleaded. No, said the marketing directors. What will everyone do with all those breaks? They need to be entertained. They'll love these midget auto races, shooting contests, and carnival acts during every time-out.

But the issue wouldn't go away, and for the 1995–96 season, the NBA promised to consider possible limitations after fans in Indianapolis during the 1995 Eastern Conference Finals twirled hypnotic pinwheel signs to distract the free throw shooters. Earlier, the Magic had handed out the signs in Orlando during the series with the Bulls, but were told to stop. So when the

Pacers handed out similar pinwheel placards in Indianapolis, the Magic protested, and a mini-rhubarb ensued. It was decided that fans would be allowed to use the pinwheel signs for the rest of that game, after which they were banned. The whole ordeal sent Pacers coach Larry Brown off on a tirade that was seconded by most of his colleagues.

"Let's just play basketball," Brown pleaded. "People who aren't involved in the sport are taking over. I've said our players are MTV guys. I just wish we could play the game and the fans could yell and cheer for good plays."

But fans are told when to cheer and how much louder. Many in the NBA worry that the emphasis on entertainment over the substance of the game, in large part inspired by NBA videos of slam dunks and wild plays, has encouraged the selfish element that's crept into the game even more, particularly from young players who demand who should coach them, come to practices when they feel like it, and leave games when they're unhappy.

"I like to see kids grow up and want to be basketball players for the right reasons," said Brown. "But the emphasis is on individual play. If they want to be in an individual sport, they should play tennis or golf. Basketball is the greatest team sport in the world. But guys only want to dunk or shoot a three-pointer. And after they do it, they want to acknowledge their own success instead of that of their teammates helping them. And the fireworks, the whistles, the music. Let's just play basketball."

And so the divisions were drawn. Can't we all just get along? Not the marketing and basketball people.

In Chicago, they had worked for years on an indoor fireworks show, but it was hard to accomplish in the old Chicago Stadium. So the Bulls' marketing people were overjoyed to be going into the new United Center in 1995. New laser possibilities, multiple fireworks.

Jackson hated it more than ever. Despite the cavernous size of the building, he still had to shout to be heard in the huddle as the music blared during time-outs. And those fireworks.

Jackson said it sometimes took him several minutes into the game before he could see through the fog created by all the smoke.

It was up to Jordan to get it stopped.

AIR JORDAN CHANGES PLANES

Everything, it seemed, would be up to Jordan. Including saving his teammates' lives.

If Jordan was a figurative lifesaver for the NBA, his teammates saw him as an actual savior—when the Bulls switched charter services on his behalf.

The trouble first started back in November on the team's Western Conference trip. A chunk of what was thought to be ice broke away from the tail of the plane in midflight with a sharp thud. In recent years it had become common for NBA teams to purchase or charter aircraft that enabled them to leave cities immediately after games, which frequently ended after the last commercial flights had already flown. Until the late 1980s, teams had flown commercial aircraft, which meant that when they were on the road, they were required to take the first flight available out of the city they were in for the next game. With the lifestyles of most NBA players, that meant little sleep. In addition, with the escalating contracts, players began to demand the amenities of private aircraft: beds, swivel captain's chairs, TV, and film rooms for the coaches.

But the charter service the Bulls were using stopped servicing professional teams, so the Bulls for the 1994–95 season switched to one that was using retired commercial aircraft. And the trips became routinely uneasy, with clumps and bangs and flumps common during flights. Players complained they could no longer sleep, and some of the more unsteady fliers, like Toni Kukoc and Scottie Pippen, gripped hard on takeoffs and landings. The feeling of the players was the team was just trying to save money.

The air-safety record for sports teams has been remarkable. With teams crisscrossing the country daily, there hasn't been a serious incident for years, since fatal crashes involving college teams in West Virginia and Indiana. But on March 4, the day after Jordan had left the White Sox for good and was contemplating joining his old team, Jordan was almost left without a team to return to.

The Bulls were coming out of Philadelphia after a win. Less than thirty minutes outside of Philadelphia, the cabin depressurized after a loud thumping sound. Players are veteran fliers, and many watch the flight attendants for signs of trouble.

"You couldn't hear the captain over the intercom," remembered Pete Myers. "It was all staticky. And then the stewardess gets on the phone to the cockpit and she says, 'Oh no! Oh shit!' and she runs down the aisle."

Myers was playing cards with Ron Harper and Pippen, a group that later was expanded to include Jordan, the foursome involved in excited games of tonk, a ginlike card game popular in the black community. (Even after Jordan had hit the Knicks for that memorable 55-point game about ten days after his comeback in New York, the players barely remarked on it on the way back home, so involved were they in their tonk game. Even Jordan only occasionally stopped to look at the overhead TV screen at the game tape while the card game went on uninterrupted throughout the entire flight home.) The plane went into a dive and the oxygen masks popped out, the temperatures in the cabin now below freezing.

"You could see your breath," remembered Steve Kerr.

Harper was panicky and yanked at his oxygen mask. He grabbed for it so hard, in fact, it came out of its holder and he was left holding the mask without any connection.

Myers laid his head down on the card table, the money and cards scattering onto the floor as the nose of the plane continued to be pressed in a sharp angle forward.

"I said my prayers," related Myers. "I asked the Lord to protect my loved ones, the ones I was leaving behind."

Myers had his oxygen mask on, Pippen had his on. They stared at one another while Harper held his in his hands. No one spoke.

Eventually, the plane leveled off at about ten thousand feet, a drop of almost twenty-five thousand feet in just over a minute.

"The captain then comes on," said Myers, "and he explains, but says we'll be going on to Chicago. We've got an hour and a half left and the plane is banging all the way. I couldn't believe it."

Pippen, especially, had had enough. That was it, he decided. Not another flight on that airplane.

The Bulls were home for the next ten days, and the players became distracted over the Jordan phenomenon. And Pippen was enjoying it most. Jordan had approached him after talking to Jackson and said he especially wanted Pippen to stay, that he'd make sure Pippen was taken care of with a new deal. Pippen had stopped talking to the media by this time, tired from his feuds with Krause all season, demands to be traded, and a welter of trade rumors in late February. Now Jordan was soon to be back, and all anyone wanted to talk about was Jordan. Pippen was relieved to be forgotten about. Perhaps they would get rid of Krause, since Jordan's presence was certainly more important than Krause's, at least in Pippen's opinion.

So Pippen was feeling good as he got on the charter out of Chicago on March 13 heading for a game with the Washington Bullets the next night. On takeoff, the plane banked hard, tossing the players about wildly. When Pippen got to the team hotel, a Ritz-Carlton in Pentagon City, he was furious. He called his agent and Krause to say he was no longer flying with the team. He called teammates, saying they all should refuse to fly back from Washington with the team. It was the only way to get results, a mutiny of sorts.

Pippen called Harper, but Harper refused to join the mutiny even though he didn't want to fly. "You're the captain," Harper said. "You do it."

"You got all the money. What can they do to you?" Pippen shot back.

He was trying to lure other teammates into his plan but not

getting results. "We got so many guys so insecure about their jobs, they're afraid to say anything," Pippen said. "But I'll tell you, Michael ain't flyin' on that plane."

The next night, Pippen stood alone.

As the players boarded the bus to the airport after the Washington game, Pippen was not there. He got a cab and went back to the team's hotel in Washington for the night and took a commercial flight back to Chicago the next morning.

Trying to quell the uprising, the Bulls had the charter president come to Washington and fly back with the team. He explained that the sharp maneuver coming out of Chicago was routine and he merely wanted to assure players there never had been any danger, even on the flight from Philadelphia.

By the time Jordan joined the team the next week, the Bulls were using their previous charter company.

Chapter 10

RETURN FLIGHT

Michael Jordan was a man who died young and then got a second chance.

Here Comes Mr. Jordan?

"Living in the nice hotels again," Jordan said after his return to the NBA, "you sort of forget about the Ramada Inns and La Quintas and the bus rides. It's good to revisit those values. It's made me appreciate where I am a little bit more. When you're living on a pedestal for so long, you forget about the steps to get there and what it was about."

The morning after his first game in Indianapolis, Jordan walked into the Berto Center and saw Bulls coach Phil Jackson. Jordan had shot seven of twenty-eight in the Bulls' overtime loss, which hardly seemed to matter to anyone.

But Jackson had one good-natured dig: "That average [.250] might have been acceptable in the profession you just came from, but we're expecting more like fifty percent here."

Jordan laughed heartily.

He was even ready to make up with his former foes, the media.

"I was glad to be back," Jordan said after the opening game in Indianapolis. "The media gave me very positive criticism and I appreciate that."

He especially went out of his way for the *Tribune*'s beat writer, Melissa Isaacson, who was pregnant. He'd soothingly touch her stomach almost every time she walked past, sometimes bringing a chair over for her when she was standing in the locker room interviewing players. During the massive interview sessions when the media stood six and seven people around him, Jordan would demand she be brought up front, parting the reporters like Moses did the Red Sea.

"He was very gallant, sincere," Isaacson said. "Very sweet."

Kent McDill, the senior beat writer who'd been covering the team since 1988 for the suburban *Daily Herald*, was perhaps the most cynical about Jordan's return. He wrote a widely quoted column about the damage Jordan could do to his legacy and suggested Jordan might be making a mistake to return.

Jordan took McDill aside one day before a game, said he'd seen the column (although it was unlikely Jordan had ever in his life seen a copy of the *Herald*, a quality but modestly distributed newspaper), and understood the points McDill was trying to make, good ones, Jordan added. But Jordan explained why he was back, what it all meant to him.

And with Lacy Banks, the *Sun-Times*'s basketball writer who formerly covered the Bulls, Jordan would joke and mock him like they were two old friends, one day arguing for almost a half hour before a game about who could run long distances faster, with Jordan playfully mimicking the burly Banks's running style, as if he were alone with his closest friend.

It was a full-court press. When national writers came in, columnists whom Jordan might have seen only once or twice a year, Jordan called them by their first names, occasionally grabbing one around the shoulder for some whispering.

Just for you, buddy.

Suddenly, it was a much more open Jordan, relieved to have returned and finally accepting the realization that despite all the controversies—the switch to baseball and back, the gambling, the rumors of suspension, his belief the media was out to get him and destroy him—the truth was that both he and his image not only had sustained themselves but had grown to never imagined proportions.

It was a new, paranoia-free Jordan who faced the media now, secure in the realization that nothing had touched him, nothing could touch him. Suddenly, he didn't have to be as careful as he had once been about where he was going or what he was doing. Where he had always tried to hide his golf games during the season and playoffs, noting how the coaches frowned on them and teammates sometimes resented them (like when Jordan golfed after that 63-point playoff game in Boston and had little energy for the next game, or when he came in coughing and hacking and weak after playing in the rain before a back-to-back set of playoff games against the Pistons), now he was completely up front. Asked by reporters after a game what he was doing that day, Jordan responded, "Playing golf. Any problems with that?"

None, it seemed.

"You know how you go on vacation and then come back home everything looks fresher?" Jordan said to reporters after his return. "Well, I'm having the best time of my life now. I'm doing what I love, and not that I didn't before, but I've had a chance to revisit my life and people don't get a chance to do that. I wasn't enjoying the game eighteen months ago. I am now."

Jordan even seemed to be tolerating Krause. He still didn't talk with Krause much, but he seemed generally unbothered by the general manager, who could drive Jordan crazy just by being nearby. Jordan used to lead his teammates in making up mocking nicknames for Krause, like "Crumbs," a tribute to what Jordan claimed were doughnut remnants on his lapels, and making swine noises when Krause came into the locker room.

Jordan's enmity stemmed from a dispute with Krause almost ten years earlier when Jordan was recovering from a broken foot. Jordan wanted to return to play; Krause insisted that he should sit out the rest of the season, that they didn't want to risk their star. But Jordan believed that the team wasn't in any hurry to win games, that they were just trying to get into the draft lottery for a better pick. The team said Jordan's health wasn't worth making the last playoff spot and being swept by the best Celtics team of the decade, which is what happened.

Both arguments had merit, but Jordan had already started testing his star muscle. Like a kid, he'd push to see how much he could get away with. It's why he came to have great respect for Dean Smith and Jackson, two men who, like his father, would tell Jordan no. He'd never like it at first, but he came to respect their authority.

Krause's problem was that he'd say no but at the same time attempt to be friends with the players. Always the kid who hung around the athletes growing up, Krause spent a lifetime desperately trying to be accepted by the cool guys, even when he became their boss. But his role with the Bulls cast him as the bad cop, the tough guy who usually makes the low-ball contract offer before Reinsdorf steps in and graciously makes a more accommodating proposal. But Reinsdorf maintains an arm's-length relationship with the players, and they give him grudging respect as the employer. Krause, on the other hand, routinely travels with the team, hangs out in the locker room, and appears in the trainers' room with the players for treatment of his chronically bad back.

He wants to be in on the players' jokes and talk basketball with the guys. But he's never understood he cannot be both, and in trying to be a friend to both the players and Reinsdorf, he'd become a symbol of the frustration players have with the organization. And very easy to mock. After all, these are kids playing a kid's game.

But there was another side to Krause that was rarely seen. In fact, in a rare occurrence, Jordan and Krause actually had a mutual interest.

One practice day, sitting in the trainers' room in the Berto Center, Jordan was approached by the Bulls' veteran public relations chief Tim Hallam. Hallam wanted to know what to tell reporters, was Jordan coming out to talk that day? No, Jordan said. Not today. Hallam started to leave when Pippen, jokingly, asked if he was "carrying." Hallam had recently been arrested on substance abuse charges, charges that were later dismissed.

"Hey, cut it out," Jordan demanded, jumping to Hallam's defense. "He's getting himself together."

The charges seemed minor at the time, a minor mistake made by a man caught up in personal problems, and had he not been a visible member of the Bulls organization, the episode would have gone unnoticed. But the Chicago TV media made it a major story, particularly the CBS-TV affiliate, which irresponsibly suggested that there was perhaps some connection to the Bulls team.

Hallam, who'd gone through a painful divorce and had been Jordan's point man on the road for nine exhausting years, was particularly vulnerable. And it would have been easy for the team to dump him, since the Bulls had shown they wouldn't tolerate such action from players. It had been Krause who, years before, systematically got rid of the drug users on the team— Orlando Woolridge, Quintin Dailey, Ennis Whatley—all of whom later went through successful treatment programs. (During his rookie year, Jordan once walked in on a bunch of teammates using cocaine and marijuana and turned around, never to hang around with that group again.)

But on the day of Hallam's arrest, it was Krause who was there to assure him that if he got the proper treatment he'd be welcomed back to the Bulls. Krause helped arrange for an attorney and a treatment facility, and almost every day, Krause or his wife, Thelma, called Hallam's new wife, Nancy, to find out about her welfare and check up on Hallam. It went on for weeks, and later Hallam's doctors would say that it was Krause's assurances and support that were key to giving Hallam the will to get himself the proper care.

Yet Krause, for all his unseen good deeds, would still continue to take abuse from somewhere, anywhere.

There was the sports radio call-in show whose topic for the day was whether a woman would sleep with Krause for $1 million. "They said it was for women only," recalled Steve Kerr, "and women are saying no, and some woman calls in and says, 'Yes, for $1 million.' And the guy on the radio says, 'Now that's all night in your bed.' It was disgusting," Kerr said, "ridiculous."

The players all laughed about it, but not Hallam, and not those who knew what Krause had done for him.

When Jordan was deciding whether to return to the NBA, he chose to ignore Krause and deal directly with Reinsdorf, since Jordan had grown comfortable with Reinsdorf and the two had discussed future business dealings. He later boasted to teammates that when he finally informed Krause of his return, it was in a brief speakerphone call with his kids making a fuss in the background.

But he was making every effort to keep peace with Krause, who had longed for the chance to rebuild but now would try to keep running in place for as long as possible. As Krause continued to take a beating from Pippen and restless fans, Jordan tried to make the best of their volatile relationship.

Jackson had noticed the unusual tolerance in Jordan immediately upon his return.

"He's encouraging with the guys, trying to tell them what to do, where he'll be on the court, 'You set this pick, and then I'll use you that way,' that kind of stuff," said Jackson. "He's taking guys and playing one-on-one, players like Dickey [Simpkins] for the fun and thrill of it. He's still involved in the shooting games and likes to make those little bets, but there's also been this acceptance, which also has helped us as coaches."

COULDN'T JORDAN BACK ME UP ONCE?

Pete Myers, like everyone else, was caught up in the excitement of Jordan's return to basketball.

Myers had worked himself back into the starting lineup in place of high-priced free agent Ron Harper after having become the answer to a trivia question: Who was the guard that replaced Michael Jordan with the Bulls?

But even after a solid season, starting all but one game and being one of the few Bulls to stand up to the New York Knicks in the Bulls' seventh-game Eastern Conference Semifinals loss in May 1994, Myers hadn't been invited back for the 1994–95 season.

Instead, the Bulls signed Ron Harper to a $19.2 million all-guaranteed deal over five years. But Harper had disappointed the coaching staff and was benched, playing most of the 1994–95 season behind Myers and Steve Kerr, and Myers was

getting caught up in the excitement of still another unlikely res-
urrection for him and perhaps another big playoff run.

"Man, think about what's it's going to be like if he comes
back," Myers had exulted before anyone knew for sure.

"If he comes back, you're not going to be starting," joked
Lacy Banks, the *Sun-Times*'s basketball writer. Banks, who was
also a preacher, had held a lonely vigil since Jordan's departure, saying it was Jordan's only destiny to return to the NBA.

"Oh, yeah," said the likable Myers. "I won't be starting."

"Starting!" roared Scottie Pippen, sitting nearby. "You'll be
lucky to be on the team if Michael comes back. They'll probably cut you."

"Not only had I just gotten back in shape," recalled Myers,
"but I was playing my best ball of the season, the team was on
a roll, I had just gotten my starting job back, and I'm thinking,
'Okay, I've got a chance to get a deal for next season.' I've
never even had a guaranteed contract for one year ahead, and
all of a sudden I look up and here he is at practice. I thought,
'Damn, here we go again.'"

The previous November, Myers was sitting at home in
Chicago, watching the Bulls on TV as they made their first
Western Conference trip. Detroit had shown some interest in
him and so had Washington, but Myers remained without a
basketball job.

He had just come off of the most productive season of his
career, but there were no offers for the thirty-two-year-old
Myers. One night that summer of 1994, he was at a concert in
Chicago's south suburbs and ran into Harper.

What was he doing here? Myers asked Harper.

"I just signed with the Bulls," Harper said.

"Oh," Myers said, "I see."

The Bulls decided to keep CBA guard JoJo English, Myers's
agent told him, because English would be cheaper, since
Myers was unwilling to play for the $150,000 league minimum.
Myers was once again out of a job.

"It's natural to want to watch the guy who replaced you,"
admitted Myers. "But I didn't see the Ron Harper I remem-

bered. I don't know if it was because he didn't know the system or he wasn't healthy, but he was struggling. My agent kept calling me and said they might want me back."

Myers had heard that before.

He was a long shot to start with, a skinny kid out of Mobile, Alabama, where baseball and football are kings and basketball is craps. And life seemed to be, too. Pete's father, with whom he was exceptionally close, was killed when a shot aimed at another man accidentally hit him, the innocent victim.

It's tough to lose a father tragically at any time, as a future teammate of Myers's would discover. Pete took it exceptionally hard, and that, combined with knee problems from an unusual growth spurt prevented him from playing sports when he was in high school. Pete was on the edge of a deep fall into the well of lost youth, but he was able to return to basketball as a senior, now almost a foot taller and a top player, though still not a star.

He went to Faulkner State Junior College, then worked himself into a basketball scholarship at the University of Arkansas–Little Rock, where he occasionally went out with a teammate's friend, a quiet kid and not a particularly outstanding player from a nearby Arkansas college, Scottie Pippen. But the Bulls chose Meyers in the sixth round—number 120—in the 1986 draft, and suddenly Myers was practicing against Jordan every day.

"All those guys I watched growing up, hearing Dick Stockton talk about, and I was there, but I was never afraid," said the wispy six-six Myers, whose feisty attitude has kept him around the game. "That was the year Mike averaged thirty-seven, so he'd play forty-five minutes and then he'd go out with a few seconds left so everyone could applaud and then I would go in."

But the next training camp, the Bulls brought in four rookies, Pippen and Grant, plus Tony White and Ricky Winslow. The latter two were cut quickly, but not before Myers. That would begin an arduous journey around the edges of pro basketball, Myers going to the CBA, to Italy and Spain for two years, to the Spurs, 76ers, Knicks, Nets, and back to the Spurs again, all brief stints. Myers was a nice addition to a team, a defense-oriented guard who didn't want to score and didn't care too much about how many minutes he played. But there was always something—a coaching change, a minor injury, a new rookie, a trade—and being at the end of the bench without a guaranteed contract, Myers was always the one lopped off.

After two seasons in Europe, Myers decided to give the NBA one more try and was ready to go to camp in Sacramento when Krause called his agent in October 1993.

Myers, of course, was pleased, since he now made his home in Chicago. He didn't know the Bulls were calling because Jordan was retiring. Jordan would later stop by in training camp and counsel and encourage Myers, who knew his life in the NBA often depended on hitting the one or two shots he'd be allowed to take in a game.

"It makes it tougher when you think you have to make every one to stay," Myers said.

Suddenly he was the Bulls' shooting guard everyone wanted to interview. In training camp, he even sat in Jordan's locker stall for a while until Pippen claimed it, one day cleaning it out in front of reporters with great glee.

Finding a hairbrush, Pippen quipped: "What was he doing with this? He had no hair. It's not like he's going to miss it." Discovering an old T-shirt, Pippen reached out toward the reporters and said, "Here, anyone want to wipe your tears?"

"I even had to put a 'Do Not Disturb' on my phone before the opening game, I got so many calls," Myers said about the hours before the opening game. "That hasn't happened in a long time."

How long, exactly? Myers was asked.

Well, actually, never.

Myers averaged about eight points per game, and even Jackson admitted it allowed the Bulls to do more in their offense than they could have with Jordan, by moving the ball so well. Not that Jackson preferred Myers to Jordan. But Myers did appreciate Jackson's egalitarian coaching method. Jackson starts every season with a team meeting, saying that once the season starts, it doesn't matter what you earn: The guy who performs best in Jackson's eyes will play. And midway through the 1994–95 season, much to Krause's dismay and anger, Jackson demoted Harper and his $4 million annual salary for Myers and his $550,000. Jackson particularly liked Myers's fire on a team that, without Jordan, often lacked the toughness and heart to fight back. Myers had fought hard his whole life, and when in just the second game of his new career with the Bulls, Miami's Steve Smith began elbowing him and taunting him about going back to the CBA, Myers drew a fine for fighting back. Later that season he would have to be separated from Smith in a hallway in the Miami Arena.

"If I didn't love to play so much, I guess I would have given up a few years ago," says Myers. "But I believed in myself, so no matter how many knocks or obstacles were thrown in my way, I felt I deserved to be here and I felt I deserved to be part of the Bulls and make a decent salary. But it's always been like that, a roller coaster."

Myers's roller coaster would take yet another plunge. When Jordan returned to the Bulls, Myers returned to the bench.

"You knew what was coming, but I was just hoping to get in that one more start in Indiana," recalls Myers. "I knew it would be the last time I'd get to start in an NBC [nationally televised] game. But then Phil came to me before the game and said he was starting Michael."

Myers's playing time diminished rapidly, and then in the playoffs, Jackson would return to playing Harper more regularly than Myers, who became one of the last players off the bench for just a few, if any, minutes per game. After the season, the Bulls would tell Myers they probably would not bring him back.

NOT WILL PERDUE, *CAN* PERDUE?

The new kinder, gentler Jordan had a tremendous impact on all the players, but perhaps none more than Will Perdue. Perdue had been one of Jordan's most frequent targets of abuse during

Jordan's first run with the team; Jordan had slugged him once in a practice after Perdue had set a hard pick on him, making Jordan angry because Perdue wouldn't do the same in games. Generally, he had regarded Perdue as ill equipped to perform on a competent NBA level.

But now it was a more humane, less critical Jordan who returned to the Bulls, at least in the beginning. "Baseball probably helped him see it from the other side a little better," said Perdue. "He needed coaching, he had to swallow some of that ego. Here he is six-six and two hundred pounds, a guy who's taken all this pounding, and he's watching hundred-fifty-pound guys hit the ball over the fence and he can't get it out of the infield. He still could be harsh, but when he came back he was a little more understanding."

For Perdue, who had been there in the early days and witnessed Jordan's wrath on and off the court, it was quite a shock. It had taken Jordan years to become comfortable with his former Bulls teammates, to believe they could perform if he gave them the opportunity. It was that ego and determination that opponents had so easily exploited in Jordan and the Bulls. Both Boston and Detroit knew that if you handled the other guys, Jordan would lose confidence in them and try to do it all himself, an endeavor that kept the Bulls from winning; even 63 points against Boston in the playoffs was not enough to win the game. But Jordan came to understand and accept Pippen and Grant and Cartwright and Paxson, and as for the rest, well, to heck with them.

"I don't know if you can say Michael gave up on guys," said Perdue. "But he would do what he could with a guy for a certain amount of time, then that would be it and he'd move on."

And usually, the player did, too.

Jordan couldn't have expected that Perdue would be around for a return in 1995. The Bulls thought so little of the veteran center they left him off the playoff roster in 1994 for a free agent out of the CBA, JoJo English.

"I was devastated," Perdue admitted.

Sure, Perdue wasn't very nimble and shot the ball like he was throwing hand grenades. But he had been there for all three championships.

"You learn," said Perdue, "they're paying you a lot of money, so you have to take care of your career yourself, and if you don't do the job they'll find someone else. They sure know how to take the fun out of the game."

Jackson had long soured on Perdue's ability to help the team, and the two repeatedly clashed. Most coaches, including Jackson, like to express themselves, sometimes rather colorfully, during games when they believe players have made mistakes. For former players like Jackson who still have the competitive urges, it's a release. Players are expected to nod and move on; most tune the coaches out. But Perdue, a kid who grew up anxious to please elders, infuriated Jackson by constantly trying to explain that he hadn't made a mistake. It angered Jackson enough that he helped orchestrate the trade for Luc Longley earlier in 1994 with the idea of pushing Perdue out.

Which is what the gangly seven-footer expected after six years with the Bulls. He was drafted out of Vanderbilt in 1988, Southeastern Conference player of the year, as the heir apparent to Bill Cartwright. But he never developed to the Bulls' liking, especially on defense, where the coaches said Perdue flinched in the face of attacks on the basket. Although seven feet tall, Perdue weighed only about 240 and didn't present a huge obstacle.

Perdue seemed destined to be another in a long line of failed Bulls centers. In the early 1980s there was Wallace Bryant asking veteran trainer Mark Pfeil to check his ears because he thought air was escaping through his head. Years later, Juwan Oldham was once playing a video guessing game with some players and the question came up: Which of these NBA centers was born in the United States? Patrick Ewing, Hakeem Olajuwon, Manute Bol, or Juwan Oldham. Oldham, a Seattle native, said he didn't know. The answer was, of course, Juwan Oldham.

Likewise, Perdue was mocked when he came to the Bulls,

regarded as clumsy and ineffective. But he'd won over the fans throughout the years, perhaps less with his play, which was steady on the offensive boards, than with an intimacy generally unseen in professionals these days.

Perdue was a true fan. He'd go to White Sox and Cubs games, Blackhawks or Bears games, but instead of sitting in luxury boxes, he'd buy a seat in the bleachers or the upper balcony, slosh down beer and popcorn, and yell for the home team. The fans loved it.

"They saw me as a normal person," said Perdue. "I wasn't on a pedestal being a Bulls player. All of a sudden they turn around and I'm sitting next to them. I've stood with standing room tickets, sat in the second balcony in the stadium, and now I'm just a normal guy who doesn't think he's better than anyone else."

The problem was, the Bulls seemed to think that, too.

After his unceremonious exclusion from the playoffs in 1994, Perdue hung around the team for a few games and practices, but he couldn't take the humiliation and requested a trade; Krause, however, liked big men in reserve. Perdue was ready to start making a fuss in the media. He and his wife, Jennifer, decided against buying a house, figuring their stay would be short.

But Jennifer had an idea. Perdue was sitting around moping over his playoff demotion most of the summer of 1994, "pretty much demoralized," he admitted, when Jennifer said he should try some different form of training.

"Actually, it was my agent who suggested it," said Perdue, "but it was Jennifer's idea. But when you're in a deranged state like I was and thinking how bad life is and your wife comes up and says she has an idea about basketball, well, you're thinking, 'Where does she come from?' But my agent [Bill Blakely] coached in the ABA. He knows basketball."

The idea was to hire a personal basketball coach, someone who played the position, knew Chicago and the Bulls, knew the abuse Perdue had taken. Jennifer suggested former Bulls center Dave Corzine.

Corzine was the center who replaced Artis Gilmore in Chicago, and though he was a Chicago native, he was another in a line of slow, awkward, white centers like Tom Boerwinkle. Corzine was out of basketball and between business ventures, so he embraced the new role, which would lead to the head-coaching job of the CBA Chicago Rockers for the 1995–96 season.

He picked up tapes of Perdue from previous years, talked with Jackson and Tex Winter about what they felt Perdue needed, got books from the library on playing center, filmed Perdue and analyzed his game against other centers and Perdue's previous play, and entered Perdue in summer leagues against varied types of Chicago competition.

"Michael always used to talk about how Bill [Cartwright] got in his way," Perdue recalled, "but he liked playing with Dave. Dave knew how to set screens, was a great shooter. Phil's idea of a center is Willis Reed, a big body who can do a little bit of everything. On this team we didn't have that, but it's not necessary to have a big body at all times. Dave helped give my confidence a boost, and with the centers we had, I felt I could start if given a chance.

"To Michael, I was one of those guys who dribbled off his foot, didn't know how to shoot, didn't know anything about the game," said Perdue. "But I learned from playing with Michael over the years that you've got to expect the pass at any time. Michael has more of a scorer's mentality and looks to score first. He'll go into a crowd intent on getting the shot off. If he can't get it off, he'll make the pass. Scottie and Toni have the intention of going to the hole, but as soon as they see an open man, they'll dump it off. With Michael you've got to be ready."

When the 1994–95 season began, Perdue found himself starting for the first time in his career, as Longley was forced out with an injury. And in January, shortly before Jordan's return, as Longley was preparing to come back off the bench, Perdue said he would ask for a trade if Jackson put Longley back in the lineup as a starter without showing he could out-play Perdue. It had been Perdue's first chance as a starter, and he was performing reasonably well. But although Perdue was a good rebounder and passer and knew the Bulls' offensive system well, Jackson believed that the Bulls would have no chance of success unless Longley could be effective thirty-five minutes per game.

It would be a touchy issue for Jackson, since the players favored Perdue and felt it was Longley, not Perdue, who wasn't tough enough or strong enough to fight back. Perdue remained the starter, although the threat of Longley hung over him like a seven-two, 290-pound cloud.

When Jordan returned, it was Longley, not Perdue, who would face Jordan's wrath.

Jordan was surprisingly public with his unhappiness toward the big center. "I told Luc," Jordan said after a few games back, "if he doesn't catch any more of my passes, I'm going to hit him right in the face with it. I'm going to start throwing them right at his head." Jordan also said he preferred playing with Perdue.

Jackson cringed. During Jordan's return, Jackson's plan had been to steadily reduce Perdue's minutes on the floor and reintroduce Longley for the playoffs, when, Jackson felt, Longley's bigger presence would aid the team defensively.

But Jackson backed off somewhat after Jordan's comments.

"Why did you have to say that?" Jackson asked the next morning after seeing the newspaper.

"I'm sorry," Jordan said. "They [the media] caught me and I wasn't thinking about it."

Later, Jordan would demand during a game that Jackson remove Longley.

It was, in many respects, the same way Jordan dealt with Bill Cartwright in their first year together, mocking him and telling teammates not to pass him the ball, firing impossible passes and then glaring at him.

Cartwright, of course, dealt with it in his own way, remaining quiet for some time before telling Jordan that if his antics continued he would make sure Jordan never played basketball again.

"You got to take him down," Cartwright said. "That's how you deal with him. Phil would never let me practice against him. He'd either be on my team or I'd be sitting. Phil knew I was taking him down."

Longley had neither the heart nor inclination for that. But after Jordan's first game back he did offer that he didn't think the savior was with us quite yet.

"He certainly elevates the performance of others, but it's not by coaching on the floor," said Longley. "People make it seem like he's waving this magic wand over us and we're all better players all of a sudden. And that's a bit frustrating."

Jordan, incredibly, was now embracing Perdue and starting to talk up the once ungainly center.

"Will has great hands," Jordan said. "He has a knack for seeing passes and he finishes pretty good. He keeps the ball high, which eliminates the ball getting slapped away, which happens when you bring the ball down around your waist. The other two guys, Bill and Luc, have a tendency to bring the ball down and guards kind of come and knock the ball away. But either way, I think it's going to take some time for them to adjust to certain passes. I've been with Will and I think he understands those types of moves, slip off the picks and look for the ball. That's always going to be the difference between us two and the other guys."

If Jordan preferred Perdue as a starter, so did the rest of the team, though not because they were so enamored with Perdue.

"A guy's got to earn his spot," said Pippen.

Chapter 11

ONE IF BY LAND, TWO IF IT'S JORDAN

The biggest farewell/welcome-back tour in sports history was under way.

With his return on Sunday, March 19, in Indianapolis, Jordan said he liked the notion of starting on the road and giving himself two games, against the Pacers and Celtics, before his big welcome home in the new United Center on Friday, March 24, against Shaquille O'Neal, Horace Grant, and the Orlando Magic, the team with the best record in the Eastern Conference.

Jordan's return became the most watched regular season NBA game in history, with two-thirds of Chicago's TVs tuned to the game. So what were those other people watching?

TNT and NBC were scrambling to add any Jordan game possible; the joke going around was that Jordan was going to appear on TNT so often that Ted Turner would want to colorize him.

The night before that first game, the Jordanaires pulled into the Canterbury Hotel in Indianapolis. Jordan would not be joining his teammates that night; the hysteria had prevented him from traveling with the team.

As they exited the bus in Indianapolis, Pete Myers, with vaguely the same build as Jordan, had teammate Larry Krystkowiak hold a towel over Myers's head as they ran from the bus to the hotel entrance. Cameras clicked madly, and hundreds of spectators screamed, "Michael, Michael!"

Then someone finally yelled, "Hey, that's not Michael."

"He wasn't Michael anymore," said Myers, who was Jordan's backup in the 1986–87 season when Myers was a rookie. "He was Michael then. Now he was Air Jordan. When I met him he was a basketball player. When he came back, he was an entertainer. He tried to be the same person, but he wasn't. There was the hype, all hype."

Despite the fantasy script that would have had Jordan scoring 100 points in his first game back, Jordan would shoot seven of twenty-eight for 19 points and the Bulls would lose 103–96. It was a precursor to the rest of the season.

Fifteen seconds into the game, Jordan swooped up behind Pacers center Rik Smits and stole the ball, cameras clicking crazily. Jordan lined his first shot off the front of the rim.

He wouldn't score until the second quarter, after the Bulls, equally nervous, missed nine of their first ten shots and fell behind 13–2. With just over four minutes left in the half, Jordan scored on an eighteen-foot jumper, his first NBA basket in twenty-one months. The Bulls were behind 47–37 at halftime.

Jordan would shoot two of nine in the first half and then three of thirteen in the second half. But after the rest of the team shot 33 percent in the first half, led by Scottie Pippen's 31 points for the game, the Bulls rallied from 16 behind with eight minutes left to tie the game in regulation on a Pippen 3-pointer with nineteen seconds left.

Jordan did hit two jumpers in overtime, but the Pacers jumped out ahead and took the game.

"It was pretty disappointing from my standpoint," Jordan would admit afterward, his first statements to reporters since he left White Sox camp two weeks earlier. "With the competitor I am, I wanted to come out and do well. That's probably one of the reasons a lot of my shots were short and my layups were long. But whatever it may be, it was good competition."

Then Jordan smiled. "The Bulls were playing good till I came back," he joked. "I love the game and that's why I came back. It's not about money or commercial things or anything else. At the time I walked away, I needed to get away, probably mentally more than anything. But it isn't like I could separate myself from the things I love. I began to realize over time I truly missed the game. I missed my friends, I missed my team-mates, I missed the atmosphere a little bit. I know what I'm doing here.

"At least I thought I did."

Still Jordan was looking ahead. "It was one of those bad games for me," Jordan admitted, "but that means I've got something to build on. If I came back and scored 60, it looks boring. Now I have to work myself back up to my caliber of play. It's disappointing I played bad, but it ain't the first time. I wish it was. I hope it's the last time."

Despite the loss, the day still belonged to Jordan. Pacers coach Larry Brown would liken it to the return of the Beatles and Elvis Presley.

The Bulls headed to Boston for Game 2 of the Jordan Traveling Show, site of Jordan's record playoff effort in 1986 and the friendly rims he'd enjoyed over the years in daring shoot-outs with Larry Bird. Bird would be there, this time as a spectator, but also to honor the memory of his late teammate Reggie Lewis. Lewis's number was being retired amid accusations in the media that he had used drugs that perhaps contributed to his death.

It was also a night for nostalgia: the Bulls' last game in the old Gahden, as Bostonians pronounced it, and memories of Bird, Bob Cousy, and other Celtics greats there for the Reggie Lewis retirement ceremony, and some fond memories of gravely voiced announcer Johnny Most, who was synonymous with the Garden and who had died recently.

Most was from the corps of legendary play-by-play announcers with a distinctive style, like Philadelphia's Dave Zinkoff and the Lakers' Chick Hearn, who probably wouldn't get jobs today because of their unique styles.

Most was a chain smoker and always had a cigarette going during broadcasts. One night he was making the call, and unbeknownst to him, some burning ash had fallen onto his pants. Most was following the ball in his distinctive growl: "Bird, to McHale to Parish to—oh, my God, I'm on fire."

But the Bulls wouldn't see much of the dingy old Garden until the game. As Jackson had done in the past when the pressure was turned up too high, he decided to shake things up. For example, after a tough loss to the Knicks during the 1994 playoffs, Jackson snuck the players away from the media and practice for a ride on the Staten Island Ferry to relieve the tension. It was even a little educational, as Horace Grant said he learned the Liberty statue depicted a woman.

A few years back during the regular season, Jackson took the team on a tour of Congress with a former teammate, U.S. senator Bill Bradley. Another time he lectured about guns when Pippen was arrested on a weapons charge, about terrorism a few years back during the Persian Gulf War, and he gave a pop quiz on Casimir Pulaski during the Polish general's holiday in heavily Polish Chicago.

"I feel a responsibility to these players beyond basketball because of the amount of time we spend together," Jackson said.

Jackson felt it was essential to incorporate humor and tension release into the team's regimen.

After Jordan left, the team was routinely having trouble after halftime, blowing many leads. Jackson said he thought he knew the problem: The team was not getting the full effect of his halftime talk. He asked for a show of hands of how many players were urinating before his talk, how many after, perhaps that division being a reason for those poor second-half performances.

"It's always a combination of humor and seriousness with Phil," says Steve Kerr. "That ferry ride. No other coach in the NBA would have done that. It would have been right to the gym and more film. The NBA season is so long and Phil understands that. It can't be all basketball. He talks about Native Americans a lot and spiritualism, burns incense to burn out the evil spirits haunting the team.

"I remember one time in training camp he says we're not

being aggressive enough on the court," recalled Kerr. "So he gets all of us, about twenty guys, to line up facing each other. And then he told us to jump up and down like gorillas with a stick of gum with the wrapper in our mouths to get the aggression to come out.

"Some guys think he's totally wacko," admitted Kerr. "But most guys realize it's great. If you've been with other teams you can appreciate the things he does. For the guys who have been around, they know, and that's one reason why I think he can last longer than other coaches in this league."

So as the hysteria and frenzy continued to swirl around the Bulls, Jackson once again changed the team's routine. Early in the day before the Celtics game, instead of going to shootaround, Jackson took the team to the hotel ballroom to meditate. He brought in a "stress reduction expert" from the University of Massachusetts.

"You know," said Jackson, "we're channeling energy through the body, stretching, consciously moving energy throughout the body and head, through the spinal cord to generate energy to other parts of the body."

Jackson knew the pressure would only be building with Jordan back, and the crowds would only get bigger, along with the demands and attention. Predictably, the celebrities were also starting to gather around Jordan. Actor Bill Murray was staying in the Bulls' hotel in Boston and had worked out earlier in the day in the hotel exercise room with former Bulls guard John Paxson, now doing radio color for the team. Afterward he sent a note to Paxson: "I am experiencing excruciating pain right now."

Jordan was experiencing pure joy. He stole center stage again with a routine 27 points in twenty-six minutes in a 124–107 Bulls win, Jordan's time limited by foul trouble. He also recorded another first, the first slam dunk of his second career on an alley-oop pass from Pippen. The Bulls won easily over a team that was a mere shell of what the Celtics' teams had been.

"It was good to be home," Jordan said, latching on to the venerable Boston Garden in its final season. "Since Chicago Stadium isn't here. This is now my home."

James Jordan was his son's best friend and closest adviser. His murder—and the negative rumors about it—contributed to the retirement of the younger Jordan in 1993. *AP/Wide World Photos*

Stunned Bulls chairman Jerry Reinsdorf sits alongside his departing superstar at the press conference announcing Jordan's retirement on October 6, 1993: "He surprised me. I should have seen the signs, the strain of that last championship year after the Olympics when he had no time off that summer, the gambling stuff." *AP/Wide World Photos*

Chicago White Sox batter Michael Jordan hits a single during an exhibition game against the Florida Marlins during 1994 spring training. "I'm curious to see if baseball is as hard as I think it is," said then Sox manager, Gene Lamont, of the Jordan experiment. *AP/Wide World Photos*

Jordan laughs during a work-out with the Sox just prior to signing his minor league contract. The smile would soon disappear, though, as the reality of his skill level hit home. *AP/Wide World Photos*

The Jordan family looks on as Bulls chairman Jerry Reinsdorf retires Jordan's number 23 at the United Center on November 1, 1994. With Jordan are his mother, Deloris (*far left*), his wife, Juanita, holding daughter, Jasmine, and his two sons, Marcus (*front left*) and Jeffrey. Looking on is talk-show host Larry King. *AP/Wide World Photos*

n November 1, 1994, twelve-foot bronze tatue of Jordan was nveiled outside the nited Center. Four onths later, as rumors a comeback began to rculate, fans began ving coins and other ementos at its base. P/Wide World Photos

On March 19, 1995, in Indianapolis, Jordan is introduced at his first NBA game in twenty-one months. Earlier that morning, he spent over an hour sitting alone on a private jet, thinking about his father and wishing that his father was there to see him through the ordeal. *AP/Wide World Photos*

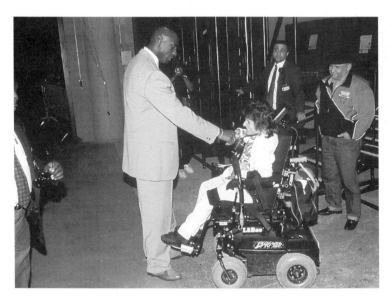

Jordan's fan and friend Carmen Villafane has, since 1988, received tickets for every home game, courtesy of Jordan. His comeback so excited her that she made the trip to Indiana to see him play. *Photo by Bill Smith*

Jordan didn't score in his comeback game against the Pacers until the second quarter, when, with just over four minutes left in the half, he scored on an eighteen-foot jumper. *AP/Wide World Photos*

Jordan didn't wait long to show his teammates who was boss on the court. *AP/Wide World Photos*

Luc Longley, the big center who became Jordan's most frequent target. *Courtesy Chicago Bulls*

Pete Myers, the guard who replaced Jordan in 1994 and lost his job when Jordan returned. *Courtesy Chicago Bulls*

Toni Kukoc, the Croatian import who cried when Jordan retired but was confused about his role when Jordan returned. *Courtesy Chicago Bulls*

Steve Kerr, the likable 3-point champion who became the most quotable Bull before Jordan's return. *Courtesy Chicago Bulls*

Ron Harper, the high-salaried "replacement" for Jordan, failed to emerge as the star the Bulls thought they had purchased. *Courtesy Chicago Bulls*

B. J. Armstrong, the sweet-faced kid who was frequently a cauldron of frustration. *Courtesy Chicago Bulls*

Bill Wennington, the veteran backup center, was another of the failing Bulls Jordan had trouble adjusting to. *Courtesy Chicago Bulls*

Jud Buechler, the NBA journeyman who, as a pro beach volleyball player, was the only two-sport player on the team. *Courtesy Chicago Bulls*

Larry Krystkowiak, the oft-injured power forward who ran afoul of Jordan early. *Courtesy Chicago Bulls*

Will Perdue, the long-maligned center whom Jordan embraced over Longley. *Courtesy Chicago Bulls*

Jordan towers over the Charlotte Hornets' Muggsy Bogues in Game 3 of the Eastern Conference playoffs. The Bulls towered over the Hornets as well, taking the series in four games. *AP/Wide World Photos*

The matchup of Jordan and Shaquille O'Neal was heralded as the battle of the century: Nike vs. Reebok, Coke vs. Pepsi. *AP/Wide World Photos*

Jordan drives past the Magic's Nick Anderson in Game 3 of the playoffs. Earlier in the week, Anderson started a firestorm by saying, "Number 23, he could just blow right by you. Number 45, he revs up, but he doesn't really take off." Jordan switched his number for the next game. *AP/Wide World Photos*

The Bulls' playoff loss to the Magic would put an end to the NBA conspiracy theories for now; there would be no seventh-game ratings bonanza featuring Jordan and O'Neal. *AP/Wide World Photos*

Scottie Pippen embraced Jordan's return in March but by June found himself frustrated over the team's failure and his diminished role. *AP/Wide World Photos*

Coach Phil Jackson felt powerless to overcome the pattern of isolation and alienation between Jordan's stardom and his teammates' mortality. "Looking back at everything, if I had it all to do over again—and I expect I will—I would have locked them all together in a room for a day and let them get this all hashed out," said Jackson. *AP/Wide World Photos*

The 1994–95 Chicago Bulls. *Courtesy Chicago Bulls*

The *Boston Globe*'s account of the game referred to Jordan as "He" and "Him," as in the biblical sense.

"I am not a god," Jordan continued to insist. "When it is perceived as a religion, that's when I'm embarrassed by it [the acclaim]."

Divine or not, he did offer guidance to Boston's rookie center Eric Montross, a fellow North Carolina graduate, who missed all eight of his free throws.

"He said I was shooting my free throws like Shaq," Montross said.

"A couple of more games and I'll be ready to play forty-five minutes where I'm not hanging on at the end," said Jordan. "Now we'll get a look at where we are with Orlando."

Michael Jordan was coming home.

"AND FROM NORTH CAROLINA . . . "

That was all anyone heard that night in the United Center, as the decibel level during the pregame introduction was recorded somewhere between the sound of sandblasting and outright pain. It was Michael Jordan's first regulation NBA game in Chicago since June 1993, and Chicago, America's biggest little city, had turned out to honor its hero. Again.

"Well," said WGN-TV announcer Wayne Larivee, who mostly does Bears games, "the Super Bowl is still bigger."

Maybe, but not by much.

It was an event, not a game. More than four hundred media credentials were issued, with TV stations sending their principal news anchors to do the news live from the arena. Spike Lee flew in (without his John Starks jersey), a Warner Brothers crew came to shoot footage for a movie Jordan was making with Bugs Bunny, and Steve Kerr said he had become a roadie in the Jordan rock opera. United Center concessionaires reported selling almost a thousand number 45 Jordan jerseys at $50 each.

No one ever got tired of it in Chicago; he had become the city's chief export. No longer was Chicago most famous for gangsters and Al Capone and Prohibition, no longer did people identify Chicago with political scandal and voting by the deceased. Now Chicago was famous for Michael Jordan, and he had become synonymous with Chicago. Jordan symbolized excellence, commitment, celebrity, perhaps also an easy mark on the golf course. But that was fine, too. Nothing wrong with a little charity.

Jordan's restaurant, with a huge three-story mural of Jordan on the outside, had become one of the principal tourist attractions in Chicago. Seen the Water Tower? The Sears Tower? Nah. Had Michael's wife's favorite macaroni and cheese recipe at Jordan's.

Billboards of Jordan modeling clothes towered over nearly every interstate dissecting the city. Jordan's statue outside the new United Center drew tourists every day, quickly surpassing the Daley Center's Picasso as the most famous sculpture in the city. Jordan could drive a Range Rover, but Chevy dealers continued to sell Blazers through his commercials. A Niketown store featuring a floor of Jordan memorabilia on fashionable Michigan Avenue became a shrine. Chicago was the Second City, and it was all due to Jordan's Bulls. They'd vanquished the Knicks. Choke on it, New York. They'd knocked out the Lakers and Magic Johnson. Michael, you made us proud.

Be like Mike?

Who in Chicago didn't want to be?

When Jordan began wearing a tam after his return, teammate Ron Harper couldn't wait to get a hat just like it.

"He's always had a unique style in clothes," admired Harper.

Jordan had become fashion conscious in his early years in the NBA and was said to own hundreds of pairs of shoes that were not Nikes.

Steve Kerr used to crunch one of those supposedly energy-boosting Power Bars before games, but after Jordan returned, they were hard to find in the locker room.

"B.J. and I were the only ones eating them," Kerr said of the team's two 170-pound weaklings. "Michael comes back and starts eating them, and now everyone's eating them."

It was a curious phenomenon, one Jordan had to laugh about in his private moments.

He had always hated his appearance as a kid, particularly his big "Dumbo" ears his brother taunted him about. Even before "the tongue," Jordan's habit of flipping his tongue out when he drove to the basket that he picked up from watching his father tinker with the family car, it was Jordan's ears that got him attention.

"I call him Mr. Spock," former teammate Orlando Woolridge would say in reference to the pointy-eared Vulcan from Star Trek.

In his youth, Jordan wasn't particularly manly, usually fumbling around while his father, a skilled mechanic, worked on family cars with his brother and always ordered Michael into the house "with the women."

And Michael, so the story goes, even took a home economics course in high school because he feared he'd never marry because of his goofy looks and would have to sew for himself as a lifelong bachelor. If there was a statue of Jordan in high school, instead of Jordan taking flight and slamming the ball as he does outside the United Center, it would be Jordan pressed back to the wall, the wallflower, thinking he'd never bloom.

From "Uh, gee," to GQ, for Mike. It was perhaps an even more remarkable achievement than what he'd done in sports, Jordan sometimes thought.

As if the presence of Jordan wasn't enough, the game itself was an irresistible matchup for an event of incomparable magnitude. Michael and Scottie versus Shaq and Horace, the NBA's proven past versus its up-and-coming future.

Phil Jackson was thinking about Horace Grant.

Grant had missed the last two games against the Bulls, and Jackson was going to have some fun. In the past, Jackson had chided Grant for missing games against whomever his twin brother Harvey was playing for, and for contracting the "blue flu" throughout his free-agent year. So he was prepared when the media predictably asked before the game how the Bulls expected to defend Grant. Jackson wasn't sure, he said, because "he [Grant] hasn't shown up to play in these games."

It wasn't hard for Jackson to get to Grant. Jackson really wanted to win this game because he knew how much pressure Jordan was feeling, and he felt that distracting Grant might give the Bulls an edge.

Grant swallowed the bait.

"So Phil thinks I sit out too many games," Grant was fuming before the game. "Well, what I suggest is you check my record and check Phil's record [as a player]. I'm surprised they paid Phil his salary, he missed so many games. [Jackson had back surgery one year.]. He should have been paid part-time.

"I don't know why Phil is saying these things about me," complained Grant, who was soundly booed before and during the game, in contrast to the warm welcome he'd received back in January on his first trip back to Chicago. "He's supposed to be an educated man, but that's hitting below the belt when you question if someone is hurt. I have nothing against my former teammates, but you can't have respect for a coach when he says things like that."

Unfortunately, Jackson's psych job was as unsuccessful as Jordan was awful—four for fifteen shooting in the first half, seven of twenty-three for the game—as the Magic pummeled the Bulls in rebounds 53–35 and held their poise down the stretch by outscoring the Bulls 29–19 in the fourth quarter. It was a relatively easy 106–99 victory for the Magic, a harbinger for the playoffs, as Jordan repeatedly failed in the fourth quarter.

Jordan was not thrilled afterward.

"I'm used to playing across the street," he said in what would become a familiar refrain, as Jordan was both dejected and relieved as he patiently answered reporters' questions. "The dimensions are the same. I have to get used to the surroundings. But I just can't turn it on as much as I want to."

In addition to clanging shots off the side of the rim as if they were Shaquille O'Neal free throws, getting shots blocked by Brian Shaw, and missing several free throws, Jordan shot the Bulls out of the game; the rest of the team shot 52 percent, Jordan 30 percent.

"It's not my nature to pass up open shots," he explained after the game.

In the postgame Orlando locker room, it was a bubbly scene as O'Neal did one of those funky little dances from his rap videos, dressed, and painted his toenails red. No one asked why.

Long after the Magic locker room emptied, Pippen, Ron Harper, and Pete Myers stopped by to see Grant.

"Same old stuff, G.," said Pippen. "I'm still playing with a guy who's got to prove he can score fifty."

It was an observation not without merit, for Jordan, although trying to simply enjoy the game and the camaraderie, couldn't escape the fact that he was still *Michael Jordan*, and that meant putting on a show.

Even when he was playing baseball in Birmingham, he told NBC's Peter Vecsey he could return to the NBA that day and average 32 per game. "That's just eight points a quarter," Jordan explained. He later told ESPN, "People are always going to judge me on thirty-two points per game."

Several teammates saw the interview and shook their heads. Did that really matter?

Jordan was now as much a prisoner of his reputation as he was of the public, fans expecting astonishing performances, Jordan trying to accommodate.

"Same old thing, G.," said Pete Myers. "Hard to get the ball."

The three Bulls and Grant talked about Jordan, and Pippen remarked that Jordan looked like he'd lost a step or two, that he couldn't finish strong at the basket anymore.

Grant said Jordan looked fatigued and wondered how Jordan would fare against the younger legs of emerging star Anfernee Hardaway. The grousing about Jordan went on for a while; Pippen said the Magic's rebounding strength—Grant had 19 points and 13 rebounds—would be the Bulls' undoing.

Harper shrugged. "I'm just counting my money," he said and laughed.

A reporter wandered in as Grant was finally leaving.

"Staying around to buy Krause lunch?" joked the *Sun-Times*'s Steve Rosenbloom.

"I don't make enough money to feed Jerry," Grant said.

Reinsdorf, too, had noticed the difference in Jordan, and was convinced it was because of lower body weight Jordan put on for baseball.

"He'll be much better next season, his old self," Reinsdorf said.

Of course, it was too soon to scrutinize Jordan, for he hadn't played competitive NBA basketball for almost two years. But Bulls insiders were saying Jordan had slowed. Following the strategy employed first by the Pistons and then by the Knicks, teams were hitting Jordan hard at the basket during Jordan's last season of what he called his first career. So Jordan had started to settle for more jump shots.

Even back then, something was happening, something was different. In Game 5 of the 1993 Finals against the Suns, Jordan was dribbling the ball late in the fourth quarter with the Bulls close to wrapping up the series. But the Suns dropped a double team on Jordan, and Kevin Johnson swiped the ball, scored, and set off a rally that sent the Suns back to Phoenix for Game 6. It could have happened to anybody. But no one had ever seen it happen to Jordan, not in that kind of situation, the game on the line, just one play to close out a championship.

"Before, he'd split the double and dunk over the guy at the basket," Bill Cartwright said. "But he couldn't. Time catches up with everyone."

It would become a stunning pattern during Jordan's comeback season.

Jordan hated the new arena. He always talked about never playing in the United Center when plans were announced in 1992 to replace the old Chicago Stadium. In fact, Jordan was furious when the Bulls asked if he'd like to buy tickets in the new arena. For all he'd done to make it possible, he said he was insulted the Bulls would ask him to purchase seats.

And immediately Jordan's worst fears were borne out. He shot poorly at home, which Jackson predicted.

"As it got closer to him coming back," recalled Jackson, "I told him to sneak down there one night and get some late-night shooting in that building, that we'd get the lights turned on for him. I said it's a tough place to shoot, the angle of the lights, the length of the tongue of the backboard, the bounce of the rims. Touch any part and the ball comes out. They were tense and unforgiving. He said, 'Yeah, yeah, yeah. You said that about the Palace in Detroit.'"

It did remind Jackson of the Palace. Jackson always felt the Pistons had adjusted one of the baskets in the Palace to make the rims unforgiving, which would aid Detroit's rebounding. This was home, though, and Jackson felt the new rims were different, the lighting and angles tougher.

But Jackson had planted a seed of doubt, which would eventually sprout into a tangling vine of uncertainty for Jordan, who would never become comfortable shooting in the United Center. Jordan, who had always faced a challenge head-on, doing what others said couldn't be done, was backing away from this one, always complaining or griping about the new arena. The thought would never leave him that he couldn't shoot there.

And there were other problems. Jordan said the floor was too slippery. No, he was assured, it was cleaned before every game as usual. Then Jackson had an idea. It was the fireworks, he said. They were leaving a light film of dust on the floor. He suggested Jordan get two new pairs of sneakers and try one at the practice facility, another in a game after the fireworks went off. Jordan did and the game sneakers had a gray coating on the bottoms.

It was a small victory for basketball. The fireworks were discontinued for the rest of the season.

The day after Jordan's return to Chicago, there would be an Epiphany in Atlanta. Anyone seen the Black Jesus of Basketball?

Of course, if there was to be a Jordan miracle, Lenny Wilkens would have to be in the building, along with Craig Ehlo.

Ehlo was the victim of Jordan's "Shot" that won the 1989 first-round playoff series and numerous 50- and 60-point efforts when Ehlo was with the Wilkens-coached Cavaliers. Wilkens had drawn criticism over the years, even from Jordan, for rarely double-teaming Jordan, who once said he took it as an insult because every other team double-teamed him. Rather than be grateful, Jordan said he tried his hardest against Cleveland because he took Wilkens's defensive strategy as a challenge to his ability.

With the Bulls trailing Atlanta by one, Jordan hit a straight-on sixteen-footer at the buzzer for a 99–98 win. Bulls TV color man Johnny Kerr screamed into his microphone, "He did it again! He is now back!"

Jordan exulted, slapping the floor after the shot and pan-tomiming shooting dice.

No craps this time.

And then on Sunday, he rested.

Earlier in the week, Ehlo had begged Atlanta management to take him off the injured list in time for the game. "It's the sequel," said Ehlo. "He can't come back without me. He can't get his sixty if I'm not on the floor."

Everyone wanted to see it. Andre Agassi, playing in a tennis tournament in Florida, hired a jet to fly in for the game.

"I was thinking I'd been screwing up this team," Jordan said in another postgame press conference in an extra-large room to accommodate the massive media throng. "They've been going pretty good before I came back. So I was glad to do something to help the team."

The gentle irony was that the dramatic game winner came as Ehlo, perhaps Jordan's most famous victim, sat watching the Hawks' Steve Smith try to deny Jordan the inbound pass.

With 5.9 seconds left, Jordan and Pippen were on the court awaiting the pass, Jordan in the backcourt, Pippen downcourt. Smith pressed close to Jordan.

"Who's going to get the pass?" he asked.

"Pippen," Jordan answered.

Smith backed off and let Jordan catch the ball easily and

run downcourt. He stopped with Smith still backpedaling and hit the winner.

"I was kind of surprised," Jordan said after the game when asked about the Hawks' endgame defense on him. "But Lenny Wilkens has always played me one-on-one."

It would be another forty-minute-plus effort for Jordan, his third in the four games back.

At the beginning of the fourth quarter, Jackson had tried to rest Jordan for the stretch run, but Jordan refused to leave the court. "I'm finally having fun," he said after hitting eight shots in the third quarter. "Why don't you leave me in a little longer?"

"What could I do?" asked Jackson.

START SPREADIN' THE NEWS

Mike was back on Broadway. The Garden. The Knicks. Michael Jordan.

Because as everyone really knows, at least everyone in New York, nothing really happens until it happens in New York.

Sure, they'd heard about the big comeback in Indiana, the effortless grace in Boston, the game winner in Atlanta. But that was off-Broadway.

Now it was time for the Show.

"Air of Drama!" screamed one tabloid before the game on March 28. "Would Jordan Show?" wondered another. "Apple Gets Up for Air!" shouted another.

Nobody in sports, perhaps in sports history, is more aware of the stage, the spotlight, than Michael Jordan, who was shooting just 39 percent going into the game. When the lights and cameras go on and someone shouts "Action!" there's no one better than Jordan. And it would be no coincidence that Jordan would have his best game of his new career—55 points— against the Knicks in Madison Square Garden (or do you say Madison Square Jordan?) that night in just his fifth game back. Jordan had pointed to this one, talked about it, was ready for it.

When Jordan walked onto the Madison Square Garden

floor that night, fans bowed in a "salaam" greeting. TNT cable would set a ratings record for the game. The bus ride in midtown traffic to the Garden was an adventure with fans running alongside the bus all the way and banging on the windows.

"Obviously, a lot of people have idle time," said Bill Wennington.

Idol time, actually.

Spike Lee and Woody were there, along with Tom Brokaw, Maury Povich and Connie Chung, Phil Donahue and Marlo in the dueling couples section, Peter Falk, Christopher Reeve, and even Al Cowlings, the driver of O. J. Simpson's famous Bronco. The joke going around was that with Jordan back, O.J. would have to confess to get back on the front page.

Sorry, Michael. Guilty in New York, of Gross Excellence.

He would have 20 points before the end of the first quarter—"I could tell then I had something special going," he said—hit almost 60 percent of the thirty-seven shots he attempted, ten of eleven free throws, and three of four 3-point field goals. His eleven first-quarter shots were more than any other Bull would attempt for the entire game, with the exception of Pippen, who would have twelve. Jordan scored 15 of the Bulls' 19 points in the second quarter, although the Bulls would be trailing at halftime despite his 35 first-half points. Only once in the seventeen regular season games would Jordan score more in an entire game than he would in that first half.

Still, he would not have a better shooting game the rest of the season. He would never score as many points.

In the end, Jordan would have 55 for the game.

"It was a joke all along," said Knicks forward Charles Smith, "him not playing well the first four games and all of a sudden he comes to the Garden and drops fifty."

In a daze, Smith must have missed the last few.

Jordan's victim, mostly, was punky John Starks.

"I think he forgot how to play me," said Jordan.

In the end, oddly enough, the game would be won not by Jordan, but by Bill Wennington, who was making his first shot of the night on Jordan's second assist. With just fourteen seconds left, Jordan spun into the middle, around Patrick Ewing, and slipped the ball underneath to Wennington for the winning basket. Not exactly the way everyone thought it would end, but good enough for the legend.

"I'd be lying if I said I came out to pass the ball," admitted Jordan.

The 55 points, which senior New York basketball writer Peter Vecsey would call maybe the greatest basketball performance in Madison Square Garden history along with Willis Reed's dramatic return in the 1970 Finals, would come five years to the day after Jordan's career-high 69 points against the Cleveland Cavaliers. It would be the most ever scored against the Knicks in the current Garden and the NBA's high for the season to that point.

And Jordan knew it.

Late in the third quarter, during a time-out, Jordan saw Jackson summon Pete Myers to go in for him. "I'm okay," Jordan sneered at Jackson.

"Go in for Kukoc," Jackson instructed Myers.

Later, Myers would grab a rebound and go back up with the shot. The cameras would catch Jordan in animated fashion yelling at Myers, Myers yelling back.

"He wanted me to get the ball and give it to him," said Myers.

Phil Jackson would even get to read about the game, since the New York Times, Jackson's only acknowledged daily media reading, would headline the game on the top left side of its front page.

Even the Times couldn't find enough hyperbole, comparing the electricity in the arena to Ali-Frazier I, the Rolling Stones, Frank Sinatra at his best.

"There are some players who are unique, who transcend every aspect of the game. No one in the history of the game has had the impact he has," admitted then Knicks coach Pat Riley, who had his former players Magic Johnson and Kareem Abdul-Jabbar to compare Jordan to.

"Best game of my second career," Jordan offered afterward.

A LITTLE MAGIC

After the win in New York, the Jordan Show returned to Chicago for relatively easy wins over the Celtics and 76ers, and then back out on the road to New Jersey for another win.

The Bulls were looking like the contender almost everyone said they would be with Jordan. But not Magic Johnson, who had told the New York media: "They're too weak on the front line. Michael can't score, rebound, and block shots. Michael can't do everything."

The great ones always know.

Johnson and Jordan were a curious pair. When Johnson learned he had the HIV virus that ended his NBA career, one of the first people he called was Jordan, who said later he almost drove off the road as he listened to Johnson on his car phone and had to pull over to the side to recuperate.

Later, in 1991 when Jordan was being pummeled by gambling allegations, Johnson would come to Chicago for a joint press conference and warn the media that they were running the risk of driving Jordan from the game and should curtail their aggressiveness. Johnson was buoyant and supporting, Jordan dark and depressed. It was a surreal night in the old Chicago Stadium as Johnson consoled Jordan.

"Who was the one with AIDS?" one Chicago columnist asked afterward.

Although there was a friendship, Jordan and Johnson had always been two cats eyeing one another. Johnson was the star who, along with Larry Bird in 1979, effectively saved the NBA, their rivalry from college transferring into the NBA. Later, with their support for a new income-sharing labor agreement, the league prospered wildly.

But it was Jordan who would come along and get the huge endorsements that Johnson felt he deserved.

Johnson, with his old friend Isiah Thomas, was part of the plot to freeze out Jordan at the 1985 All-Star game. And as Johnson collected accolades and championships, Jordan bristled over talk that Johnson was the complete player because his teams won while Jordan was merely a talented scorer.

When Johnson won his third MVP award in 1990, Jordan, who had won only one at the time, whispered afterward that he wished it were anyone but Johnson.

Jordan remained jealous of Johnson's acclaim among basketball experts and of his basketball achievements; Johnson envied Jordan's popularity and endorsement deals.

In 1991, a promoter came up with an idea for a Jordan-Johnson one-on-one game. The NBA immediately shot it down, saying it was outside the bounds of their contracts. But Jordan savored the idea. "He knows I'm a far better one-on-one player," said Jordan. "He wouldn't score a point."

Eventually, there would be a healing around the summer of 1990, as Johnson's friendship with Isiah Thomas began to splinter in the heat of their Finals battles and Jordan began coming to Johnson's summer All-Star games. After all, Jordan was the star and Johnson liked stars to be around.

Nobody loved the game like Johnson. Even after his stunning retirement, he would try a comeback, be thwarted by hysterical players worried about contracting the disease, and then put together a barnstorming team to tour the world playing basketball.

After being named MVP of the 1992 All-Star game, in which he treated the fans to a spectacular display of one-on-one against Jordan and Thomas, he starred in the 1992 Olympic games, and later he would apply for the 1996 Olympic team.

Jordan often talked about his love for the game, but it was never as pure as Johnson's, who thought of little else, certainly not baseball or golf, playing pickup games when he couldn't play in the NBA. And so as Johnson offered his prophetic observations about the Bulls' chances with Jordan, the hunger within him to play grew even more acute; watching his friend play was excruciating. Here was Jordan, enjoying the attention, the adulation, everything Johnson yearned for. Johnson, some close to him said, wondered if it had been a mistake to publicly admit his condition, that he could easily have gone on playing. Surely Johnson, in a sport overpopulated with rich young men and willing young women chasing them, could hardly be the only NBA player to have the HIV virus, just the most public.

Johnson began to test the waters with the notion of yet another comeback in an era that was perhaps more forgiving of AIDS than it had been several years earlier. He talked to reporters from other cities, feeling them out. The Lakers were baffled again. Would he or wouldn't he? They chafed under Johnson's indecision after his initial retirement, and now they had put together an exciting young team with Nick Van Exel looking like a star at point guard.

Johnson, much heavier but in excellent condition and with the virus apparently in check, said he would play forward. Lakers coach Del Harris said Johnson would be the perfect sixth man for the Lakers given the circumstances of a young starting corps, Johnson's versatility, and the need to limit his playing time.

Johnson wanted to play. One more time. As the summer of 1995 wore on, the Lakers seemed open to the idea. Perhaps by 1996 or 1997, God and health willing, it would be Jordan and Johnson in the Finals, one more time, the two greats of their era going out together again.

One could only dream.

But in late July, Johnson said his business interests—particularly a complex of movie theaters named for him—were too compelling to allow another comeback, as much as he imagined taking one more shot at Jordan in the Finals.

Of course, whether Jordan himself would ever make it back to the Finals again remained a separate issue. He was just five of nineteen shooting against the 76ers on April 1 for 12 points, and thirteen of thirty-one against the Nets on April 5 after coming up two of thirteen by halftime, while his teammates often stood open, waiting for a pass that would never come.

At one point against the Nets, Jordan, who would be eleven of eighteen in the second half, came twisting down the left side, then angled toward the middle where three Nets waited. Jordan tried to duck under and come up for a shot.

Meanwhile, Steve Kerr stood in the left corner, unguarded,

waving his arms like he was signaling for help on a desert island.

While Jordan was at the free throw line, Scottie Pippen wandered over to Kerr.

"You open?" Pippen said smiling. Kerr looked up and said he was.

"I'll get you the ball next time down," Pippen said, and sure enough he did.

"Scottie is one of the best teammates I've ever had," said Kerr, who had played with Phoenix, Cleveland, and Orlando before coming to the Bulls as a minimum-earnings free agent in 1994. "Everyone loves him. He's so unselfish the way he plays and plays so hard. He knows where you'll be and where you want the ball for a shot. And he'll consciously try to get you shots. He'll be aware when you're struggling in a game, or when you've gone awhile without a shot. He cares about everyone like no star I've ever played with. It's a shame he has the reputation he does."

It was a fact: The media and fans loved Jordan; the players loved Pippen.

"I'd say, with the players, Scottie was the most popular," said Jud Buechler, who joined the team for the 1994–95 season. "No question, if you had a problem, it was Scottie you would go to."

How ironic, considering Pippen was the one always embroiled in the controversies, uncooperative and uninteresting to reporters. Not like Jordan, around whom even veteran columnists swooned when Jordan flashed the smile, the eye contact, the knowledge of the first name. But it was Pippen who charmed the players. "Scottie always has a kind word for you, a 'hello' at practice," said Buechler, another player Jordan didn't talk to. "He's a really nice guy."

And Pippen passed first. In fact, he preferred that. Asked which part of the game he most enjoyed, Pippen said without hesitation passing.

Jordan, indeed, had thrown the Bulls' offense for a loop.

"We had to make a huge adjustment," agreed Steve Kerr. "Everyone's role changed."

And Jordan would concede after the season he didn't adjust to the team as much as he should have.

Jackson saw what was developing between Jordan and the others.

"I kept emphasizing that, 'You guys are going to have to step up and execute situations,'" said Jackson. "Michael is penetrating and going up against all these guys and they're going to take him out. And there's Steve Kerr, what is he, a fifty-four percent three-point shooter, standing in the corner wide open.

"I said to Steve after that play, 'Were you open?'" related Jackson about watching Jordan charge into the middle with Kerr standing lonesome as a cloud in the corner.

"He said he was.

"I said, 'Did you tell that to Michael?'

"And he said, 'What, me go tell Michael? You've got to be kidding.'

"And I said, 'Yeah, tell him you're open,'" said Jackson.

But there would never be that communication bond, not with the godlike status being bestowed on Jordan and his general uncertainty about just who these guys were.

"I had to say to Michael," related Jackson, "'Steve Kerr is a fifty-four percent three-point shooter. You might make a three-point play getting fouled. But you're going to get crushed. Why risk that if there's a higher percentage to pitch out and give a guy a shot?' But Jordan liked those challenges.

"That was the problem with this club," said Jackson. "We had the inside-outside game. Pippen was tremendous, a very unselfish player, and when Michael came back he could take over things down the stretch when we needed it and they had their own little things going. My effort was to get guys to step up and say, 'Give me the ball. Don't try to do it all yourself.' That was where the chemistry had to come together and in the end it didn't. That was the hardest thing over the course of the year. I felt that was my responsibility and maybe I didn't fulfill it. I was maybe able to do it better last time with Michael."

So one of the victims was Kerr, whose opportunities and

production fell off markedly after Jordan's return. "We went from Pete Myers getting six, seven shots, to Michael taking twenty-eight," noted Kerr. "It's got to be taken away from someone."

Everyone was trying to adjust, to cope with the new situation, and everyone agreed to one thing: Jordan would take more shots. But when you did get a shot—if you were lucky enough—at least you'd get a good look because everyone would be looking for Jordan. It seemed obvious to everyone— except Armstrong, who bristled about the notion that he might flourish with Jordan back.

In fact, Armstrong felt he flourished most with Jordan gone because he no longer had to run into the corner and wait for Jordan to pass. He could try some one-on-one or screen/roll plays, even if Jackson demanded otherwise. Armstrong felt great ambivalence with Jordan back. Jordan had embraced Armstrong when he retired. Armstrong was Jordan's only link to the team when Jordan went to play baseball and the only Bulls player or member of the club that Jordan allowed to attend his father's funeral. But Armstrong's feelings about playing alongside Jordan were deep-seated, going back to the days when Jordan said he preferred playing with John Paxson and Armstrong had asked for a trade when he wasn't starting. He just couldn't figure out how to adjust to Jordan.

"It doesn't improve my looks at the basket," Armstrong simmered when asked how much easier it was going to be for him now. "Everyone says, 'You'll be open.' But I haven't gotten an open look at the basket since high school. You don't get open shots in this league. You don't get great looks. You get opportunities in key situations where you have to knock them down. You may only have two looks a night and you have to make them."

Players rolled their eyes when they saw the quote in the newspaper, and the joke became whether anyone in the league would ever dare leave Armstrong open.

"Sure," someone would offer, "Michael's on the floor, but you never leave B.J."

OPIE TAYLOR WITH A JUMP SHOT

Kerr was a pragmatist, and he knew it was to be expected, for Jordan had to average twenty-three to twenty-five shots per game. Who else was going to take those shots? Kerr? But there was always a delicate balance between what players like Jordan could do and what players like Kerr had to do. In the end, Jordan and the players like Kerr wouldn't be able to mix well enough. Ironically, though, they had something very vital in common.

Their fathers were both murder victims.

The death of Steve Kerr's father made worldwide news, but not because of who his son was.

Malcolm Kerr, president of American University in Beirut, Lebanon, was assassinated on January 18, 1984, by a gunman from the extremist Arab group, Islamic Jihad. A lone gunman, with a silencer on his pistol, snuck up behind Malcolm Kerr as he walked from an elevator in the university administration building on the way to a meeting. Steve was a freshman at the University of Arizona at the time.

"My dad had the same passion for the Middle East that I have for sports," Kerr related. "I remember clearly the Camp David peace talks with Sadat, Begin, and Carter. Dad was so excited. Middle East peace. That's what he lived for. There was a strict rule at our house. You couldn't watch TV during the week, only Friday, Saturday, and Sundays. He didn't like TV. He felt we should read books, instead, although I was usually out shooting baskets or reading a book about Dr. J. or somebody like that.

"World affairs was always being discussed, but Dad was a big sports fan and he used to take us to UCLA [where he taught before returning to Beirut less than two years before he was killed] basketball and football games," recalled Kerr. "I became a ball boy at UCLA for a couple of years. Dad and I were tight.

"It was during my freshman year when it happened," related Steve, a boyish-looking six-three and about 180 pounds with a little bit of backwoods Opie Taylor about him, a freckle-faced kid with a broad jaw and friendly eyes. "I was the only one of the family in the U.S. at the time. My mom and brother Andrew [now on the staff of the National Security Council] were in Beirut. I was kind of alone, really too young in some ways to really understand the gravity of what happened. I was hurt, angry, but the way you deal with it is to continue to live your life.

"I never had any feelings about revenge," Kerr concedes, echoing what Jordan would say about his own father's murder. "I guess that's maybe because of living in the Middle East and my dad's feeling about the area. He knew the risk when he took the job, but when he did things seemed to be settling down. I still think about it a lot. They never arrested anyone. We heard a few stories. I had visited the campus in August of the year before right before school started for that semester. So I could picture the whole thing."

Steve owed Malcolm much. Steve admits he wasn't the most cooperative of the kids when his father would take sabbaticals and go off to Europe or the Middle East to live. Steve was born in Beirut, one of four Bulls, along with Luc Longley, Bill Wennington, and Toni Kukoc, born outside the United States.

"We were in France when I was five, and then Cairo when I was in the sixth through ninth grades," recalls Kerr. "I probably was the most rebellious because I wanted to stay and play Little League. But it was a great experience; being in the same boat with a lot of American kids, I developed great friendships."

Steve and friends would climb the pyramids, bribing guards to get into sacred areas, and cruise the Nile; he played on a basketball team that toured in Europe. Now he wanted to play on a basketball team against better competition.

Kerr returned to California for most of his high school education, but he was barely recruited: too little, too slow, jumped too low.

"I wasn't that good, frankly," Kerr admits. "Think I'm slow

now? I was really slow then. I could always shoot it, but I didn't have much feel for the game. After my senior year, I didn't get any scholarship offers."

Quite a Bulls team that would have been back then: Pippen a walk-on at Central Arkansas without a scholarship offer, Kerr no scholarship offer, Bill Wennington a gangly high school player in Canada, Pete Myers playing at Faulkner State Junior College, Jud Buechler more celebrated for his beach volleyball play than his basketball, Luc Longley an Australian party kid coming to the United States to play basketball on the coattails of a friend who had drawn scouts' interest.

Kerr played some summer league basketball and got an offer from nearby Cal State Fullerton. Arizona showed some interest but wasn't committing. It wasn't until his father tracked down Lute Olsen, who was taking over the program, that he learned he would be offered a scholarship.

Kerr, who in the 1994–95 season won his second 3-point shooting title and remains the NBA's all-time percentage leader, was brought in by Arizona as a zone buster for the 3-point shooting rule in college. It was at Arizona that loudmouthed fans from rival Arizona State sat in the stands during a game, yelling at him, "PLO, PLO! Hey, Kerr! Where's your dad?"

But luck played a major role for him: He hurt his knee one season and was eligible to play a fifth year, the year Arizona went to the NCAA Final Four. He received plenty of national exposure, and when a drug scandal rocked his home-state Phoenix Suns, they took a chance on good-guy Kerr in the second round of the draft, even though he was a player who had less NBA potential than most of the guys on his high school team.

Later, in Cleveland, Mark Price got hurt, so Kerr got substantial playing time there and won his first 3-point shooting title and learned what it takes to remain in the NBA for players like him.

"I was on Cleveland teams that went to the Conference Finals, won fifty-seven games and thirty games," said Kerr. "I learned you have to be prepared for anything, and I found out my place was going to be somewhere between fifth man and twelfth man. Role players could have a spot in this league."

He was traded to the Magic in December 1992 but didn't play much and then decided to take a chance and try to make the Bulls in 1993. He liked the idea of getting a chance to play with Jordan after being on so many of those Cavaliers teams whose hearts were broken by Jordan, and he thought he could eventually fill the shooter's role then occupied by John Paxson.

"If there was one guy in the league I always compared myself to, it was John," said Kerr, who was embraced and befriended by Paxson even as he hovered as a threat to the Bulls veteran. "I wasn't a consummate point guard nor big enough to be a two [shooting] guard. I felt I could thrive in that situation."

Oddly, he would thrive more with Jordan gone. With Jordan back, he was having difficulty finding a place to help or gaining Jordan's acceptance as Paxson finally had.

Paxson had tried to help Kerr and the others adapt to playing with Jordan. "It took a long time for me," agreed Paxson. "I told the guys all season they had to gain Michael's confidence as players. And that takes time. For years, you have to prove to Michael you can make critical plays, that you're not going to take any crap from anybody. Until you do that, he's going to be apprehensive about you when you're on the floor and whether he'll be willing to give you the ball. That's all a part of Michael. Seventeen regular season games and ten playoff games isn't much."

SWEET HOME CLEVELAND

Any one game with Jordan, meanwhile, was always enough for the Cavaliers as the Bulls pulled their road show into Cleveland's new Gund Arena for a nationally televised game on Sunday, April 9, and perhaps the most hostile crowd Jordan faces anywhere.

The Bulls were now in that late-season jockeying-for-play-off position and trying to move up a notch to avoid the Knicks in the first round, that nerve-wracking three-of-five series, to get a shot at wounded Charlotte, which already had lost starter Scott Burrell for the season. This was the second of two straight games between the Bulls and Cavs, after the Bulls won the first in Chicago on Friday, April 7.

The Bulls always felt Jordan helped neutralize any home team's crowd advantage because he had so many fans around the NBA. In fact, once in 1990, Jordan's number 23 jersey was stolen before a game in Orlando, and the Bulls thought about borrowing a number 23 jersey from someone in the crowd because there were so many. Unfortunately, they couldn't find one large enough because all the jerseys were being worn by kids, and Jordan ended up wearing number 12, the only other number he wore before switching to 45, briefly, upon his return.

In Cleveland, though, Jordan was worth one loud boo from the home folks.

The Cavaliers had assembled a talented team in the late 1980s, and although injuries had wreaked havoc, it was Jordan who was generally blamed for their disintegration, beginning with his shot in the 1989 playoffs. "If he hadn't made it," said Ron Harper, then the Cavaliers' high-scoring shooting guard, "I don't think they would have traded me. He changed my life. He changed everything for that team."

Jordan also hit Cleveland for his career-high game, and the Bulls knocked the Cavaliers out of the playoffs five times between 1988 and 1994, the penultimate time in 1993, a sweep in which Jordan hit the game winner at the buzzer in the final game, signifying the end of Lenny Wilkens's run as the Cavaliers' coach.

Now Mike Fratello was the coach, but fate hadn't been any kinder to him. All-Star center Brad Daugherty was out for the season—and perhaps his career—with back problems. Starting shooting guard Gerald Wilkins blew out his Achilles tendon and would miss the season and be left unprotected for the new

Canadian expansion teams in June 1995. All-Star forward Larry Nance retired, and Mark Price would again miss almost two months with a broken wrist; late in the season his backup, Terrell Brandon, broke his leg.

"I think there's a cloud over Cleveland. It picked one city to hang over and it's us," said John Battle. "I just wish it would go away."

"It's not just the Cavs," said Steve Kerr. "The Indians have the best team they've had in forty years and the baseball strike happens [in 1994]. The Browns get within one game of the Super Bowl three out of four years and first it's Elway and the Drive and then it's the Fumble by Earnest Byner. It's actually made me into a real Cleveland sports fan because you have to have so much sympathy for them. There was always so much heartbreak involved."

So Fratello had adjusted as best he could, but in the process produced an ugly slowdown game to try to offset the Cavaliers' lack of talent. For a time, it worked, especially against the Bulls because it deftly exposed their weakness at a power game; Cleveland would hold the ball almost the entire shot clock, then throw up a shot and send the stronger power forwards smashing through the Bulls' weak front line for the ball. The Cavaliers would win a 77–63 snoozer in December in Chicago, while the Bulls were booed angrily at home. In January, Cleveland would win at home, 92–78. They were the surprise team of the league.

And then came Jordan.

"I remember when word of his return came," lamented Cavaliers general manager Wayne Embry. "I said, 'I guarantee you we'll play them in the first round.' I think all Cleveland fans have the same reaction and feeling. They can't get away from the guy."

The Bulls had won rather easily in Chicago the previous Friday, leading by 14 after three quarters. But back home Sunday, Fratello had succeeded in slowing the pace, and Jordan was working through a nine for twenty-six shooting day. Once again, it came down to Jordan with the ball, taking the last shot with two seconds left and Cleveland ahead by one.

"I could picture Craig Ehlo falling down," said Bobby Phills, who was nervously guarding Jordan. "I did not want to be a part of that highlight film."

Jordan's 3-pointer from the right side went long off the back of the rim. History would not repeat itself.

Jordan smiled. "I was saying, 'See, I'm not that bad, Cleveland.' I had the chance," said Jordan. "I knew everybody was watching and I guess that's the thrill of it all, that you have the opportunity to make people sad or happy. That's the fun position to be in."

Scottie Pippen, on the other hand, was not smiling. He had decided to break his six-week media boycott that day. He didn't say much, though, just that he was tired of answering questions.

With 9.8 seconds left and Cleveland ahead by one and taking the ball out of bounds, Toni Kukoc tipped the ball to Pippen, who headed toward the basket with only Price ahead and Jordan running down the left side waving for the ball. One-point lead. Pippen at almost six-eight against six-foot Price going to the basket. Jordan wanting the ball. Pippen stopped and called time-out.

"He thought he had a shot at getting the ball to Michael, but didn't," said Jackson.

The specter of Jordan was looming very large, indeed.

THE NEXT MICHAEL JORDAN

Everywhere Jordan looked there were old rivals and new pretenders to the throne.

The Bulls moved into Detroit on April 12, where this year's "next Michael Jordan," Grant Hill, was playing. Of course, there was already another next Michael Jordan waiting in the wings after Hill, North Carolina's Jerry Stackhouse.

"Every year there's a new one," conceded Hill.

But Hill had some credentials. The quick first step, the explosion, the acrobatic plays, the all-around game, a little of the charisma. Which suggested to Hill's coach at Duke, Mike

Krzyzewski, that Hill might be in for some trouble when he finally met Jordan.

Krzyzewski, who was Chuck Daly's assistant with the Dream Team, remembered what Jordan and Pippen did to Toni Kukoc at a time when people were calling Kukoc the next Jordan. Pippen, with a little help from Jordan, embarrassed the young Croatian headed to the Bulls, denied him the ball, harassed him all over the court, made him look like a junior college player compared to the NBA players.

Krzyzewski saw much the same treatment coming for Hill, who was being featured on the cover of the current *GQ* with the question: "Can Grant Hill Save Sports?"

"He just said, 'Be careful,'" related Hill.

But Hill was not all that concerned. He was thrilled finally to be playing against Jordan. He didn't even care about the result. It was going to be a great story to tell the guys back home, where he had been raised in fashionable surroundings in Washington, D.C., the son of All-Pro football player Calvin Hill.

Grant Hill remembered playing on the practice team for those 1992 Olympians, coming out to line up against Jordan. Jordan came out, looked at Hill, and said, "You know I can get the ball whenever I want. And when I get it I can do anything I want with it."

Wow. It reminded him of Jordan's "Come Fly with Me" video when Jordan says, "When I'm on my game, I can play you like a puppet."

So when Hill was coming out of Duke, touted as one of the top picks in the 1994 NBA draft, he called Jordan's agent, David Falk, saying he was thinking about retaining Falk. Actually, Hill admitted later he had no such intention but wanted the chance to talk to Jordan. So Falk gave Hill Jordan's private phone number.

"I'm in my car," Hill recalled, "and I'm talking to my friends, trying to decide what to call him. Michael? Mike? M.J.? Mr. Jordan? I had the phone on speaker so my friends could hear and I think I called him M.J.

"You know, M.J., this is G.H.," Hill said, laughing uproariously. "I was like, 'Wow, I'm on the phone with Michael Jordan.'"

And now he would be on the court with him. The Bulls had now won eight of eleven since Jordan's return; the only mystery against Detroit would be how many the Bulls would win by. The Pistons hadn't come close to beating the Bulls this season even without Jordan; it didn't seem likely they'd fare any better now that he was back. Reports were already circulating that both general manager Billy McKinney and coach Don Chaney would be fired after the season (they were), as the Pistons skidded to the bottom of the East.

The massive Palace at Auburn Hills rarely sold out anymore, but Jordan's appearance produced sales of six thousand tickets within hours of his announced return a month before. On hand, sitting first row baseline under the basket near the Pistons' bench, were former rivals Isiah Thomas and Bill Laimbeer, with entertainer Bill Cosby between them. And when Hill blew by Jordan twice in the first quarter with crossover dribbles for baskets and later for a slam on a lob pass, Cosby leaped up and exchanged high fives with Thomas and Laimbeer.

The Cos a Bad Boy? Couldn't be.

Jordan hit more than half his shots for the first time since the New York game two weeks earlier, and even with Pippen home with the flu, the Bulls won easily, 124–113.

So when the Bulls showed up for practice the next morning at home with three days off before playing the Knicks in Chicago (for another Sunday-afternoon NBC ratings blockbuster), Jordan was in an airy mood.

"No triangle today," Jordan playfully yelled to Jackson. "Let's scrimmage."

The Bulls were probably the most fundamentally sound team in the league because they worked on basic fundamentals: how to make an inbound pass, how to throw a bounce pass, a chest pass, as well as their triangle offense.

Jackson was quick to note other teams' bad habits. A month

later during the playoffs, Jackson would be laughing over the Indiana Pacers' improbable comeback in Game 1 against the Knicks, when Reggie Miller scored 8 points in eighteen seconds, the game winner occurring when Anthony Mason lost his balance throwing an inbound pass that Miller intercepted.

"Serves them right," Jackson said. "That's something we work on as much as anything. You've got to stand there like a quarterback with your feet set. You've got to break them of bad habits."

So Jackson liked to practice about twenty minutes of triangle offense every day. The players detested it, moving to spots they'd memorized for years, Jordan especially. But the system had proven its usefulness during the season Jordan was gone, as the Bulls won fifty-five games and appeared every bit as dangerous as they had been with Jordan.

The Bulls' triangle, or triple-post offense, relied upon quick passing and cutting to get players open for shots. Jordan long resisted its "equal opportunity" concept, feeling the Bulls had a better chance to win if he had the ball, as opposed to say, Stacey King or Horace Grant. Jackson, though, always emphasized to Jordan that there were ample opportunities for him but that the system provided a structure for the others, something they could fall back on to produce offense when teams shut down their options.

Jackson also convinced Jordan that his headlong rushes into Detroit's defense over the years were fruitless, that it was the contributions of the others that would eventually make a difference, as long as he adhered to the system.

It was in 1991 after the Bulls defeated Detroit in Game 1 of the Eastern Conference Finals, the year the Bulls won their first NBA title, that Jordan coined the term "my supporting cast" to describe his teammates, who had provided the cushion for victory in that pivotal game. Earlier that year, Jackson had given Jordan a speech: "These guys might not be as talented as you'd like them to be, but this is as good as they're going to be. If we run a system, everyone is going to have an opportunity to perform. They can't do what you can do, but they can have some level of success and perform even in critical situations."

Now Jordan had seen enough of the triangle. He just wanted to play in practice.

"You're not leaving any fun for the coaches," Jackson chided in return. "That's our fun."

"Look, Phil, you've had these guys for eighteen months," Jordan said, pointing to Toni Kukoc and Corie Blount and laughing, "and they still can't get it right. So what's the point?"

Jackson had to laugh, too.

Players like Steve Kerr, Jud Buechler, and Bill Wennington were proving nice fits, quick learners, and adaptable. But Blount would never get it, and after the season he would effectively be given to the Los Angeles Lakers to take the four years remaining on his contract. The Bulls' principal condition of the deal for "future considerations" was that the Lakers not let it be known what those considerations were, since they were so insignificant.

In almost two years with the Bulls, Blount never mastered even the simplest terminology of the offense and forever was out of position, drawing the abuse of other players. Yet it was not an uncommon concern around the NBA. Many players coming into the NBA these days had not been well coached, if at all, allowed to perform because of their great athletic abilities. Blount was a player like that. He rebounded and blocked shots in college and didn't seem to be asked—or taught—to do more. He couldn't play for Jackson, that was for sure, and he was soon gone.

As if there weren't enough issues swirling around the Bulls, now there was something new: The team's racial mix was drawing attention and comments that the Bulls favored white players over black players and complemented their stars with whites. The notion was that the Bulls hired white players to be smart and black players to be athletic. It was the old stereotype, although Jordan generally disproved it by being the most aware player on the court.

Although there seemed to be reasonable racial harmony on the team, the influx of white players had formed definite groups.

Previously, there hadn't been any definable large cliques on the team. In years past, the rookies who came in together, such as Stacey King, B. J. Armstrong, and Jeff Sanders, would hang out, as would Pippen and Grant. But after Charles Oakley and Rod Higgins left the team and Jordan's celebrity grew, Jordan drew apart from the group. Players generally went out individually, usually having friends in visiting cities from previous trips.

But Buechler and Kerr had played together in college, and they'd latched on to the playful Bill Wennington. Longley and Larry Krystkowiak became friends and joined in, as did Perdue on occasion. It was the first time in perhaps a decade that large groups of Bulls players could be seen out together.

That group, along with broadcaster John Paxson and Kukoc (who was thrilled to be invited and trailed along like a puppy dog), would grab a bunch of tee times, play golf, then get together for dinner and go back to the hotel to hang out together.

"It's the best group of guys I've ever been around in the NBA," Kerr would say. "It made it a fun season."

Pippen, on the other hand, had gravitated toward Harper and Myers, and sometimes the three would be out together. As for Jordan, he stayed with his bodyguards on the road and usually had a large entourage of hangers-on from back home.

"The entourage, the security, kept Michael pretty much apart from his teammates, especially in the postseason," Jackson noticed. "It's just too much of a crunch. He doesn't have the ability to mingle and kind of get that community feel we like to have as a team. The problem as a team was because of the way we play basketball, depending on one another, moving the ball, the fluidity and function and intuitive nature. When he came he saw how everyone fit it, but he wasn't able to make that transition."

Jackson, while uncomfortable and resentful of the charge that the Bulls were selecting players on the basis of race, didn't wholly dismiss it.

He told the *Chicago Tribune*'s Melissa Isaacson he was aware people were saying that he was trying to make the Bulls a predominantly white team not unlike his Knicks team of the 1970s with Bill Bradley and Dave DeBusschere.

"The style of basketball we play," Jackson conceded, "and the system we use happens to be conducive to a lot of skills white players have—spot shooting, ball movement, cutting. As opposed to power basketball usually indigenous to the skills black players have—one-on-one moves, quickness, jumping ability."

Of course, this didn't account for Kukoc, who was baffled by the offense, although Jackson often attributed that to Kukoc's stubborn nature.

"He's understood about five of the hundred plays he's gotten since he's been here," said Jackson. "Like with Scottie before the play when he sat out of the game [in the playoffs against the Knicks]. He goes to the wrong spot and then shrugs."

What Jackson felt was that Kukoc employed a tactic used by many non-English-speaking athletes. When he didn't like a play, Kukoc simply claimed he didn't understand. It made for frequent vivid displays of anger on Jackson's part, as Kukoc, playing the role of the cute little foreigner, would wander off the court shrugging his shoulders.

Veteran sportswriters who'd been around many Latin athletes, like boxer Roberto Duran, found that they were bright and often spoke and understood English well. But some used the language barrier as a tool to avoid an embarrassing situation or question.

Kukoc, though, said the problem was in the translation. His. He said he'd understand Jackson's English, but then he'd have to translate into Croatian for himself to be sure, and by then Jackson was already talking about something else.

So Kukoc would say he understood even when he didn't. But the crowd was roaring and Jackson was shouting instructions and, well, "Okay, coach, whatever you say."

"It's easier," said Kukoc, "just to say I understand."

But Kukoc was baffled upon Jordan's return. Jordan had come to accept Kukoc after being outspoken and opposed to the Bulls' pursuit of Kukoc in 1991, but Jordan remained uncomfortable that Kukoc had become a power forward.

Which meant there would be no screens for Jordan, and no protection, another reason Jordan embraced rookie Dickey Simpkins. Kukoc had longed to play with Jordan and was devastated when he retired, but he flourished and began to develop with Jordan gone.

To be effective, Kukoc needs to handle the ball.

Kukoc's European habit of getting to the basket and instead of powering in, flipping the ball out to a perimeter shooter, exasperated Jackson. Kukoc opened the 1994–95 season coming off the bench and seemed on course to rank among the league's best sixth men.

But with scoring a problem for the team, Jackson moved Kukoc, the Bulls' highest paid player, into the starting lineup in December. Jackson enjoyed holding the team's highest paid player in reserve, as he felt it showed the team money would not determine playing time. Krause wanted Kukoc to be the starting point guard.

But there was no true position for Kukoc as a starter.

So Jackson put him at power forward, figuring the team could take advantage of his offensive strengths against certain power forwards. Kukoc bothered little with defense, which also infuriated Jackson, and when Kukoc didn't score early in a game, he would be hopeless on defense.

Kukoc was thrilled when Jordan returned, and Jordan admired Kukoc's penchant for taking last-second shots, one standard by which Jordan measured players. Jordan felt Kukoc was the only Bull—other than himself—who really wanted to take the game-winning shot and then could live with the consequences. But with Jordan back, there was even less opportunity for Kukoc to handle the ball, and as the playoffs approached, Jackson began to think of returning Kukoc to the bench.

ANYONE GOT SOME DYNAMITE?

The phone call was what every expectant parent fears.

Jimmy Sexton, Scottie Pippen's agent and close adviser, had gone to the Taco Bell near his Memphis home. He would just be gone for a few minutes. His wife was due with their first child any day now, and Sexton was bringing home a quick, late-night snack.

Sexton's car phone rang.

It was Dr. Drummond from Baptist Hospital's emergency room, the voice said.

"What's the problem?" Sexton asked nervously.

"I can't tell you on the phone," the doctor said, Sexton's line crackling with static, his heart pounding.

Sexton stuttered.

"We have to make some decisions," the doctor said.

Sexton gunned his car out of the drive-through lane, his bag of food flying out the window, when he heard Scottie Pippen on the other end of the line laughing.

"Sorry, sorry," Pippen was saying. "But I couldn't resist."

Pippen has a lot of the practical joker in him and enjoys playful pranks and taunts with teammates and friends, but he was positively giddy that Sunday night, April 16, as he drove to the airport for the Bulls' flight to Miami.

The Bulls had absolutely crushed the Knicks that afternoon back in Chicago, and Pippen had been the star on national TV. He scored a game-high 29 points and was the key in staking the Bulls to their 20-point halftime lead, from which the Knicks never recovered. So bad was the beating that Knicks coach Pat Riley never brought his starters back even when the Bulls' lead shrank to 10 (they would win by 21) in the fourth quarter. And Pippen was even starting to believe a little as the Bulls, 11–3 since Jordan's return, now had the league's second-best record since the All-Star break after San Antonio.

It was Easter Sunday, and not only was Jordan's second coming a success, but it seemed Scottie Pippen had been resurrected as well.

"We were starting to play better before Michael came back," Pippen said. "Then, when he came back, it was kind of a setback for us, you could say. He was trying to get himself going and the team had been going in the other direction [toward team play]. But it seems like we're starting to play together again. There's room for improvement, but I like our chances right now. We like our chances of winning another title."

This time, though, it was Jordan who had to improve.

Once again, against the Knicks, he'd failed to shoot 50 percent for the ninth time in his thirteen games back. And this from a career 51.6 percent shooter who hadn't shot worse than 49.5 percent in any season since 1987.

Jordan was now convinced it was the rims in the new United Center, and before the game against the Pacers the week before, he had come out early and was hanging on one of the rims, trying to loosen it. Jordan said he thought it might be a personal mental block because he always said he'd never play in the new building. Whenever he had the chance, he bemoaned the destruction of the old Chicago Stadium, which by now was almost completely torn down and being made ready for parking space.

Jackson was cynical about Jordan's reaction.

"He built it," Jackson said in reference to Jordan's popularity that resuscitated basketball in Chicago and created a demand for a new arena. "He should like it."

Jackson had never before seen Jordan back off from an obstacle like this.

That had always been the Bulls' edge with Jordan. No matter the odds, the view of the experts, or the circumstances, Jordan said he could overcome it, and he'd drag the team along. They could beat the Lakers in 1991, Jordan promised as the team flew to Los Angeles tied 1–1. He'd take care of Clyde Drexler in the 1992 Finals, he promised. The Suns wouldn't win a game at home, he said in the 1993 Finals, and they didn't. Jordan had predicted and delivered improbable victories. His confidence was legend. Often, he didn't even realize it, like the time the Bulls were playing the Bucks and Cartwright had rolled in for a shot and was called for traveling. A time-out was called, and as the players walked back to the huddle, Jordan bellowed at Cartwright to give him the ball.

"You had two guys on you," Cartwright reminded Jordan.

"But one was Fred Roberts," Jordan snapped.

A double team? So what?

Before the Bulls played the Knicks that Sunday in late April, Jordan was shooting jumpers left-handed.

"What's the difference, the way I'm shooting here," he said.

Earlier he'd come onto the floor and the lights were still off. "Maybe that's the way I need it," he said, "shooting in the dark."

It had become almost like a vigil for a sick relative. Fans were sending shooting remedies. Before one game, an usher found an old chair from the Chicago Stadium and placed it by the Bulls' bench for Jordan to sit on for good luck. Candles were being lit in churches and prayers were being said.

The week before, after playing in the new Gund Center in Cleveland, Jordan said, "It's very nice, better than ours." Asked the next day if he felt like he might be ready to explode in the United Center, Jordan said, "Could be," although it was unclear whether he was referring to himself or the building.

Perhaps, someone dared to suggest, the problem was not the building or the rims, since other players were doing just fine there, and Kerr, after all, was the league's leading 3-point shooter there. Maybe the problem was Jordan himself, that he wasn't jumping like he used to and didn't have the strength in his legs anymore.

"A lot of people said you don't have your height back," a reporter queried.

"I'm still six-six," replied Jordan.

BEATING THE HEAT

Vanquishing the Knicks sent the Bulls off to Miami in a giddy mood. Miami is one of the more inviting NBA cities, particularly for the Bulls, who stay at the posh Mayfair House. All the rooms have Jacuzzis and many have pianos. And those aren't even the suites. Across the street is Hooters, which attracts many of the players. But this was just a one-day trip. Jordan would pose on the roof of the Mayfair, where the cover for his book *Rare Air* was shot. And then he would try to produce some more legend.

Jordan was always good for that against the Heat, the mouthiest bunch in the league who hadn't done anything. The Heat, in many respects, represented the new NBA that Jordan resented and the league elders shielded their eyes from. The Heat were among the four expansion teams admitted in 1988 and 1989, and unfortunately, they weren't bad enough or lucky enough, like Orlando and Charlotte, to get top picks in the lottery and land star centers. So they had a bunch of high draft picks, mostly athletic guards and small forwards, not good enough to be winners but cocky enough to think they were.

The height of their arrogance was on full display a few years back in Chicago Stadium with Jordan, not atypically, a little sluggish with the flu. Seems he'd been out playing golf again as winter approached and had gotten sick. "I never knew a pro athlete who got sick as much as he did," recalled Bill Cartwright of Jordan, who played golf in the morning almost no matter what the weather.

Jordan was coasting through a close game when Willie Burton blocked a Jordan shot and started taunting him. Mistake number one. Then Glen Rice jumped in to say the Heat were going to beat up Jordan at home.

That was enough.

Jordan stole the ball from Burton on the next possession and dunked. As he ran back, he passed Heat coach Ron Rothstein and said, "Now you've done it. I was tired. I played eighteen holes of golf today and I didn't feel like playing. But now your babies got me upset."

He blocked an Alex Kessler shot and threw to Pippen for a breakaway layup, then stole the ball from Sherman Douglas, was fouled, and hit two free throws. And suddenly a narrow Heat lead with four minutes left became a 7-point Bulls lead with two minutes left on the way to a Bulls win. Later Rony Seikaly said that Jordan hadn't been totally honest: He'd told Seikaly he had played thirty-six holes that day.

But that was the stuff of legend, not the Michael Jordan of 1995, a jump-shooting Michael Jordan who rarely dunked. Sure, he had that remarkable first step, but now it was mostly good for getting free to get a shot anytime he wanted, no small feat in the NBA. But he didn't frighten anyone as much anymore. Opposing shooting guards ran into the post against him and asked for the ball. That had never happened before. Excuses were made for Jordan's shooting. Slippery floor, fireworks, poor lighting in the new arena, tight rims, extra weight from baseball. Where Jordan used to focus completely on the game and block everything out, now it seemed there were mental lapses when Jordan's concentration seemed to wane, his mind wandering. It would prove a fatal lapse against the Orlando Magic in the playoffs.

But all that was almost incidental as the regular season and the celebration of Jordan's return continued. It didn't matter that Jordan wasn't producing miracles regularly anymore. It was enough just to witness the man himself, a chance to see Sandy Koufax finish his career, Jim Brown rush for a touchdown, Ben Hogan with that two-iron again, Muhammad Ali sharp as ever, Babe Ruth bandy-legged on the way to home plate. The thrill was simply in seeing Jordan.

Jack Nicklaus came to Miami on Monday, as did fellow golfing great Ray Floyd. A bunch of major league baseball players showed up along with a bunch of Miami Dolphins football players, and so did actress Debra Winger. Before the game, Heat forward Kevin Willis came into the Bulls locker room with two basketballs, asking for Jordan's autograph.

"What do I get for these, a free layup?" Jordan joshed, not that it would matter against the short-armed Willis.

Jordan again shot erratically, nine for twenty-one. But he made a bunch of free throws, including one with forty seconds left that allowed enough for the final margin. The Bulls were feeling good.

Then Steve Kerr missed one of two free throws with twelve seconds left to give the Heat a chance to tie with a three-pointer.

Jackson started yelling at Kerr when the Bulls got to the sideline.

"If you would just have a little confidence in yourself for a change you'd have made those free throws," Jackson spat.

The normally placid Kerr shot back.

"What the hell was your free throw percentage in your career?" Kerr accused.

Everyone broke up laughing and then went out to shut off the Heat's first two scoring options, as little-used Brad Lohaus took the potential tying shot and came up way short. Jordan had 31, including a neat baseline reverse layup, and he had shut down Glen Rice, who the game before had scored 56 to break Jordan's league season high.

NOT TOO SPECIAL K

While a championship danced in the minds of Jordan and the other starters, guys like Larry Krystkowiak were mostly concerned with where to eat after the game.

Krystkowiak, the veteran power forward, had been brought in for just this purpose, to show some toughness at playoff time. But the coaches feared that Krystkowiak, injured on and off all season, might break down again and leave them shorthanded. Jordan was lobbying for Dickey Simpkins, and the staff was leaning toward Corie Blount; someone would have to provide the athletic key to playing Horace Grant in the second round of the playoffs.

Krystkowiak didn't hold out much hope anymore; it had become painfully clear that Jordan had no use for him.

In the beginning, Krystkowiak had been thrilled when Jordan first began practicing with the team, before anyone had any inkling he was making a comeback. He knew something was up as he saw Jordan run the offense, watch films, and run postpractice sprints.

"It was then I knew he was coming back. It may sound corny, but I felt it was like being back with Babe Ruth. I felt looking back on it I'd be able to say when I was eighty I was a part of it, like a musician playing with Elvis. It rejuvenated the way I was looking at things. Everyone had a hop in their step and was holding their heads a little higher knowing he was on our team. I thanked him for coming back then. I said, 'For those of us who never got a chance to play with you, it's a great opportunity.'"

But it wouldn't be for Krystkowiak, who was a victim of Jordan's sharp tongue and lack of confidence in his new teammates. Krystkowiak's balky knees and creaking body sentenced him to the injured list and then the inactive list for the playoffs.

At one time, Krystkowiak thought that Chicago might be a savior for his career, especially now that Jordan was back. Regarded as future coaching material, Krystkowiak had impressed Jackson for years. He wasn't fast, nor could he jump much, but the Bulls thought they could bring him in as sort of a salvage project, just as Reinsdorf had done with his baseball team for previously injured players like Julio Franco and Ellis Burks.

Krystkowiak had been a Bulls draft choice in 1986, but he was traded on draft day to Portland and then a few days later to San Antonio. He stayed there just a year and then moved on to Milwaukee, where he became a solid contributor in 1988–89 before suffering a severe knee injury in the 1989 Eastern Conference Semifinals.

"Sure, there's a lot of what-if," said the six-nine, 240-pound Krystkowiak. "I always wondered what would have happened if not for that play, a pick and roll, I was open for a dunk. But I also wonder if I'd had a normal childhood, would I ever have worked hard enough and gotten a chance to play in the NBA."

Krystkowiak was one of several Bulls with particularly dysfunctional childhoods. In fact, both he and Bill Wennington were thrown out of their homes as teenagers by stepmothers and forced to live with other family members.

"My mom died when I was eight," Krystkowiak explained, "and my dad got remarried when I was eleven and I couldn't deal with my stepmother."

One night, according to Krystkowiak, there was a confrontation. She threw a glass at him and said he was never to return.

He never saw her again.

He moved in with an older brother who raised him, then buried himself in basketball, going to the University of Montana near his Missoula, Montana, birthplace and almost made Bobby Knight's 1984 Olympic team, where ironically he would have played alongside Jordan.

The knee injury was a virtual death knell for his career. Krystkowiak played a few games the following season, but then sat out the entire 1990–91 season, drifted off to Utah and then Orlando, and was cut loose by the Magic after playing just thirty-four games in the 1993–94 season. His recent history read like a medical journal, with stress fractures, sprains, and knee, foot, and arch injuries.

"It seemed like every time I was on the brink of something exciting and positive happening, it hasn't turned out that well," admitted Krystkowiak. "I've been happy to be in the league, but I always felt there were more things to prove."

Jackson had long kept an eye on Krystkowiak from fairly close. Jackson spends his summers in Montana on a ranch on one side of Flathead Lake. Krystkowiak lives on the other side, and in the summer of 1994, Jackson motorcycled over and wondered if Krystkowiak had another run left in him.

Jackson knew there was no replacing Horace Grant, but he felt a good backstop would be a player who did the kinds of things Grant did—box out, grab an offensive rebound, settle within the Bulls' system without needing to shoot much, and most important, stand up to the other teams' toughest players by throwing a body, knocking someone down. Krystkowiak was known as a tough guy who would battle anyone, as he did the previous season in Orlando where he almost came to blows with Shaquille O'Neal, saying O'Neal wasn't practicing seriously enough.

Jackson was impressed. "I'd watched him in the playoffs against Indiana," Jackson said. "He was fronting [Rik] Smits to let Shaq rest or let someone else get the rebound, letting Shaq run the break, the subtle things, and I said this guy is a valuable player. Orlando let him go because they needed the salary cap room to sign Horace."

So it was a philosophical trade of sorts: Grant for Krystkowiak. Jackson targeted Krystkowiak as the team's starting power forward, with a chance to develop the young power forwards, Corie Blount and Dickey Simpkins.

But Krystkowiak's body would fail him again in a bizarre series of injuries that even included an attack of appendicitis, although no injury would hurt him as badly as Jordan's dissatisfaction with him.

Shortly after Jordan's return, Krystkowiak was offering some tips on mistakes the starters were making during practice.

Jordan was enraged. "Who the fuck are you?" Jordan spat at Krystkowiak. "You've got no legs and you don't even play. Who are you to be telling us what we did wrong?"

Krystkowiak wouldn't back down.

"Screw you, Superman," Krystkowiak said. "We're not all Supermen here, but we know what we're doing."

Not long after that, the Bulls brought Krystkowiak in and asked him if he'd prefer to go on the injured list or be released. It seemed Simpkins, the rookie power forward, wasn't happy about being on the injured list without any injuries. Rookies were generally expected to "take a hit for the team." But Simpkins was threatening to go to the league about his noninjury status, and Jordan had befriended the rookie. Jordan saw Simpkins as something of a modern-day version of Charles Oakley, a burly player who might come to Jordan's defense, something of a policeman. Jordan looked around and didn't see any other candidates for the job and began to embrace Simpkins, taking him aside in practice and getting into little games with him.

Once, late in the season, Jordan came off the court seething about being knocked around.

"He looked at me and Jud [Buechler]," recalled Krystkowiak, "and he said, 'The only fuckin' guy on this team who'll set a pick is Dickey.'"

Jordan would be furious weeks later when Jackson and Krause picked Blount over Simpkins to go on the playoff roster.

Just before the team meeting to announce the playoff roster, Jackson called Jordan into the kitchen in the Berto Center to inform him and avoid an embarrassing session in front of the team.

"Whose fucking idea was this?" Jordan demanded loud enough for several teammates to hear. "Is this Krause's idea?"

The Bulls would end up buying out the second year of Krystkowiak's contract and releasing him.

ANYONE SEEN B.J.?

The Bulls were heading home to finish off the regular season with just one game of any interest, a playoff preview with the Charlotte Hornets on Saturday, April 22, in Chicago, with NBC getting one more national appearance out of Jordan in the regular season, even if the game meant nothing to the season standings and playoff seedings.

Two days earlier, the Bulls had whacked the Pistons again at home, and then Charlotte came in. The Hornets sat out Muggsy Bogues, who was injured, and Alonzo Mourning, who wasn't.

Jackson had hoped that Mourning would play, since one of Jackson's favorite tactics come playoff time is to point out obvious violations of certain players, such as Patrick Ewing's traveling, the Knicks' holding, the Pistons' brutalizing. Although referees try to ignore such obvious ploys, they do remember, and the Bulls have evened the playing field in years past in that way.

"We just let the guys play and hope the best team wins," said Jackson, "but we do want the referees to stop Mourning from running with the ball."

It was a reference to Mourning's driving move in which he travels, much like Ewing does when he goes across the lane with his right hand to the basket. But in a league built on its stars, the stars are allowed exceptions. Jordan travels quite a bit, as does Ewing. Karl Malone commits dozens of offensive fouls per game, as does Charles Barkley. It's an accepted practice. Jackson was just seeking an edge, which is what a playoff game can come down to.

The Bulls beat the Hornets, then lost their final game of the season, an uninspired loss to the Milwaukee Bucks and an aggressive Glenn Robinson. Kerr won the 3-point shooting title, but couldn't say enough about Pippen, whose passes against Charlotte put him in position to hit four 3s to move ahead of Seattle's Detlef Schrempf.

"I hadn't gotten a shot in the first seven or eight minutes, and Scottie comes over to me during a free throw and says, 'We got to get you some shots,'" said Kerr. "We came down on the next play on the break. He had the middle and a five-foot finger roll if he wanted it, but he threw it back out and I got an open shot, then another and another and I was hot. That's the way Scottie plays. We play so well when he has the ball."

But now it was playoff time. The ball would shift into Jordan's hands. And that would pose the greatest challenge to the Bulls throughout the playoffs.

Jackson said if there was an obstacle in the playoffs, "It's telling Michael, Scottie, and Toni to get B.J. and Steve involved. Also to get the ball in the post once in a while so we get all five guys involved. We need dispersal of the ball so the Kerrs and B.J.s can be a threat."

Especially Armstrong, who was in full funk now.

"Phil is messing with my head," he was telling teammates.

Armstrong felt he wasn't getting any shots, that Jackson was yanking him for Kerr too quickly, that he was being left on the floor with players who wouldn't get him the ball.

He was feeling sorry for himself, as was Perdue, who kept insisting that Longley was about to start in place of him. He sounded paranoid, like Doug Collins did when he used to rave about then Bulls assistant Jackson replacing him. Of course, that's exactly what did happen, just as Perdue would be replaced by Longley as a starter in the playoffs even as the team rallied behind him. Perdue would continue to seethe, one time throwing the ball the length of the court after Jackson yelled at him, coming to the bench and kicking over some chairs and slamming down a towel.

Armstrong had taken a new tack.

He refused to shoot much in games. He wouldn't shoot in practice. Even when Jackson would call a play for him, Armstrong would pass the ball off.

"I'd told him to be more aggressive, but he wouldn't take the shot," Jackson said.

In practice during the last week of the season, Kerr was instructed to play off Armstrong and see what happened.

"I was about ten feet off him, and he had a bunch of wide-open fifteen-footers, but he wouldn't take them," recalled Kerr.

Then Armstrong would glare at Jackson. It appeared to Jackson that Armstrong was taking some sort of retaliatory measure, getting back at him by not shooting.

But while many of the players viewed Jackson's actions and methods as original and fresh, Perdue and Armstrong in particular found them tiresome. They were ready for a divorce. To Armstrong's credit, he never allowed personal feelings to become public; he realized, even as he suffered with his personal situation, how good it was to be living his dream.

"You see players complaining and people are asking, 'What's his problem? Why is he complaining with all that money and everything?'" Armstrong would note.

So he seethed internally, for the most part, although he'd occasionally offer reporters cryptic hints about finally seeing "what this is all about."

Armstrong had been more self-assured in Jordan's absence, especially in 1993–94, standing up to Pippen, for example, after Pippen had been suckered into an ejection by Rick Mahorn; Armstrong said Pippen had to be smarter if he intended to be a leader.

Armstrong finally felt that with Jordan's departure, he would have his opportunity to run a team; it was his longtime dream. But Jackson felt Kerr played better in the Bulls' system and was starting to use Kerr more in certain game situations instead of Armstrong. It was one thing to sit behind John

Paxson, who had hit big shots and was a starter for championship teams. But Steve Kerr?

Jackson had made Armstrong a co-captain in 1993, but Armstrong remained a loner on the team, especially after Cartwright's departure.

Cartwright had been Armstrong's primary mentor, encouraging him and playing a major role in Armstrong's inspired defensive play that was a key in the 1993 championship run against Mookie Blaylock, Mark Price, and Kevin Johnson. Whenever Armstrong became depressed or sulked about perceived slights, Cartwright would be there to tell him, "Screw them. Do what you know you can do."

Cartwright was also a model of composure in the face of slights and snubs, and Armstrong admired him for it. But when Cartwright left after the 1993–94 season and the team continued to change over, Armstrong withdrew more. There was no one else he was particularly close to.

Armstrong had also been inspired by his mother, who had multiple sclerosis, rarely complained, always remained stoic. Armstrong tried to maintain the same demeanor, but he was overcome by the need to stretch himself as a pro. It wasn't happening with the Bulls, and it seemed like it never would. He could run an offense, he believed, if just given the chance.

After Jordan's retirement, Armstrong had kept in contact with him, so when the rumors about Jordan's return were exploding and few players really knew anything, Armstrong seemed to enjoy the association; it made him feel involved and in control, something he couldn't achieve in Jackson's offense.

But after Jordan's return, everything seemed to be slipping away, harder to reach. Jackson liked the way Kerr ran the plays to precision, and Jordan was taking on so much responsibility, trying to shoot himself back to where he had been two years before.

Some of the players felt that both Armstrong and Perdue were acting a little spoiled, and they attributed it to them being only children, kids who grew up pampered by their parents, both from stable middle-class homes, kids who went to good schools in good neighborhoods, who learned to occupy them-selves at home and who faced lots of parental control and feel-ings of guilt. No one admitted to having a psychology degree, but that was the in-house diagnosis.

Jordan was well aware of what was going on and felt he could salvage Armstrong. In the end, though, Jordan, too, would give up, doing nothing to prevent the Bulls from putting Armstrong on the expansion list for Toronto and Vancouver. He said he couldn't understand Armstrong's attitude.

In that last game of the season, as the Bucks beat the Bulls and rookie Glenn Robinson outdueled Jordan with 36 points to Jordan's 33, Jordan made every attempt to help Armstrong one last time. Every time Jordan got the ball, he looked across court to find Armstrong. He'd tried it with some success the preced-ing Saturday against Charlotte, helping get Armstrong fourteen shots, the most Armstrong had taken since Jordan's return and just the fifth time since Jordan had been back that Armstrong attempted at least ten shots.

Thanks to Jordan, Armstrong took five shots in that final game before Jackson brought Kerr in.

But the message was clear to Jackson, who was starting to see resentments rise and bravado fall at precisely the wrong time as the Bulls headed into the playoffs.

"This is not a particularly close group," Jackson admitted as the playoffs were imminent. "They feel for one another, but they're not supportive. There's a lot of anger out there, a lot of frustration and resentment. I'm concerned about this team and its ability to get along and to play in sync."

Chapter 12

CRUNCH TIME

If divine intervention would have anything to say, the Bulls' playoff script would have gone like this: Jordan returns home to North Carolina, the hero conquers the Hornets. Then the Orlando Magic: Jordan takes care of Generation X, the Fu Schnickens' lovin' kids of today, jammin' and basket wreckin'. Bye-bye Shaq and Penny. You weren't ready. Then it's the Knicks, finally, the stake through the heart. So long, Pat, you guys had your shot. Then on to clean up in the Finals against whatever emerged from the Western Conference.

In the beginning, it was perfect, and Jordan was enjoying it all. He talked about the burden of having to get so many extra tickets for his first playoff series in North Carolina, where he grew up and attended college and where the license plates, "First in Flight," apparently were named for him.

There was no limit to Jordan's love affair with his home turf. When the All-Stars came to Charlotte in 1991, Jordan reminded them to wipe their shoes before they got off the plane. There's a stretch of federal highway named after him, and back home in Wilmington, the Cape Fear Museum opened a Jordan gallery that includes such items as Michael's middle school certificate for good humor (Michael was the class clown because of his insecurity about his looks), a box he made in shop class, gym bags and uniforms from his youth, a letter from Dean Smith thanking his mother for a meal on a recruiting visit, a cake recipe from his home economics class, and his Christmas stocking.

The Hornets were about to be the next item in Jordan's bag of goodies.

"I think everyone is considering us as favorites because I came back," said Jordan. " But [without home-court advantage] we're underdogs. In truth, we're probably somewhere in between. But I wouldn't have come back if I didn't think we were capable of winning."

After the Bulls' regular season finale in Milwaukee on April 23, Jackson gave the team Monday off, so Jordan flew down to North Carolina for the day to play golf with friends. But when the Bulls arrived back in North Carolina on Thursday, April 27, to prepare for the playoff opener the next day, Jordan got hit with a battering ram of reality.

Larry Demery admitted guilt in the murder of James Jordan.

"Any reaction, any reaction," reporters yelled to Jordan as he left a Bulls practice at the Charlotte Coliseum that afternoon. Jordan wore dark glasses, a black T-shirt, and sweatpants. The guilty plea came as somewhat of a surprise, so Jordan didn't have the six-man security force with him that would surround him for the remainder of the playoffs.

"No reaction," Jordan said as he hurried past reporters. "None at all."

At least for the public.

But no event in Michael Jordan's life, before and probably subsequently, would draw as much of a reaction as the death of his father, whom he affectionately called "Pops." Michael Jordan is American royalty: rich, successful, beautiful, revered. He lives as close to Camelot as there is for us. Sure, there were the minor irritations, the gambling accusations, battles with the NBA over sponsorship, the Olympic commercial disputes, occasional petulant media boycotts. So perhaps sometimes the July and August of Jordan's Camelot was a little too hot. But life still was a most congenial spot. Despite the controversies, his fame grew and multiplied. The Bulls won, Jordan won every award. Life was a pretty picture. But every picture has a negative. Jordan's picture went dark in July 1993.

James Jordan, then fifty-six, was taking a rest along U.S. Highway 74 near Lumberton, North Carolina, on the way back home to the Charlotte area from a funeral in Wilmington, where Michael was raised. He had stopped to take a nap, and the sight of his red Lexus on the side of the road, windows down, apparently gave ideas to Larry Demery, who pled guilty, and Daniel Green, who maintains his innocence. Demery says that Green shot James Jordan in the chest, they took the championship ring James had gotten from Michael, along with some other items, then dumped the body over the state line in South Carolina.

James Jordan's unidentified, decomposed body was found several days later and cremated, the local coroner saying he had no place to keep and preserve it. But dental records were kept. Later, the red Lexus was found nearby. Demery, nineteen, and Green, twenty, were traced through the use of James Jordan's cellular phone.

Demery claimed he only helped dispose of the body, reportedly telling police in a statement: "When we picked the body up from the car, the body made a gurgling sound for about five seconds. The sound scared me so bad I almost dropped the body."

Michael was James's son in every possible way.

No, Michael wasn't mechanically inclined like his father, who always was tinkering with a car or some household appliance. But Michael was his dad. He looked like James, and their habits were similar, right down to the hanging tongue when they were deeply involved in a project.

At first, no one was alarmed when James didn't show up for a few days after that funeral.

"He would go off on his own a lot," Michael said, such as when the parents had a fight or James wanted to be with the boys, hang out, play some cards. He was a man's man, with huge stores of energy, a high metabolism, and an appetite for adventure, just like Michael. Michael's life was a constant series of games and challenges, card games late into the night, golf early in the morning, a pro basketball or baseball game worked in somewhere in between. And James enjoyed the race with Michael.

Friends smiled and nodded knowingly when Michael said at his October 1993 retirement from the Bulls that he was going to stay home and cut the grass, relax with the family. That wasn't Michael. Because it wasn't James. And sure enough, Michael was soon riding minor league buses with a bunch of nineteen-year-old kids, trying to live out one dream when he wasn't golfing and trying to chase another.

James, perhaps more than Michael, enjoyed the public, the attention, the life. He was gregarious and friendly; no one was a stranger. Seconds into conversations with him, you were lifetime friends. He laughed easily and didn't take much seriously. He wouldn't be defensive with those who upset Michael in the media or the league. He sympathized with his son, protected him, advised him, but treated everyone as a friend.

He had retired from a supervisor's job at General Electric at about the same time Michael came into the league with that first contract of less than $1 million per year for seven years—big money in 1984. He became his son's companion. He was there in 1993 when Michael went through his depressions and bouts with the media, talking to reporters almost daily when Jordan was being buffeted by gambling allegations. "I'm glad to talk for my son," he would say, always the protective father.

In 1990, when Michael had stopped talking to reporters during the Eastern Conference Finals, James would come to the pressroom and explain. "He's not mad at you guys," James would tell reporters. "He just wants to win so much, and that's all he wants to concentrate on."

And it was Michael who bought James that red Lexus. It was only when the car turned up stripped in the woods outside Fayetteville that Michael knew something was desperately wrong. He flew back to North Carolina from the West Coast, where he was playing golf, for the chilling news.

In the mythic land of Camelot, the fog always disappeared at 8 A.M. But the fog that descended over Jordan's Camelot that day would settle in for a long stay, turning his life black and cloudy.

Before long, he was out of basketball, crying, searching, alone.

Sometimes the tears came, and they wouldn't stop coming. Once, during one of those interminable road trips with Birmingham in 1994, Jordan said he sat in the team's motel, watching a movie on cable TV. It was raining.

"It was a Wesley Snipes movie," Jordan told the *Tribune*'s Melissa Isaacson. "And at the end, the father died. The room was dark and I was lying in bed and I guess it hit the right buttons because all of a sudden I couldn't stop crying. I talked to my wife [at home]. I called everyone I knew. And I still couldn't stop crying."

Jordan would have little to say about Demery's plea.

"It doesn't really make a difference to me or the way my life goes right now," he said. "I committed to let the thing take its course and let the judicial system take over. I'm not going to get wrapped up in it. I'm happy the situation is taking care of itself and the judicial system is taking care of it. But, in terms of my life, it doesn't make a difference."

Demery, who appeared in court handcuffed, wearing wire-rim glasses, a white shirt, and paisley tie, said he would testify against Green. He was trying to avoid the death penalty.

"[His attorney] was looking for a way to save their client's life," Johnson County, North Carolina, district attorney Johnson Britt told the *Charlotte Observer*.

But Jordan was grateful the absurd notions being aired by defense lawyers would finally be put to rest. There had been accusations that James was still alive and had faked his own death. A national magazine published a story suggesting James was involved in drug running and was killed in some sort of botched drug deal.

Jackson had talked to Jordan about gun control a few years back when he discovered that Jordan was one of several players carrying pistols into the locker room. But Jordan felt, as he did after his father died, that he needed a gun for protection. He knew his father might not be dead if there had been better handgun control, but he also knew criminals always find a way.

As to whether he felt the death penalty was appropriate punishment for his father's killers, Jordan was indifferent. "It won't bring my father back. I was thankful to have had him."

The week before the playoffs started, when the Hornets were in Chicago for that meaningless penultimate game of the regular season, former Bulls assistant John Bach got a chance to see Jordan for the first time since Jordan's gala farewell the previous November.

"Good to see you," Jordan said, smiling at Bach.

"I wish I could say the same," Bach replied.

Bach, who was now the defensive guru of the Hornets, had the toughest task in town: to stop Jordan, or at least harness him. A thankless job, one that had given Bach fits back when he was with the Bulls, drawing up defenses to stop other teams. Bach would use Jordan as sort of a guinea pig, figuring that if the Bulls could devise a defense to stop Jordan, they could stop anyone.

"He'd challenge me in the morning when he walked in and said, 'What have you got for me today?'" Bach recalled. "We'd practice doubling on him from different angles, we'd try to defend him in every unusual way, but he saw everything and beat everything we threw at him."

In many ways, Bach represented the premature conclusion of what could have been a Bulls dynasty. He was a league-renowned defensive genius, fired by Krause.

Jackson took the blame. He always liked and respected Bach, but he knew he couldn't win another battle with Krause to keep Bach.

"Johnny was everything Jerry wasn't," said one member of the Bulls organization. "He was handsome, well liked by the public and the media, charming. Krause hated it."

The two fought often, Bach picking up the name "Dr. Doom" for his negative forecasts of the team's ability and for harsh criticisms of favored Krause draft picks like Stacey King, Jeff Sanders, Will Perdue, and Brad Sellers. Finally, with so few players under contract after the 1993–94 season, Jackson felt he had to win his battles with Krause over acquisition of players, so he sacrificed Bach.

Bach understood why Krause wanted him gone, but he was hurt Jackson didn't put up more of a fight.

"He just said, 'Johnny, this is best for you,'" recalled Bach.

Bach's firing was stunning. He was one of the key ingredients behind the "Doberman defense" that the Bulls put together between 1991 and 1993 in their championship run, and when the Hornets and Bulls met to open the playoffs, Pippen walked up and said, "I don't fear your players. I fear you."

Sure, the Bulls had Jordan and Pippen, but it was the defensive spurts, Horace Grant trapping, the subtle funneling of offensive players, the disguised double teams and traps that left teams truly afraid to play the Bulls, more out of fear of embarrassment than losing.

And Bach often argued on behalf of the players against elements of the triangle offense, which he felt was stultifying. Jordan and Pippen, particularly, gravitated to Bach over the offense, and Jordan often called Bach his personal coach with the Bulls. "When I'm having trouble, I go to coach Bach."

In that next-to-last game of the season, Pippen walked by Bach early in the game, made a pyramid with his two hands, and then stuck his middle finger through it and smiled.

Bach also was adept at reading other teams' tendencies and had compiled a book of other teams' plays throughout his career. NBA plays are rather simple, unlike those in football, with simple hand signals and verbal calls of numbers usually relating to that player: "5," for example, might mean a play for the center, or a balled-up fist would mean some sort of power play in the post. There were variations, of course, and Bach's study of the league was invaluable. It was not unusual to see Bulls players signaling the opponent's next play just as the other team was calling it. Once, when Sherman Douglas was with Miami, he couldn't hear a call and strained toward the bench for more information. "He wants a high screen roll," Jordan told Douglas.

Now Bach and his priceless insights were gone, leaving the well-trained assistant Jim Cleamons to pick up the pieces.

Within days after Bach was fired, NBA commissioner David Stern called and asked if he could help the veteran coach find a job. But Bach would have no problems: Charlotte leaped to grab Bach, signing him to a longer contract than he'd ever had with the Bulls. Later, Detroit tried to hire him away for a contract twice as long as Charlotte's two-year deal. Quite a tribute to a seventy-year-old man.

"We have a habit of letting good coaches get away," Bulls chairman Jerry Reinsdorf said after Bach was let go.

Bach had played for the Boston Celtics in the early days of the NBA in 1948 after a stint in the navy, which shaped his life and coaching. He was a collegiate head coach for two decades, the youngest head coach in the country when he took the Fordham job in 1950 at age twenty-six. He then coached at Penn State before coming to the NBA as head coach of the Golden State Warriors and then spending eight years with the Bulls.

His films were indicative of his military background; he spliced scenes from Vietnam-era war movies, like *Full Metal Jacket*, into his defensive tapes. He urged Grant to be a warrior, and he gave Grant books about military heroes and tactics. He became renowned for drawing an ace of spades on the team's chalkboard, the ace the symbol of battlefield death for an enemy.

And Bach admired no player more than Jordan, the way Jordan was capable of stopping anyone in the league, the way he attacked opponents, the way he brutalized teammates in practice like it was a Civil War battlefield. But more than anything, Bach wished Jordan hadn't returned from retirement.

It wasn't that he didn't want to face him in the playoffs; he just didn't want to remember Jordan any other way than he had been before. He recalled Julius Erving, who late in his career was goaded into a fight with Larry Bird when Bird kept taunting the aging Erving about their respective points during the game: "Forty-two to six, Doc, forty-two to six," Bird kept repeating. Bach didn't want to see that happen to Jordan.

"An awful lot of us who have watched sports heroes go were glad he was leaving on a great note," said Bach. "There was nothing more to be done in basketball, and I thought people would remember him as the greatest player ever. I would have liked to have seen him walk away. He always said he didn't want to walk away like Larry Bird, injured, rookies yelling in his face, 'Larry, you can't play me,' like Dr. J., with his best behind him.

"There is risk involved," Bach added. "You know, none of us is immortal. I found that out the hard way."

Because John Bach had died on August 15, 1994.

Flat line, they call it in hospitals.

That's what Bach's monitor read at Anne Arundel Medical Center in Annapolis, Maryland, in August after he had a heart attack. Bach had had a minor heart attack in 1992 and then an angioplasty to clear blockages. But it hadn't worked as expected. He was at a friend's house when he experienced sharp pains, sweating, weakness. He contacted his cardiologist in Chicago, who didn't hesitate.

"He said call 911," recalled Bach.

When Bach got to the hospital, his heart stopped. For more than a minute.

In that time, his doctor would later tell him, Bach fought desperately, as hard as the doctor had seen anyone fight his fate.

At that same time, Bach saw stairways and light, something over his shoulder, vivid recollections of the door to death.

He refused to pass through.

"Maybe, like a lot of people," Bach said, "I needed a jolt."

There had been a divorce and a bitter battle after decades of marriage, and the separation from the Bulls.

"I learned you can work too hard," said Bach, still a handsome man with a silvery mane of thin hair, a flat stomach, and a wardrobe of clothes selected from stores around El Paso. "You can be too intense, too emotionally wrapped up in things. I'm not charging up hills like a battalion ranger anymore. I'm seeing a lot more. I learned a few things."

Like not to worry so much about games, even against
Michael Jordan.

The *Charlotte Observer*, tapping all angles for the big show-
down, asked students at an elementary school how to defend
Jordan.

"Charlotte can win by ten points," one wrote, "if two people get on Michael Jordan and the rest get on B. J. Armstrong
and Scottie Pippen. Let the other players alone."

That was the strategy of most teams.

"Hornets, be joyful," another wrote. "Don't get mad at one
another."

Added still another with perhaps the most appropriate
advice: "Don't get scared when Michael walks on the court."

Besides Jordan, the Bulls' edge in the series was their depth.

"Allan [Bristow] just doesn't have as many weapons," Bach
lamented, particularly referring to the season-ending injury to
Scott Burrell, who was in the running for the most improved
player award. And that depth could have been less if the
Hornets had let the Bulls steamroll them as they'd tried a few
years before.

Before the series opened, Hornets owner George Shinn
revealed that Bulls general manager Krause had tried to extract
a draft pick from the Hornets in exchange for playing an exhibition game in Charlotte with Jordan.

"I said, 'Are you insane?'" recalled Shinn, "and he said, 'Do
you know how much money you can make on an exhibition
with Michael Jordan in North Carolina?'

"I said, 'Forget it.' But that's how they did business. In
some of their deals, they'd try to throw in an exhibition game
with Jordan."

Jackson saw Shinn's comments and shook his head. It was
just another reason the Bulls had so many problems making
trades anymore: Teams didn't want to deal with the Bulls
because the Bulls were always trying to get something for
nothing, trying to "win" the deal. Krause delighted in trying to
show up other general managers, something that was coming

back to haunt the Bulls, not only when Utah got Jeff Hornacek for a badly declining Jeff Malone, but later when the Bulls couldn't deal B. J. Armstrong. Instead they let him go into the expansion for nothing, and then watched the Toronto Raptors turn around and trade Armstrong to Golden State (a deal that was pending the new player agreement in July 1995) for two players and two draft picks.

Also, Krause's insane secrecy had limited the team, Jackson believed. Krause would often size up a team's ability or interest in making a deal, then decide unilaterally whether they could or not. He wouldn't let teams know if he was willing to trade a certain player for fear the talk would leak out to the media. The result was the Bulls couldn't get in on three-way deals and other options teams were considering, another reason the Bulls couldn't get anything for Armstrong while rookie general manager Isiah Thomas in Toronto could get two players and two draft picks.

Yet despite Krause's suspicious nature, the Bulls had remained competitive, and Krause had brought players into the system through the quirky methods that had benefited the Bulls.

Toni Kukoc had been one of those players, and ten minutes into Game 1 of the opening playoff act of Michael Jordan's second pro basketball career, Phil Jackson was cursing out Kukoc so loudly one could even hear it above the constant hornet buzzing over the speakers.

The Hornets were leading by 8 points, and Kukoc, who was in foul trouble throughout the game although he played reasonably well, was late on getting back for the ball to throw inbounds for a five-second-call turnover.

"Wake the fuck up," Jackson bellowed as Kukoc came off the court.

Kukoc shrugged.

Jordan laughed.

It would be a mirthful night for Jordan, really his last for the rest of the playoffs, although he would not know that then.

He would score 48 points, including 10 in overtime, shooting a dazzling eighteen of thirty-two, as the Bulls took back home-court advantage with the 108–100 overtime win.

Jordan couldn't help feeling for Kukoc.

"I had to laugh," said Jordan. "The kid is trying so hard—he's just lost out there sometimes."

Jordan took pity because he saw possibilities.

"He's getting killed by P.J., by other players," noted Jordan. "You don't want to yell at him. Toni's my project. I have the chance to get him to understand basketball is simple. He makes it too complicated. There's a lot of potential there, a lot of expectations on him, and I'm trying to get him to understand that it's simple. Just play."

So with rookie power forward Dickey Simpkins inactive for the playoffs, Jordan took to working with Kukoc in practice, Kukoc's heart practically fluttering at the prospect, with Jordan asking Jackson and the other coaches to lay off a little.

But Kukoc was in a vital position at power forward. The Hornets were attacking him, attacking the basket and the backboards, and Kukoc was not standing up.

"You've got to fuckin' stand up and hit someone," assistant Jim Cleamons screamed at Kukoc after one play. "Knock someone down."

Kukoc's response? "He looked at me like I was crazy," laughed Cleamons.

The Bulls didn't see the fire in the droopy-eyed Croatian, who always seemed to wear the look of a frightened fawn.

Bach, from down on the other bench, smiled.

He always used to tell Kukoc that he had to fight. The Serbs fought, Bach would taunt Kukoc. "Fight!" Bach would demand. Like his people at home, Bach would tell him, Kukoc was having the bombs dropped on him.

Into all this stepped Jordan. He knew Kukoc wasn't about to set a screen for him, but he felt Kukoc might step up and take a big shot. And he liked that.

"Michael is serving as his protector," Jackson would say. "I've got a warrant out on Toni abuse from Michael."

Jackson could have served one on Jordan for Longley abuse.

Jackson was getting closer to going with Longley, after playing Perdue just sixteen minutes as a starter in Game 1, and although Longley would have his best game of the play-offs with 14 points and 5 rebounds in a reserve role—his only playoff game scoring in double figures—Jordan had unloaded on him as the team came off the floor for a second-half time-out.

"It's not really personal," insisted Jordan to reporters in a rare admission of public anger at a teammate. But Jordan cared less now what others thought.

"I'm just trying to make sure they understand that in crucial situations in the playoffs, execution is the most important thing," said Jordan of his tirade against Longley. "He screwed up a very simple play, and this is when you really have to focus on execution."

It had become somewhat personal for Jordan with Longley by now. Jordan preferred Perdue in the lineup and saw the inevitable. So he would combat it in his own way.

A few days later in practice, during a scrimmage, Jordan had tossed the ball ahead on a breakout to Pippen. Pippen took one dribble and passed ahead to Longley, who lost the ball out of bounds.

"I told you," Jordan yelled at Pippen, "don't ever pass him the fuckin' ball on the break."

Then Jordan walked off the court, muttering loudly: "I'm tired of playing with these fuckin' stiffs."

The mild-mannered, polite Australian hung his head.

It was the Jordan Test for Longley. Cartwright and Grant survived it. Brad Sellers, Dennis Hopson, Steve Colter, Rodney McCray, and Dennis Hopson had not.

Pippen, too, had been in foul trouble in Game 1, scoring just 8 points and playing just twenty-seven minutes. And Jackson was exasperated.

"The first time I put him back during the third quarter, he gets a charging foul," lamented Jackson. "Then I said, 'Can I trust you not to take a silly foul?' And he gets another. Somewhere in the fourth quarter, I say, 'Is it time now?' But he said, 'You better wait until five minutes are left. I might make a stupid foul.'"

Actually, none of it mattered, because Jordan was brilliant.

"I felt like a shark in the water. I just had to attack and hope I'd bite the right person," he said.

"Michael bailed us out," Jackson said.

Especially Pippen.

"You owe me one," Jordan said to Pippen as the two ran off the floor after Jordan's stunning overtime act.

The Hornets had had a chance to win at the buzzer in regulation, but five-three Charlotte point guard Muggsy Bogues missed a runner when the principal options broke down. Jordan was his old self again in a stunning overtime display: jumper for a 94–92 lead, drive for a 100–95 lead, quickstep move past Hersey Hawkins for a slam dunk and wide-mouthed scream: "Aahhhhhhh!" Another jumper and a pair of free throws, with an assist on a Longley basket thrown in there and a steal.

But the Hornets, the second worst rebounding team in the league and the worst offensive rebounding team, had pounded the Bulls on the boards, 18–7 on the offensive boards as Alonzo Mourning had 32 points and 13 rebounds. Charlotte's atypical rebounding success had roused Jackson's suspicions.

Before the game, Jackson noticed the league-imposed seal that prescribes the uniform amount of pressure for the backboard and rims was broken. No problem, said the Hornets, the league inspected and said the baskets and supports were fine. Jackson had doubts, though.

He knows, as do NBA insiders, that home-court advantage comes less from all that nonsense about sleeping in your own bed, eating at home, and having a regular routine than from the way home teams can manipulate equipment.

Jackson had long suspected the Detroit Pistons of tampering with one basket during their championship years, removing a piece of cushioning. The effect, Jackson believed, was to make it harder to shoot at that basket. Knowing that, the Pistons would keep an offensive rebounding team on the floor under that supposedly tainted basket to get offensive rebounds.

Likewise, Jackson also carried an air gauge with him to test the poundage in the game balls. Years ago, the Lakers, Jackson believed, used to sneak in inflated balls because Magic Johnson liked a high dribble, while teams with slower guards might remove some air from the ball to slow the Bulls' quicker guards.

Jordan, too, had his suspicions about the Hornets. Before the game, Jordan yelled to Jackson, "Hey Phil, got your gauge?"

Jackson had left it back at the hotel.

Jordan suspected the Hornets had pulled the old Lakers trick and pumped up the balls, knowing that their guard, Muggsy Bogues, likes to push the ball and dribble high.

But Jackson was more concerned with the broken seal on the backboard. The Bulls had shot there the day before and found the rims inviting. But Jackson also knew what that would mean: A softer rim was better for rebounding. The ball would stay on the rim rather than bouncing out and allowing perhaps for a fast break, and the team that went to the boards harder could take advantage.

Sure enough, in Game 1 Charlotte had more than twice as many offensive rebounds than the Bulls.

The Bulls would inform the league.

The Hornets were equally unhappy, though. Jordan, in forty-seven minutes of playing defense like an octopus and virtually demoralizing Hersey Hawkins, had picked up one foul.

Hawkins, in thirty-four minutes, picked up six and David Wingate helping out had three more.

A chant rose up in the fourth quarter from the partisan home crowd: "Don't touch Michael, don't touch Michael."

"When you touch Jordan, it's a foul," complained Hornets backup forward Kenny Gattison. "When Jordan touches you it's a steal."

Another poorly kept secret in the NBA: star treatment. Jordan shot a game-high eleven free throws.

"People said he's earned the right to get certain calls," acknowledged Hawkins. "But he doesn't need any help."

Already, the theories were starting to form: The NBA

wanted Jordan in the Finals because he meant ratings, which equals money, which the NBA loves. So send in some deferential officiating crews, make sure Jordan gets to the free throw line, the opponents get enough over-the-back calls to aid the Bulls' weak front line, and, hey, it's not like the game is fixed.

"Deep down in my heart, I don't believe it," said Hornets coach Allan Bristow. "If I were to find out it's true, I'd have to weigh my options, it would be adios, amigo, and more power to this league. You're talking about referees and things like that and I don't think the NBA has sat down with anyone in advance and said, 'Hey, we have to advance the Bulls.' Just think of the reality of that. Wouldn't you think that eventually would come back and haunt somebody? Eventually a referee could hold that over their heads and say, 'Hey, I want to tell the world.' Let's use a little common sense. How can this happen?"

Bristow's team wasn't convinced.

A TRIP TO THE LAND OF ZO

Hornets All-Star center Alonzo Mourning, known to teammates as "Zo," had done all he could in Game 1.

The frenetic Hornets center even hit back-to-back 3-point field goals late in the fourth quarter to give the Hornets a lead with less than three minutes left. But it would not be enough.

"This one took the life out of us," Mourning lamented after the Game 1 loss in which he typically played as if needing tranquilizers to slow down.

"Yeah, it hurts!" he shot back at a reporter after a tentative question about how it all felt. "What do you think? If someone came into your house and stole your TV, would that be a big loss for you?"

The ultimate response of the MTV generation.

Mourning was among that new breed of player that some in the NBA worried about: angry, loud, bombastic, barely holding on to reality.

Anyone who's seen Alonzo Mourning play basketball knows he has a passion for the game, if not an outright desperation. The Hornets, while supporting and protecting Mourning, long privately worried about his banshee screaming rages directed at basket supports, himself, opponents, chairs, walls. They thought bringing in laconic veteran center Robert Parish would help calm Mourning. But Parish was so ineffective he could not gain Mourning's confidence.

Bach called him "the Tasmanian Devil" the way he'd whirl around in a frenzy, spasms of rage exploding like Mourning was fighting himself as much as his opponent.

It seemed he was always angry, hitting a backboard support, screaming at himself, almost without perspective or a sense of humor. One time, veteran referee Jake O'Donnell came to the Hornets' bench and said if Mourning didn't stop talking to himself he was going to throw him out of the game.

Mourning talked plenty to the Bulls, too, when he was hitting those 3-pointers in Game 1, and particularly later in Game 2, when the Hornets won easily and Mourning had 23 points and a dominating 20 rebounds.

"He'd talk mostly to Michael and Scottie," said center Will Perdue, "not much to me. He said he was on a level with those guys. He kept yelling at them, 'We're taking this series.' 'You can't stop me.' 'We got this game.' Then in Game 3, he kept talking to Michael, saying they weren't getting any calls, that Michael was playing illegal defense, yelling, complaining."

The controversies off the court were becoming more interesting than the games.

When Jordan returned in March, he had condemned the youth of today's game for not respecting the game, for doing what they wanted no matter the rules, a charge that would come back to catch Jordan when he would later break a few rules himself. Back then, though, Jordan's comments were embraced by the media, especially the print reporters for the major publications, who were having increasing problems with continually decreasing access to guys like Charlotte's Larry Johnson, who had huge, long-term contracts and felt little responsibility to anyone but themselves.

Jordan was what the media wanted: approachable, friendly,

talented. Not the boorish antics of characters like Johnson, Derrick Coleman, even Mourning, who early in his career clashed with the media, once trying to throw Atlanta writer Ailene Voisin out of the locker room because he didn't feel women had any place in sports locker rooms.

Mourning had cooled considerably since then, but to many, players like Johnson and Mourning represented the puerile, churlish ways of the so-called Generation-X players of the current day.

Larry Johnson wasn't all that impressed with Jordan, it seemed, noting that Jordan had plenty of his own problems to begin judging others.

"Michael Jordan's not perfect," noted Johnson before the series. "Just because Michael thinks people ought to be a certain way doesn't mean that everyone else is going to do it. Everybody ain't Michael Jordan. Everyone has their own personality."

The players would joke about just who it was telling them how to behave, the man who draped a flag over himself—and a Reebok logo—in the Olympics; who, as one columnist wrote, would have been a great American patriot, saying, "I have just one life to give for my shoe company"; the man caught gambling with drug dealers, blowing off the media in the playoffs for weeks, out gambling before games.

"Michael Jordan is entitled to his opinion," said Mourning. "He was young, too. He made mistakes. You can't please everyone out there. Michael Jordan has been a big asset to the league. His presence alone makes the game more enjoyable to watch. But he's made mistakes like we have."

Jordan did get that message. He said he hadn't meant anyone in particular, he was just making general comments about the game, that he wasn't talking about Johnson or Mourning or anyone specifically.

Because Mourning did what Jordan wouldn't: He went out into the community, becoming something of a foster father at the Thompson Children's Home in Charlotte, a residential treatment facility for abused and neglected children.

Mourning spent off days there, had Nike send the kids shoes.

"You feel the warmth when you're around them," Mourning said. "You can feel them saying, 'Hey, I want you to be here for me.' And I wish I can all the time. In a way, you don't want to be around them because you don't want to leave."

Mourning could be a cauldron of rage, swirling round and round, ready to bubble up and explode.

Except when he was with the kids.

"I got involved," Mourning said, "because children are being led astray. It's a simple fact of guidance, parental guidance. So there's a pressure on all us athletes. They see us and admire us because we play the game of basketball. But that's unfortunate it happens. That's why people say we have to be role models, but we're going to make mistakes. Who are we not to?

"I remember going to a neighborhood barbershop," recalled Mourning, a glowering six-ten 240-pounder. "A boy's mother waited outside when she heard I was coming by. She asked me if I would talk to her son and tell him how important it was to do well in school. In a way, I felt bad. I felt it was good because she cared about her son, but I felt bad inside because her son wouldn't listen to her when she told him things like that. Since I do have some influence, whether it's right or not, I have gotten involved."

Especially in national campaigns against child abuse. Mourning is doing a series of ads for the NBA.

"It's not just for the kids," explains Mourning. "It's society in general. Society needs to wake up and understand that we do have a problem with child abuse. Every minute, some child is being locked in a closet somewhere. It's something we can control if we put our foot down."

Mourning knows all about it because he's been there.

When Mourning was eleven and then an only child, his parents divorced and he entered the Virginia child care system, living in several foster homes before finally being raised by an elderly woman named Fanny Threet who would raise forty-nine children during her life as a foster parent.

"I wasn't comfortable with the situation that was evolving," Mourning said in an interview in 1994. "I didn't want to live with my family. I went into the foster care program."

He refuses to discuss his situation any further. But it's clear something terrible happened in that home, for eleven-year-olds just don't opt to go into foster care. A North Carolina newspaper wrote in 1993 that Mourning had been abused growing up, although there was no mention of the nature of the abuse. Mourning denied he was physically abused, and after many years he has recently tried to reconcile with his family.

"It makes you sick to your stomach just to think about it," says Mourning, clearly growing angry with the thought, his face starting to contort with the mark of rage he wears while playing basketball, "that someone would abuse or jeopardize the future of a child by assaulting or abusing them, mentally or physically. Children are the keys to our future."

Tom Haselden is the director of the Thompson school where Mourning helps out.

"He gets close to the kids," says Haselden, "and they like that because these are kids who haven't been dealt with appropriately by adults. He's very different than you may have seen him on the basketball court. His heart goes out to them. And they can relate because they know he went through some of the things they did."

"Most people can't imagine what those kids have been through," says Mourning. "But I can. It makes me feel good to know I can put a smile on their faces sometimes."

After Pippen's poor Game 1, he said, "We didn't come down here to get just one game, we came down here to get two of them."

But that wouldn't be the case, as the Hornets won Game 2 of the series rather easily, 106–89. They again dominated the Bulls in the rebounding department behind Mourning, who outrebounded the entire Bulls front line.

Jordan again shot the ball well, thirteen of twenty-five, and scored a game-high 32 points. But Kukoc was horrid, hitting three of twelve shots for 9 points and getting run over by Larry Johnson, who had 25. Bach had urged Johnson to attack Kukoc after Game 1, and Johnson went right at the Croatian, which had been one of the Bulls' principal fears. Once again, Perdue didn't look to score, allowing Mourning to roam on defense.

And as Jordan continued to be openly hostile toward Longley, yelling, "Catch the ball!" at him in the second quarter after a quick pass went off Longley's hands, Jackson had already made some decisions.

That was it, Jackson decided, for Perdue and Kukoc. The heck with Krause. Jackson felt Kukoc was better coming off the bench, and Jackson liked the way Jud Buechler had attacked Johnson in limited minutes, holding him to six for eighteen shots in Game 1.

After Game 2, Jackson called the team together before practice. "Toni was allowing us to be penetrated," said Jackson. "I said we were going to be making some changes for Game 3, we weren't coming out aggressively enough and we were going to be starting Luc and Jud."

Jordan rolled his eyes.

Of all the players who made him impatient, he probably was least patient with Longley and Buechler, treating the two of them the harshest. He had little enthusiasm for their play or potential. He felt more comfortable with Perdue, and he liked Kukoc's ability to produce in clutch moments. What was Jackson doing? he wondered. He practiced lethargically and left. He would do it his own way.

Jackson figured that the humbling loss in Charlotte, the Bulls having been dominated by Mourning, would cool the team's ardor for Perdue. Perdue had long seen it coming, although he was still upset.

"I don't know why Phil made the change," Perdue said afterward. "With Phil, it depends on what dream he had last night or something like that. Maybe if he gets one of his visions or images he'll change again."

The interesting change was Kukoc, the highest paid player on the team, for Buechler, not only the lowest paid at the league minimum $150,000 but a player on the injured list much of the season and only activated for a look-see with about a week left in the season.

"My jaw dropped," recalled Buechler, the lantern-faced journeyman who was with his fourth team in five years in the NBA.
"I walked out of the room and I was in a fog for fifteen minutes.
I couldn't believe it. I tapped Steve [Kerr] on the shoulder and
said, 'Did he just say something about me starting?'"

Jackson had, and for two hours it would be one of the high-
lights of Jud Buechler's crazy-quilt NBA career.

Buechler was the only true two-sport professional on the
team, a southern California beach kid who was also a world-
class professional volleyball player. At six-six and 220, he was
the ultimate NBA fringe player. Coaches liked him because of
his hustle, his willingness to dive for a loose ball, to take on
any defensive assignment. But he couldn't actually do much in
basketball. He was a decent but not special shooter, good but
not great defender, adequate but not great ball handler, willing
rebounder, but not big or strong.

He'd been cut by the Nets when they needed more money
to sign first-round draft choice Kenny Anderson, and released
by the Spurs when he got injured and they didn't want to pay
his medical bills. But he thought of himself as "the Forrest
Gump of the Bulls." "Good things seemed to happen to me,"
Buechler said.

Like many of the other Bulls, particularly the new ones, he
was just as excited as the community when Jordan returned.

"I remember the first day he came back," said Buechler.
"He threw me a pass and I hit the shot and ran back and he
gave me a high five. A high five from Michael Jordan! I thought
I was larger than life. I was ready to dive for loose balls, run
through a wall. I was ready to do whatever. One little compliment from a guy like that is huge."

But it wouldn't last long for Buechler, as Jordan quickly
discounted him as a presence and began his lobbying cam-
paign for Dickey Simpkins. Jordan saw Buechler as one of the
obstacles.

"He gets on guys," Buechler admitted. "He's always saying, 'You gotta do this that way.' He is kind of hard on some of
the guys. If you're Michael Jordan and you come to practice

and start giving guys compliments, it goes a long way. I saw that with Dickey and Toni. You can really build a fire under a guy. But it was still just a great season. Remember, I started off the year not guaranteed and when I get to camp I find out there's twelve guys with guaranteed contracts," said Buechler. "I'm one of fifteen guys in minicamp with no contract and I'm going back to the hotel thinking, 'What am I doing here?' But I thought I'd stay around. The guys were fun to be around and Phil was great to play for. Jerry [Krause] had always been great to me, so they say they can waive me or put me on injured reserve. So I said, 'What the heck.' I'd stay around on IR and see what happened."

It is the life of the NBA journeyman. Hope you're on a team where someone gets injured, a trade is made, and you can get a chance.

When Buechler was drafted in 1990 and his rights traded to the Nets, he hung around for a season and then was told they couldn't sign him because Kenny Anderson wanted more money. As a result, the Nets would cut three players. Coach Bill Fitch was furious and told Buechler to refuse to help out the Nets, but Buechler was waived and picked up by the Spurs, where he thought he broke his wrist. The team doctor said the wrist was fine, and Buechler continued to play. But it still hurt badly, and he finally asked to see the team doctor again.

"[Fellow Spur] Tom Copa was there [seeing the doctor], so I pull up next to his car," Buechler recalled. "I've got an appointment, but the secretary says the doctor isn't in. I say, 'No, I know he's here. I just parked next to Tom Copa.' She leaves and comes back and says he can't see me, would I come back next week? I said I just needed an X ray, that my wrist was killing me."

So Buechler left, and the next day he was waived and eventually won a settlement from the Spurs.

Still, Jud loves this game.

He was picked up by the Warriors, but after one decent season didn't play much.

"Nellie's [coach Don Nelson] coaching style is to exploit

guys one-on-one. It's all isolation plays," said Buechler. "But going one-on-one is not one of my strengths. He'd put me on the wing and clear a side and say, 'Jud, take this guy.' That's not what I do."

So he was released by the Warriors after the 1993–94 season, which didn't mean Buechler was out of pro sports: There was always volleyball.

Buechler's father, Don, was a top beach volleyball player in San Diego, where Jud was raised. Jud then went on to play in two Olympic festivals and was invited to join the U.S. team.

"I put so much work into basketball as a kid, I wanted to pursue it," remembers Buechler. "Volleyball just came so easy. I never really had any coaching, but I could step out any day and be really competitive. Every summer, after the NBA season was over, I'd be home a day or so and someone would call and say, 'Jud, we need you to come out.' I'd say I hadn't played in eight months and it wouldn't matter."

And these were no recreational beach games. This was the beer-sponsored pro beach tour, where the top players could make several hundred thousand dollars a year.

"I was thinking about doing it last summer [1994]," said Buechler. "ESPN would have it on late at night sometimes and guys from the teams would call me and say, 'Jud, I just saw you on ESPN. I didn't know you played volleyball.'"

On the volleyball circuit he was known as a two-sport guy. "The guys would always kid me about being Bo Jackson or Deion Sanders. It's something I'm very proud of. Not too many guys get to play two sports at the highest level. But I do miss the beach during the season."

Especially the season with the Bulls. Buechler was activated in November when Krystkowiak was hurt, and he scored his season-high of 17 a few weeks later against Boston. But after the All-Star break, his playing time diminished and he was put back on the injured list to accommodate Simpkins.

"I thought my season was over," recalled Buechler.

It was a dark period. Unsure how long he might be with the team, he lived in a motel for several months before he and his wife moved into a house. But the Chicago winter, a relentless period of gray, dank, cold days, finally got to her. She left in March to go back to San Diego.

"She couldn't stand the weather anymore," Buechler said. He thought he'd follow soon, for different reasons.

"When I heard he was coming back, I was truly excited," said Buechler. "And then I thought, 'Uh-oh, I could be in trouble.' I didn't think they'd let me go that late in the season, but his coming back definitely hurt me. Playing time for everyone changed. Shot distribution changed. The first game he played back in Indiana, Steve and I are sitting on the bench and we look at each other and say, 'Did we just get traded to another team?' It was eerie. Everyone had a new role. You come so far into the season, then everything changes. It felt really strange.

"But friends are calling all the time and asking what's he really like, everyone is so excited," said Buechler. "Practices were great. He really changed that for us. Everyone felt good about our chances with him there. But it did hurt some guys. You could see with Toni, especially. When he's not scoring early, he gets down and then in crunch time if he hasn't shot in twenty minutes, it's tough. Toni plays better defense when he has a chance to score, he gets into the game more.

"And there's extra pressure when you're out there with Michael," Buechler admitted. "He gives you the ball and you want to make that shot so badly. You want to show him what you can do. You want his trust. Some of us thought being in baseball, batting .202 in the minor leagues, going through that experience, might have made him understand some of us better. But he's so confident, so self-assured, so good.

"Then he throws you one of those bailout passes and you really want to make it, to please him as well as doing it for the team. And you're thinking if you don't make it maybe he won't throw you the ball again. He was tough on me, but it was such a great team to be with, such a great group.

"And then Phil said he was going to activate me for the last four games," said Buechler. "I kept telling myself it wasn't a tryout, they knew what I could do, but I knew it was and I'm thinking I've got to play my best ball or I'm done for the season. And I keep seeing Michael with Dickey, having fun with him, encouraging him, helping him. If Michael Jordan says, 'You're my guy,' that's got to give you confidence. But I thought it was a fulfilling year, anyway, that I'd overcome so many obstacles. And then I make the playoff roster. And I'm going to start a playoff game.

"I went down and practiced with the starters and the first fifteen minutes I was going crazy," recalled Buechler. "Then I felt pretty relaxed about it. But Phil called me later that day and said he felt it was too big a change to start two new guys. I understood and everything. But it was really exciting."

THE CROATIAN SENSATION

Practice went badly that day after Game 2 for Kukoc.

He was crushed by Jackson's decision to start Buechler, a demotion, and his psyche was again becoming as fragile as blown glass.

Jackson had planted some seeds of doubt, and no one quite knew what they would become at harvest time. Kukoc was assured he'd play the same amount of minutes, but he wanted to start. He had even gotten used to Jordan being gone and the fact that Pippen might be traded. After he signed his new record-breaking $25 million six-year deal in August 1994, he was ready for NBA stardom.

"It's nice to know you're the star of the team," Kukoc said then. "It's going to be a new team, but this is not a problem for me. I will be happy to build a new team with the guys who come in. Yes, it is some kind of pressure on me. I don't know how good I will be, but I will try to be one of the All-Stars."

And now he was playing behind Jud Buechler in the team's most important game of the season.

"Toni moped through that whole practice," Jackson said, "and I was really concerned about it. When I went home, I started to reconsider everything, and later that evening I decided I would stay with Toni. I was going to call that night, but then I decided I'd let him spend the night thinking about it."

But even when Jackson called him the next morning to say

he would be starting after all, the news didn't cheer Kukoc as much as it should have. There were bigger problems on Kukoc's mind that day.

That day, word had come that Serb rebels had bombed the Croatian capital of Zagreb; Kukoc was unable to telephone his parents in Split some thirty-five miles away.

The fighting had not yet come to Split, a beautiful seaside town, so Kukoc's parents didn't want to move. Before deciding to come to the United States and play for the Bulls, he had decided to stay in Europe to play, in part to be closer to home because of the unrest in the former Yugoslavia. But now he found the fighting creeping closer to home.

"It is so close, if they bomb a couple of towns in Croatia, they can bomb any other town," Kukoc said. "When we tried to call and I couldn't get ahold of them, I said, 'Oh no, something dangerous could be happening.'"

Kukoc, an avid fisherman as a kid, really didn't take up basketball until he was a teenager.

But by age sixteen he was a star, playing for the junior national team, and at nineteen, he helped lead a strong Yugoslavia team to the silver medal in the Olympics. Kukoc was not expected ever to play in the United States, but Bulls general manager Krause took a chance on him with a second-round pick in 1990, a coup for Krause.

The year before, Jackson had urged Krause to draft Vlade Divac with the Bulls' third first-round draft pick, but Krause said he hadn't scouted Divac, so he wouldn't draft him. Krause would surprisingly admit his mistake and even hire a special European scout, not coincidentally a former teammate of Kukoc's, to help ease Kukoc's transition. Krause, who prided himself on his intimate knowledge of every top basketball player in the world, would make sure not to make the same mistake.

Divac, who went to the Lakers, is Serbian, and Kukoc's first NBA meeting with his former teammate in November 1993 would be a little awkward.

"Maybe I'll say hi. Maybe I won't talk to him," Kukoc said

before the game. "But if he comes and asks about cars and jew-
elry, that will mean he doesn't care much [about the war] and if
he starts with this, 'You started this war first,' I have an easy
way to explain the war. It is a Croatian defending his country
and a Serb attacking a Croatian country. We cannot be friends
because it's a war. A lot of my friends are on the front lines. It's
a very bad situation. We were good friends [and teammates].
But now is a very difficult situation. I'm not a political man. I
am a basketball player. But I will help my country because I am
Croatian. Everything about me is Croatian."

Krause, a fine scout and judge of talent, would go to see
Kukoc several times. Kukoc played in the Goodwill Games in
Seattle in 1990 and was spectacular, whetting Krause's appetite
for his "find" and leading to the turmoil on the team as he pursued Kukoc in 1990 and 1991 while Pippen stewed about a contract extension and Jordan seethed as Krause called Kukoc the
next Magic Johnson.

Jordan had already dethroned one Magic Johnson. Now,
Krause was saying there would be another, right on his team.

Jordan told Krause he was setting Kukoc up for failure, that
it takes European players several years to adjust, that Drazen
Petrovic didn't mature in the NBA until he was traded from
Portland, and that Krause was setting expectations too high.
But Jordan later softened after he and Pippen shut Kukoc down
in the Olympics and then Kukoc was so moved, even crying,
when Jordan told the team he was retiring.

One day, Kukoc's American attorney, Herb Rudoy, asked
his client which city in the world was his favorite, since he had
played all over the world with the Yugoslavian and European
teams.

"Jerusalem," he had said, without hesitation.

"He started telling me about this 'crying wall,'" said Rudoy,
"that he always went to. It was the Wailing Wall, but that was
his translation. And he's explained that it was this wall, where
men and women are on different sides and you make a wish
and it will come true.

"He said that he had done so every year of the European

championships, and each year his team had won," said Rudoy. "I happened to be going [to Israel] in the fall of 1993, when he was starting with the Bulls, and he asked me to make a wish for him that he would have a good season. So here I am over there and the newspapers are reporting Michael Jordan is retiring.

"I called and talked to Toni, and he said, 'Have you made that wish for me yet?' I said I hadn't," related Rudoy. "He said not to write a note for him, that the team would need a whole book of wishes now."

Kukoc had been paid about $4 million per year to play in Italy, but he decided to come to the Bulls in 1993 to play with Jordan. He had been scared off a little by the stories of anger toward him by Jordan and Pippen and had decided he was too young to sit on the bench with a team like that.

But Kukoc dominated in Europe, winning player of the year three times. And after being shown up in the Olympics, he felt he had to try the NBA. What better place to try than with the Bulls?

Now that he was a teammate, he was sure he would be embraced by Jordan and Pippen. After all, that was what teammates did, Kukoc reasoned.

But when Jordan left, he was alone in many ways.

The team asked him to bulk up to handle the pounding he'd get in the NBA, but it hurt him, costing him quickness. Score one for Jackson in his ongoing battle with management over weight training. Jackson thought it helped cause injuries, especially back injuries, and hurt quickness. Kukoc would lose weight for the 1994–95 season, but he would never regain the stamina to become an effective player for more than thirty minutes per game.

He hated the bitter Chicago weather after growing up in temperate Split. Jackson derided his defense and didn't think him capable of starting, something he'd done since he was sixteen. Pippen even singled out Kukoc when Pippen claimed Chicago fans were racist, suggesting the fans needed to boo Kukoc when he had a bad game. Kukoc was stunned, but remained hopeful.

"Maybe we do not go to dinner," he said, "but on the court we are together."

No one befriended him on the team other than Krause, who lived within a block of Kukoc. Kukoc was accustomed to the camaraderie of his national and European teams instead of the Bulls' individuality, and some Bulls theorized Kukoc might return to Europe after that rookie season.

"Sometimes I did feel out of place," Kukoc admitted.

"Here, after practice everyone goes, so it was bye-bye and I went home to my wife and kid," Kukoc offered with a shrug.

So Kukoc stayed home with his wife and infant son, existing on a diet of fast food and making almost daily trips to toy stores to shower his son with gifts.

His relationship with Krause did little to ease the feeling of displacement Kukoc had in the United States. He was mostly uncooperative and suspicious of American reporters, his closeness with Krause poisoning his relationship with the press.

A friend of Kukoc explained it this way: "He comes from a country that had a dictatorship. He sees the media as the secret police after his indoctrination from Krause. Every time he sees the media, he feels like it's the state police coming to take him away."

So Kukoc swore off pregame interviews, like many of his teammates, and liked to make a quick exit after the game as the Bulls usually defied league rules and kept their locker room closed for up to twenty minutes after the game—instead of the league-mandated ten—so Jordan could be showered and changed before the media were let in.

But Kukoc did delight in conversations about children, admitting he let his son sleep with him and his wife, and relating their daily schedule of *Sesame Street* and postpractice trips to the zoo, kids' gyms, and playgrounds. And he happily joined in when the players got to discussing their fatherhood experiences with pregnant *Tribune* writer Melissa Isaacson. Ron Harper was graphically describing his birthing-room experience, and Pippen, who'd just had a child (with his fiancée, who would later charge him with battery and with whom he would

split in the summer) was offering tales of early-morning feed-
ings and walking the floor for hours. Luc Longley talked about
the use of midwives in Australia.

"What are you having?" someone asked Isaacson.

"We don't know," she replied.

"Girl," said Kukoc. "Trust me, you have a girl."

And then he went on to explain: "When boy, stomach go
out, but with girl, stomach go out like ball. Also girl when you
have puffy cheeks, face like that."

"Oh, thanks," Isaacson said about Kukoc's observation of
her appearance.

Two months later, Isaacson gave birth to a seven-pound, fif-
teen-ounce girl.

The highlight of Kukoc's first season, apart from a few
incredible shots at the buzzer, was an off-day visit to the White
House with Steve Kerr, whose brother works for the National
Security Council. Kukoc was stunned about being able to see
the council's "situation room" and the Oval Office. Kukoc sat
in the president's chair in the cabinet room and thought about
leaving a note.

What would it say? "Save all the kids who aren't guilty for
this war," Kukoc said.

Kukoc was ready for Game 3.

He hit nine of ten shots and scored 22 points, 14 in the third
quarter when the Bulls broke the game open, to lead the Bulls
to an easy 103–80 victory. The Bulls were leading the series two
games to one.

Jordan would have 25 points and just barely miss shooting
50 percent back in the United Center, but his defeatist attitude
about the home court was becoming a growing concern to the
coaches and the community.

When the woeful Celtics surprisingly won Game 2 of their
opening-round series against the Orlando Magic, there was
some happy scoreboard watching in the Bulls locker room: An
upset by the Celtics would mean home-court advantage for the
Bulls.

Jordan didn't see it that way. "Go, Orlando," Jordan said. "I don't want home-court advantage. I want to play as many games away from the United Center as possible. It's going to take me another year to really get comfortable in that place."

Jordan also admitted he was still having problems getting used to his teammates.

"I can't find Kerr," he said. "He hides out there. I always knew where Paxson was. Before we had eighty-two games to get to know each other and get a rhythm. Now we're in a crash course to try to blend in and play together well enough to win."

And the scoring was getting just a little too concentrated. The centers weren't getting shots, and Armstrong and Kerr would combine in the Charlotte series for half as many shots and half as many points as they averaged during the entire regular season. It would catch up to the Bulls soon.

But the story for now was Kukoc.

"It's nice to play good and wake up not thinking about the game," Kukoc told reporters, who were unaware that Kukoc had almost lost his starting role. "It's not like the second game in Charlotte."

In more ways than one. Jackson always liked to hold something back in a playoff series until a loss, so it was time now to spring yet another change.

Charlotte point guard Muggsy Bogues, who fired the Hornets' running game, is a poor and, worse, reluctant shooter. So Jackson assigned Jordan to Bogues with orders to double-team Mourning in the post whenever Mourning touched the ball.

Jackson would feel a little badly for Bogues. He knew that the strategy would work. But he also knew it could effectively end Bogues's career, showing once and finally why a team could never go anywhere in the NBA with a five-three lead guard.

"I felt badly for the kid," said Jackson, who knew how ultrasensitive Bogues was and how he'd have to answer these questions the rest of his career, however long that would be.

Mourning, meanwhile, would have just 13 points and 7 rebounds on two of nine shooting, and find himself complaining to Jordan and the referees about Jordan playing illegal defense.

Jordan fired back in the game as the two jawed, although Jordan reminded Mourning they both had the same agent, David Falk, so none of this should be taken too seriously.

Jordan was now thrilled with Kukoc, his project, especially after seeing Jackson abandon the Buechler strategy.

"The only thing he lacks," Jordan said of Kukoc, "is the knowledge of how to play in this system and [how to play] here in the United States. There's a lot of things you have to adapt to, the physical beating, the consistent play. He's coming from a country where they play once a week. He's had a tough time bouncing back from game to game."

Scottie Pippen was more cautious, though.

"Toni played well," he said, "but let's see him put two games together."

Kukoc thanked Jordan: "Once out of five times [in practice] you can handle him. It is two or three of five times against other players. If I can reach the aggressiveness of these guys, M.J. and Pippen, that will be the best thing I ever did in basketball as a personal goal."

IT'S ALL A CONSPIRACY

And then it was over. By the end of Game 4, it was clear, at least to Mourning, what had happened: The Jordan Conspiracy.

"The NBA got what it wanted," Mourning yelled as he left the floor of the United Center after the Bulls won Game 4—and the series, 3–1—by a squeaky 85–84 despite another atrocious shooting game by Jordan, just eight of twenty-one.

On the last play of the game, a Larry Johnson jumper for the win, Hersey Hawkins flashed across the lane, grabbed the air ball, and tried to lay it in. But Jordan held down his arm and the game was over.

"Michael pulled my arm down," the classy Hawkins agreed.

"You could tell he knew by his reaction [looking at the referees after Hawkins's shot came up short]. The referees didn't make the call. So give him credit."

But Mourning wasn't quite as gracious.

His rage flooded the locker room, and he didn't care who knew. The NBA wanted Jordan playing the Magic and Shaquille O'Neal, and nothing the Hornets were going to do would make that much difference.

"We're playing against the Bulls, not the league, not the referees," Mourning ranted, his face contorted and twisted in anger and emptiness over the loss. "We know everyone wants to see the Orlando Magic and the Chicago Bulls. They want to see that matchup. But treat people fairly. Especially when we work our butts off. I'm willing to take any type of criticism the league might hand out. They can fine me, but I'm speakin' my mind because I'm hurtin' inside. It hurts when you're working so hard. This game was taken away from us. It's politics. The calls were horrendous."

It was nonsense, really, because probably the league's best official, Joey Crawford, was the lead referee, and the Hornets shot thirty-four free throws to the Bulls' twenty.

But the charge would linger, and Jordan would surprisingly admit Crawford had missed the call.

"I probably got his whole arm," Jordan said. "You make them make those calls. If that's what they're crying about, let them cry. The refs missed calls all night."

"Hey, the way the NBA game is officiated is basically a caste system," chimed in Steve Kerr, who had studied the country of India. "If this were India, Alonzo and Michael would be the Gandhi family and guys like me would be untouchables [commoners]. That's the way it works in the NBA. Guys like Michael and Alonzo get calls. Me and Joe Wolf don't."

But something more ominous happened in that game. In the third quarter with the Bulls trailing by five, Jordan asked to be taken out of the game. The strain of trying to perform at his previous level was starting to take a toll.

Heroes, it seems, can fail.

"I've never been in a situation like that before," said Jordan, who missed four of five shots and committed a turnover, glaring at Perdue when he didn't get out of his way. "It made me feel pressure. I feel pressure in my life all the time. On the basketball court, I've always been able to thrive on it. But this was the first time I felt pressure from my teammates like this.

"Everyone was throwing me the ball," said Jordan. "The team had been successful before I came back. If they weren't, I wouldn't have come back. So I asked out."

It was a stunning move. Not since his fit with former coach Doug Collins during the 1989 playoffs, when Collins said Jordan was shooting too much and Jordan responded by taking only eight shots the entire next game to show both Collins and the rest of the team what would happen if he didn't shoot—Try it on your own, boys—had Jordan backed off in a crucial situation like this.

That he was doubting his ability to do what he wanted, what he could do before, was obvious.

"They were not running the offense, not executing," said Jackson. "We were relying on Michael to do his one-on-one thing, not getting inside, and then they'd look to Michael to bail us out. It was a concern about whether this team could get along and play in sync. And he was having one of those shooting nights he'd been having since his return. So he wanted a blow."

Jordan did score 7 of the Bulls' last 9 points, but the Bulls scored a franchise playoff low 11 points in the third quarter, and Charlotte would have three shots at winning the game, much as they had with that Bogues shot at the end of regulation in Game 1. The Bulls had just barely beaten a team that was both injured and undermanned.

"Even though the city wants it, for me to do everything, I felt uncomfortable in the position I was put in," Jordan offered in his surprising admission. "I didn't feel comfortable.

"We won the game," Jordan said. "But it's not something we should totally forget."

It would be hard to, as the much anticipated Jordan-Shaq matchup finally was about to become a reality.

Chapter 13

FINAL ACT—OR IS IT?

The Bulls traveled to Orlando for the Sunday, May 7, game, which was moved to prime time even though it was on the East Coast as the last game of the NBA triple-header, and the only joy for Jordan was watching the replays of Reggie Miller's interviews about how the Knicks had choked in giving up a big lead to the Pacers with just seconds remaining.

"What's up?" someone asked Jordan as he sat uncomfortably in his locker stall before Game 1 of the much anticipated series with the Magic, intent on his video poker.

"Whatever it is, it's a conspiracy," Jordan said without smiling. "You can be sure of that.

"This is really pissing me off," Jordan would admit later to a friend. "At first, I didn't think about it. But now it's starting to get to me. It's bullshit. Everything's a conspiracy now. Everything I do. It's all a conspiracy."

Someone then said maybe Oliver Stone, who directed the controversial, conspiratorial thriller, *JFK*, would direct a movie on Jordan's life.

"Right," Jordan spat.

SOMEONE PASS THE POPCORN

The projector whirred almost silently as the Bulls watched. Shaquille O'Neal missing a free throw, Michael Jordan dunking. Anfernee Hardaway throwing a ball away, Steve Kerr hitting a 3-pointer. Tim Robbins giving Morgan Freeman a harmonica.

There was hope.

Hope was a good thing, maybe the best thing. That was the message Phil Jackson was sending as the Bulls prepared silently for the series everyone had waited for—the young Orlando Magic, owners of the best record in the Eastern Conference, perhaps the best starting lineup in the NBA, against the Bulls, stitched together over the last twenty-one games from Michael Jordan's will and ability and a team with desire. Jackson didn't know if that would hold together against the Team That Would Be a Dynasty, the Magic, or whether everything would come apart at the seams.

But he had hope. The Bulls had life after defeating the Hornets, so they also had hope, according to Cicero and that other classic philosopher, Phil Jackson.

Jackson believed that despite the two narrow wins against the Hornets in the opening-round playoff series and not much of a front line to compete with O'Neal and Horace Grant, the Bulls had a chance, had hope against the odds.

It was something inside all of them.

So Jackson had picked the film *The Shawshank Redemption*, a story of a prisoner's hope against seemingly insurmountable odds and what he would do to keep that hope alive, the little miracles he could produce along the way.

Jackson hoped for one such miracle over these next two weeks.

"It's a dream," Jackson admitted. "But we had hope that we could accomplish this and that was the theme to that movie.

"Hope was the dream," said Jackson. "There's a number of instances where this guy has to persevere, against abuses, the things that go on in prison. But he's also got to survive and connive. He uses education, books, a number of things that parallel what we needed to do. But the ultimate thing was hope.

"I thought this team was in a depression of sorts this season," said Jackson. "We kept trying to lift their spirits, but they kept hitting a wall. February and into March was a very difficult time with so many road games. We blew big leads in the second half, the fourth quarter. And then we went on a little bit of a run before Michael came back and then we started to come along and Michael came back and I kept saying to them we could win a championship, that it was a dream, a hope."

Jackson had become well known among his players for his creative editing sessions with a message. A few years back in the playoffs, he'd shown films of Joe Dumars slashing by the defense for a basket, then a snippet from *The Wizard of Oz* of the Tin Man. There was Bill Laimbeer drifting behind Scottie Pippen off a screen for an easy basket, then the Scarecrow. Finally, Isiah Thomas untouched down the lane for a basket, followed by the Cowardly Lion.

Standing up, John Paxson sent the message to some of his confused teammates: "He's telling us we've got no heart, no courage, and no brains."

Jackson called this his human behavioral laboratory, the notion that ideas lead to buildings and bridges, that a player could take the right message with him and expand the mental aspect of his game as well as the physical.

In 1994 during the playoffs against the brutal Knicks, Jackson had spliced in scenes from the movie *Slap Shot*, about these hockey goons who go straight, the message being you can play hard and tough, but you don't have to be a barbarian.

The year before against those same Knicks, Jackson wasn't quite as subtle. Before the first game, the team watched clips from a movie set in a South African prison, where a prisoner is surviving a brutal beating by the guards and never losing his determination or resolve.

"Rudy Tomjanovich [whose Houston Rockets, with the same forty-seven-win regular season as the Bulls, would win the NBA title in 1995] had said at the beginning of the playoffs that his team had the most to grow of all the teams in the playoffs," noted Jackson. "I told the team the same thing. Playing with Michael, we were a team coming together, and with him coming back by all accounts he should have fresh legs and be ready to play.

"We felt good about our season," said Jackson, "and we felt good about the playoffs. We knew the eighty-two-game season gets you playoff position, one extra home game. We always were a good road team in the playoffs. If we were a little more resilient, a little physically tougher, if we learned to fight together, we could do this. We were growing and learning together, but we felt we were just starting to make progress as a team. We knew the Indiana–New York [playoff series] would be a grinder and whoever came out of that would be susceptible. And when Dale Davis separated his shoulder, we saw that as a possibility for us moving by Indiana. I was not impressed with what was going on out west. I had no qualms in saying we could win a championship if we could get by Orlando.

"Of course," said Jackson, "that was a big if."

The projector went on. The prison would finally get books and music. If one tried, anything was possible.

PULLING HARMONY OUT OF A HAT

While O'Neal versus Jordan was the marquee matchup, the specter of Horace Grant remained just as big in Chicago. Fans didn't know anymore whether to hate Grant because he changed uniform shirts or to hate management for letting him go.

Grant knew whom he didn't care for, that being Jordan. And on the eve of the playoffs, after the Magic squeezed by the pathetic Celtics in four games and began to look vulnerable, Grant seized on Jordan.

"He's not the same," Grant jibed. "He used to be smashing down dunks; now he's finger-rolling the ball. Maybe he doesn't have the legs he used to. He doesn't look the same."

Grant also took on Krause and Reinsdorf again, as he would at every opportunity in the series, saying they could make Mother Teresa sin, that he'd never bought a house in Chicago because he was lied to so often he couldn't trust anything management said. "The fans treated me well," Grant said. "The organization didn't. I got tired of being stepped on."

For Grant, the remarks were mostly bravado on behalf of his team. In the decisive Game 4 over the Celtics, Grant had hit two free throws with fifteen seconds left to seal the clinching victory, the Magic's first playoff series win in franchise history. And had it not been for Grant's high-wire act under pressure, the Magic could have been facing a deciding game at home against a lesser team that already had won in Orlando. Collars would be tightening, and Grant knew the young Magic didn't need that.

They'd stumbled down the stretch, losing eight of thirteen; Anfernee Hardaway and Nick Anderson seemed particularly tentative, coach Brian Hill tightening up, O'Neal and Grant fed up.

Hill had apparently started to come apart after a loss to the 76ers in April; the *New York Post*'s Peter Vecsey reported Hill scolding O'Neal over a missed assignment in practice and Hill getting hard-nosed.

O'Neal then exploded, saying, "You can't coach, anyway. That's the problem. Every time there's a big game, your drawstrings tighten up."

It was a problem Hill had to face, much like Pat Riley did a decade earlier in Los Angeles. Nothing but success would be acceptable for Hill with the talent the Magic had accumulated. But Riley had a veteran like Kareem Abdul-Jabbar and a unique youngster like Magic Johnson. Hill didn't feel he had that kind of maturity.

Hardaway, in particular, was acutely sensitive, a kid brought up by relatives, who couldn't get over his desperate need to please and yearning for acceptance and approval. His talent was breathtaking, but it didn't appear the Magic had the team maturity to mount a challenge led by Jordan, whose picture had at one time decorated the bedroom walls of all those young Magic players—all but Grant's.

"They were really going at it," Grant recalled about the Hill-O'Neal flare-up in practice. "There was all this 'bitch' and 'pussy' yelling and it lasted like five minutes. You had to laugh. But it was like with me in Chicago. Brian felt Shaq could take it. I don't think he'd ever try that with Nick or Penny. Like with me, Phil always yelled at me, but he'd never say anything to Michael or Scottie.

"We were lucky to get past Boston the way we played," Grant admitted on the eve of the series with the Bulls. "I know this team is going to win some championships, but I can't see us getting by the Bulls. We don't play the defense for the play-offs yet, and these guys don't understand. It took us so long in Chicago, all those years with Detroit learning what it takes. I hate to agree with M.J. But they should knock us out."

Back in March, after that first game back in Chicago against the Magic when Jordan had shot so poorly, Jordan had made a vow.

"He said after that game, 'They got me when I was just coming back, but wait until the playoffs,'" recalled Pete Myers about Jordan's vow to teammates after that game. "That first game was the game he'd been aiming for for months. He didn't say a word to any of us after the [playoff] game, not the next day at practice, on the bus, anywhere."

Jordan had been just so sure. Even a few weeks after that Orlando game back in March, with Jordan beginning to bask in the glow of game-winning shots and that double nickel against the Knicks, with the Bulls winning thirteen of seventeen with him back, Jordan had pretty much dismissed the Magic.

"Orlando won't be a problem," Jordan reportedly told NBC-TV friend Ahmad Rashad, a quote that was pasted on the bulletin board, highlighted in yellow, in the Magic locker room for Game 1.

At the end of Game 1 of the Eastern Conference Semifinals between the Magic and the Bulls, Horace Grant was still rubbing his eyes and scratching his head, trying to figure out how the Magic had won, how Jordan had turned into that blockhead Charlie Brown, how it all had turned in Orlando's favor so quickly, how Jordan had tried to be Curly Neal with the basketball and instead came out looking like Curly taking a slap to the head from Moe.

"Maybe, just maybe," Grant thought.

Phil Jackson was still dumbfounded and asking, begging

his coaches to explain to him why the Magic didn't foul Jordan at the end of the game, why Jordan didn't just pull up with the ball after he crossed midcourt and let them foul him.

"What were they thinking about?" lamented Jackson, who did admit that when the Magic didn't foul Jordan with eighteen seconds left and the Bulls leading by one, he was sitting on the bench thinking, "Okay, we stole one."

"I thought we had it gift wrapped," Steve Kerr would say later.

The common strategy in that situation would have been for the Magic to foul and get a chance for a field goal if the Bulls missed a free throw or a 3-pointer to tie if both were made. Instead, the Magic were allowing Jordan to dribble away precious seconds and perhaps the game. It did look like the Magic bench had panicked.

But then Nick Anderson came up from behind Jordan and poked the ball away to Hardaway, who flipped downcourt to Grant racing in for a slam dunk. And then with one last chance, Jordan would dart into the middle against the collapsing Orlando defense and, to the shock of everyone in the building, especially Scottie Pippen, pass up an attempt at the game-winning shot and fire the ball to Pippen.

Pippen, who along with everyone in America, was anticipating that Jordan would shoot, ran toward the basket for a possible rebound. Jordan's surprise pass went behind him and out of bounds. The Bulls had lost the game, the game they thought would demoralize the Magic, the game that Jordan had promised they would win.

First games on the road as an underdog—that had been Jordan's playoff specialty. Now he had had the chance, and he couldn't deliver.

Jordan was stunned by the game's outcome, yet he was polite and gracious after the game.

"I take the blame as I would take the credit," Jordan said. "It was a mistake on my part down the stretch. It happens to the best of us. It's not a great feeling to know you could have changed the outcome of the game by taking care of the ball."

If Jordan was in a state of disbelief, Jackson was outright shocked.

"We hadn't even planned to have Michael catch the ball," said Jackson. "It was supposed to be B.J., who is a stellar free throw shooter.

"With Michael handling the ball and them doing nothing, I thought we were home free," said Jackson. "I was totally taken aback. I'd never in eight years seen Michael so disoriented and unaware of another player. I'd never even seen it once, that he wouldn't know where a player was. He has such good radar. I said to my wife it must have been the loudspeakers and the music playing that was so disorienting. But something happened to him. Maybe he was too tired."

THE THREE-HEADED MONSTER

That first game had been rather uneventful until its stunning ending.

The lead bounced back and forth like the last game of a tennis tiebreaker, and neither of the marquee stars, Jordan and O'Neal, was particularly memorable.

Jordan would finish with 19 points on just eight of twenty-two shooting, and while O'Neal had 26 points and 12 rebounds, the Bulls had contained him reasonably well with Longley, Perdue, Wennington, and anyone else who was near, invoking the league-favored hack-a-Shaq defense in which O'Neal, one of the league's poorest free throw shooters, was fouled whenever he was close to the basket.

Only this time, O'Neal made twelve of sixteen free throws, including two improbable ones with less than a minute left. Although he shoots them like they're seeds squirting out from between his fingers, O'Neal stood up to the ultimate challenge for a big man, the one Wilt Chamberlain could never master: making that uncontested shot from fifteen feet with sixteen thousand people praying for you.

"We did a good job on him," said Jackson. "He just made too many free throws."

The Bulls didn't slay the giant, but he would not dominate.

And so that was the message that Jackson had sent his so-called three-headed monster—Longley, Perdue, and Wennington—in their battle with the gargantuan Shaq.

"I liked the fact we had three centers, which gave us three different varieties of play," said Jackson. "Luc, who could block the lane even though he was maligned for his play, but he had a physical presence. Will was the good offensive rebounder and he knew our system of offense as well as anybody and could play the backside of our offense, and Bill with his shot away from the basket."

The monster could triumph, Jackson insisted, even though the odds—and history—were against the three-headed monster.

At least that was the message in the movie *Monty Python and the Holy Grail*, which appeared amid the films of Shaquille O'Neal in the team's preparation.

There was O'Neal, the brave one, the one who was supposed to triumph, like Sir Robin in the Monty Python version. And then the three-headed monster would pop up, a broad, large man with three heads, the heads arguing amongst themselves over who would slay the knight.

"You snore," one head said to another.

"You have bad breath," another said.

They argued some more and the Bulls players laughed.

"He showed Shaq beating up on all these guys," related Pete Myers, "and then there's the three-headed monster in the movie winning."

Eventually, the knight from the Round Table would run away in the face of the threat from the three-headed monster.

"It was a joke," admitted Jackson. "But there were also some items in there to say maybe three heads were better than one."

Nick Anderson had been the star for the Magic. Not only was there the steal from Jordan, but Anderson hit for 20 points in showing off a playoff trend that no one had ever done before. He would go into the post against Jordan and demand the ball. It became humbling for Jordan, as he could no longer fight off the youngsters. Before, no one would have dared. But Grant had counseled Anderson to go at Jordan, and Anderson had backed Jordan in alone several times for baskets, a tack Anfernee Hardaway would use successfully later in the series.

Anderson was a native Chicagoan, an often troubled young man, likable, but sensitive and insecure. He still wore the number of high school classmate Ben Wilson, who was murdered outside their Chicago high school with Nick nearby. He had escaped the streets and was in the process of bringing an older brother to Orlando after the brother was released from prison. He'd long before settled his mother, Alberta, in Orlando, and she had been a source of inspiration.

"Make him work," she told Nick about Jordan as Nick left for the game that Sunday morning.

Alberta had persuaded Nick to be patient in Orlando a few years back when he'd tired of losing, before O'Neal came. He'd wanted to be traded then, but she counseled perseverance. "Mother knows best," said Anderson. "I'd say everything she told me was right."

And she had told Nick to be careful what he said.

A sign that day in the stands read: NO. 23 WAS GREAT. NO. 45 IS JUST AVERAGE.

When asked about Jordan that day, Anderson said, "I just try to keep him in front of me and contest every shot. I'm not going to say I'm going to hold him off. I don't want to get him pissed off."

REMEMBER WHEN JORDAN WAS GREAT?

The Bulls would make a nice run to briefly take the lead midway through the third quarter of that Game 1 loss, but B. J. Armstrong was watching from the bench. When Jackson pulled him out, he asked Jackson why.

"Because you weren't being aggressive enough," Jackson said sharply.

Armstrong stalked to the end of the bench, and before the

week was out, he'd engage Jackson in another angry confrontation. Armstrong would get just six shots despite the Magic's poor rotating defense, and Pippen would have fewer shots than Jordan and Kukoc while leading the team in rebounding and assists. And he was not happy about it.

"I've got to be able to do more offensively," Pippen said.

When Pippen was asked about that last Jordan pass skipping behind him, he shrugged. "With Michael, you really have no idea what he's going to do," Pippen said.

Jackson was at a complete loss to explain Jordan's failures. The only similar situation he could point to was the fourth game of the opening round of the 1989 playoffs when Jordan missed three of six free throws down the stretch, the game before Jordan's miracle shot defeated the Cavaliers in Game 5.

"I checked the lunar charts and the celestial stations of the stars and figured something had to be awry. We felt that was a mirage we were seeing rather than reality," said Jackson.

"It's happened before," Jordan added with just the slightest hint of a smile, the last one anyone would see from him for days. "I've been personally responsible for a lot of baseball losses. I won't make any excuses. With the game in my hands, I couldn't deliver. The next couple of days I'll think about it. But then I'll let it go. I'm strong enough mentally to put it away. It happens to the best of us. It probably won't happen again."

It would, of course, as Jordan didn't seem to have the same powers of concentration he once did. It had been one of the elements that separated him from mere great players. Many players had the competitive drive, but Jordan's will would overcome everything in his way, his personal drive and mental acuity refusing to allow anything to interfere with his determination. But his mind wandered more now. It was harder to concentrate, and he would let fatigue get the better of him at the end of games, his waning energy pulling him into a dark, deep abyss he could not pull himself from. He couldn't fight it off anymore whenever he wanted. It was just so much harder.

Was it the time away from the game, or just simply age catching up to a legend?

The scoring totals of all the great guards had diminished after their thirtieth birthdays, which is one reason the Bulls elected not to pursue players like Derek Harper and Byron Scott in 1993 and 1994, players who had seen too many minutes in their careers. Bob Cousy, Jerry West, Oscar Robertson, Earl Monroe, Walt Frazier—all Hall of Fame guards—also suffered constant and dramatic downturns in their scoring averages after turning thirty.

"Age catches up with everybody," sports medicine specialist Dr. Charles Bush-Joseph of Rush Presbyterian–St. Luke's Medical Center told the suburban *Daily Herald*. "Theoretically, he may have a harder time summoning up those high-scoring games."

Even Michael Jordan?

"It turned out," said Jackson of the botched play, "to be one of those events of fate and momentum that changed the course of the whole series."

IS THE PRESIDENT SECURE?

The day after Game 1, Jackson saw Armstrong and Pippen huddled together.

"I know they're commiserating about their situations," said Jackson. "I've seen them off talking like that, feeling sorry for themselves."

Jackson knew and understood. "It is hard not to be a little bit resentful of a guy who's got so much, who has so many people do things for him, going out of their way for him. It's Jordan's life. It's different. But that's the way things are for him," noted Jackson.

It was an impossible gap to bridge. Before Game 1, when the team went for shootaround, the players walked across a tiny park to the arena, about a half block from their hotel. All except Jordan, who went with six bodyguards and two hangers-on in a van with smoked-glass windows. Later that night, before the game, the players took a bus across the street, since crowds had begun to gather outside the arena by that time. But Jordan opted again for his private van with his personal security.

Jordan would also travel privately to practice Tuesday, the day before Game 2, and then bolt straight from practice to Isleworth Country Club, where he planned to buy another home.

And Jordan did look like a good neighbor, patiently signing some autographs and chatting by the fence with a widow and her three small children. But again, he would leave practice without talking with reporters, angry already at what he perceived as unfair treatment in the media for his Game 1 gaffe.

"He was a mellower Michael when he came back as far as working one-on-one with some guys and helping out," Jackson said. "But when the pressure came up during the playoffs and some things happened . . . And with the entourage around him and the security factor, Michael was pretty much apart from his teammates most of the postseason. But he took as strong a hit after Game 1 as anytime I've seen in the playoffs. It was easy for people to point the finger and for him to be down about it."

Jordan, by nature of his celebrity, of course required extra protection, but this was still a team sport, after all, and the security guards, a phalanx of off-duty Chicago policemen playing secret service agents, had become something of a distraction at times for the rest of the team. They were hard-boiled Chicago police types used to cursing in the faces of drug dealers and living life on the dangerous, ugly side of the city's streets. In Jordan's early days, a few had escorted the Bulls' star from the stadium, where they were hired for security, to his car. Some had provided security for local figures like Jesse Jackson and the Gary-bred Jackson Five, and they'd traveled with Jordan to Birmingham and Sarasota while he was playing baseball. When Jordan returned to the Bulls, they recruited some friends for a virtual security force. Mostly, they were discreet, friendly, and serious about their work. But occasionally some liked to play Kevin Costner in *The Body-guard.*

Tom Hill, a reporter for the *New York Post,* was returning to his room on the top floor of the Marriott Hotel, where the Bulls were staying the night before Game 1 of the Orlando series. Two middle-aged couples, who had just been to dinner, were standing talking outside the elevators before heading to their rooms.

Jordan was staying on that floor toward the end of the corridor. One of his security men came out and approached the two couples.

"What are you doing here?" he wanted to know.

They explained they were guests and just talking.

"You can't do that here," the security man said. "You'll have to move."

Obviously rattled, they moved to their rooms.

Another threat thwarted.

A few days later, the Bulls had moved to a resort hotel, and several players were eating at the restaurant when two of Jordan's bodyguards appeared at the front entrance. They looked left and right, then hurried through to a back room, where Jordan would be eating privately. When they got to the entrance of that room, they stopped, then waved back to the front door. Jordan, with two bodyguards on each side, hurried through the restaurant to the back room. The only ones in the restaurant at the time were Bulls players.

Why did Jordan need six guards? *New York Daily News* writer Mitch Lawrence was asked one day.

"Four to carry the litter," Lawrence explained, "and two to scatter the petals."

Jordan did travel to practice Monday with the team, but he remained quiet, not speaking to any of the players and leaving practice without speaking to the media. He would later send his security guards back into the high school gym the team was using for practice to get the rest of the team, which was doing postpractice interviews.

"Michael's ready to go," one security guard said, breaking up a group of reporters around Pippen.

IT'S JUST A GAME

Practice was somber that day after the Game 1 loss, and Pippen, particularly, was despairing.

He'd had enough of this second-fiddle stuff, this role-playing. He'd been asked to guard Grant for most of Game 1, which took him inside to rebound and play defense much of the time.

"It's a lot to ask me to double-team and then go guard one of the top rebounders in the league, a guy like Horace, trying to contain him and then haul the ball up court. It's a lot of work for me. And it's taken me out of the offense," Pippen told reporters. "I'm trying to fit in, but it's taken a lot from my style of play. I've made the adjustments. Nobody has adjusted to my style of play."

Grant would get his digs in after talking with Pippen after the game, telling reporters how sorry he felt for Pippen, the best small forward in the game having to play power forwards and even centers. The Bulls would ruin Pippen's career, Grant said, misusing him and taking advantage of his unselfish nature. It was too bad for Pippen, Grant said. He felt sorry for him.

Jackson had told Pippen a few weeks before that he thought management wanted to trade him after the regular season, that he should just play well and keep quiet and everything would work out. But Pippen, as evidenced by previous actions, is not one to allow things to fester.

Before Game 2, Pippen sat agitated in the locker room, watching the tape of Game 1.

"I'm going for forty tonight," Pippen sputtered. "The heck with M.J., the heck with Phil. This is ridiculous. I'm supposed to be a premier player, but they're making me a role player."

Pippen, of course, could not just look to score. He was too conditioned to looking to pass, to moving the ball. But it was sort of his fantasy when he'd get angry. He'd say he was through watching everyone play and he'd dream of basket after basket. It never would happen, though, and in Game 2

Pippen would attempt just fourteen shots, fewer than half as many as Jordan.

Jackson had wanted to return home Sunday after Game 1, since the Bulls had two off days before the next game. With their own plane, Jackson said, the team could be home by late Sunday night, practice at home out of the glare of the media, who would not pay the airfare to return to Chicago, and then return for Wednesday's game. But that was vetoed by management as being too costly, so Jackson tried to divide the media troops.

"I thought I'd make them make a decision on where they wanted to go so at least they would be split," Jackson admitted.

So the Bulls scheduled practice at about the same time as the Magic, but about fifteen miles outside Orlando at Dr. Phillips High School, where the NBA sometimes goes because there are few available gyms in the Orlando area. It was a school day, but the principal agreed to let the Bulls use the gym. On his terms.

Two years earlier, in the Bulls' third championship season, the Bulls used the gym, but when the principal tried to come in to watch practice, the Bulls barred him from his own gym. Few teams are as secretive or as paranoid as the Bulls. But this time there would be conditions.

"Get those kids out of here!" Bulls general manager Jerry Krause, still fuming over the Game 1 loss, yelled when the Bulls entered the gym.

Uh, Jerry, there are some changes this time.

If the Bulls cared to stay they'd have to allow some student journalists not only to watch practice but do some interviews after practice.

Krause shuddered with rage.

Jordan, of course, bolted out quickly after practice, speaking to no one and stewing on the bus for a while before he sent his bodyguards back in to hurry the team.

Jackson was last to leave, and as he was answering a few final questions and inching toward the door, Amar Shah, fourteen, nervously started to speak. Who was he, Jackson demanded, and who did he work for? Before the kid could answer, Jackson spotted the youngster wearing a Knicks logo on his shirt, and Jackson put his hand over it.

"Turn that shit around," Jackson demanded with a chuckle.

The kid was stunned for an instant, but then stammered out his question, which Jackson answered in detail.

"I wouldn't have worn this if I'd have known I'd be doing this," Shah said.

TOSS ANOTHER LONGLEY ON THE BARBEE, MATE

The next day, several of the players got together with Luc Longley.

Jordan again had been tough with Longley in practice. Jordan had been running into the post, Jackson having told him earlier after his return that he could save energy by stationing himself inside and working for the short fadeaway jump shot.

"Maybe he got into the habit too much," said Jackson. "I said this would save him steps and this was where he was most comfortable with his shot, the best shot he had, the most consistent. This was where he threatened the defense most, and he got some easy layups."

But it had been scouted well, and Jordan was becoming frustrated.

"Why don't we run some pick and roll?" Jordan demanded. "Is it because our big guys can't set a screen?"

Jordan then stared hard at Longley and Kukoc.

Jordan's attitude had always been a source of discussion and consideration among the team. Many, especially the ones who hadn't played with him before, were surprised at the seeming anger and sporadic hostility; others were more sympathetic, like Bill Wennington, who had played in a high school All-Star game with Jordan and knew this was how Jordan's competitive desire manifested itself.

"First time I saw him when he came back, he remembered that game, and I said all I did was rebound and throw the ball to half-court to him," recalled Wennington. "He said, 'We won, didn't we?'

"There's a fine line in being a great player sometimes," said Wennington. "Michael got to be arrogant and a little tough, but sometimes that's what distinguishes an ordinary player in the NBA from a great player."

Still, several players took Longley out to breakfast before Game 2 and said he had to challenge Jordan, to stand up to him. They told him the stories of Jordan and Bill Cartwright, stories that mirrored Jordan's behavior toward Longley.

"You've got to go after him," Krystkowiak instructed.

But it was not his way to get angry and fight back, perhaps a reason the Bulls were able to obtain Longley for merely the underachieving Stacey King a year before. Longley was the seventh pick in the 1991 draft out of the University of New Mexico, a strapping seven-two and nearly 300 pounds but with this kindly disposition. As angry as he ever seemed to get was over American stereotypes of Australians.

"Most of what they get is from *Crocodile Dundee*," Longley complained. "They all want to throw another shrimp on the barbee. We don't even call them shrimp. We call them prawns. They know Olivia Newton-John, the outback, and Fosters. It's rare I get an intelligent question."

No doubt Longley was intelligent. He often dreamed of the days after basketball when he would finish studies in marine biology, but not before he earned enough money, he said, so that he wouldn't have to apply for government grants. He would move back to Australia, where he had a three-hundred-acre farm and where he could get away from the violence in America.

"I don't know how you can bring up a child in this country," he would often tell other players, noting the daily onslaught of urban horrors, boys thrown out of high-rise windows by other boys, kids getting gunned down daily in gang crossfires, the *Chicago Tribune* chronicling children being murdered every day. Longley, like the other Bulls, lived in the far north suburbs of Chicago away from the violence and madness, but he remained stunned at the continuing brutality and longed for a return home someday.

He wouldn't waste much time after the 1994–95 season, even after Krause demanded he remain in Chicago to work out all summer because he'd had such a poor season. As a restricted free agent, and a big (though unproductive) center, Longley knew that with the Bulls unhappy with their other centers, he had tremendous leverage, so he went back to Australia.

Running away, or leaving, had always been the knock on Longley, that he would avoid the physical play, the battles in the NBA, much as he was avoiding any confrontation with Jordan.

Jackson saw it, too. He knew Longley was growing depressed over his own play and the beating he was taking in practice. But Jackson didn't know how Longley would respond.

"He's beating himself up now about his play," Jackson admitted during the playoffs. "He's been struggling like crazy."

That had never been the case before for Longley, who was big in basketball in Australia, mate. His father, Richard, played for the national team and in a professional league, and Luc played with various basketball clubs in the country throughout his teens. He went to the state-sponsored Institute of Sport to refine his game, then got himself a scholarship to the University of New Mexico. Scouts had come to see another player, and here was this giant who could dunk, although with both hands, and had a nice little touch around the basket.

The University of Hawaii was interested, but Longley knew himself too well. He liked to hang out at the beach, body-surf, and knew if he went to Hawaii he wouldn't work hard at school or basketball. So he chose to be landlocked in New Mexico.

He was a holdout when he was drafted by the Timberwolves, who couldn't accept his relatively passive nature. They eventually grew frustrated trying to make Longley something he wasn't rather than accept what he was— a hard-working center with reasonable skills, though not a physical player or a future star—and dumped him on the Bulls. Jackson was pleased with Longley, though, because he liked the potential of having a wide-bodied player in the middle, something the team didn't have anymore without Cartwright.

And somehow, despite the harsh beating he was taking from his newest teammate, Longley was sympathetic toward Jordan.

"I know that attitude of his is what helps make him a great player," Longley said.

Game 1 of the Conference Finals with Orlando had been the highest rated second-round playoff series game in NBA history, just as Game 2 of the Charlotte series the previous Sunday had been the most watched first-round playoff game in NBA history. Yet Jordan was feeling that the league was lacking in appreciation for his return.

His high-powered and successful agent, David Falk, had repeatedly counseled Jordan on how much he meant to the league, that he practically was saving it with his return, and that the league owed him. And the results seemed to back him up.

Before Jordan returned, 1994–95 NBC ratings were lagging just behind those of the previous season, which was a down year. After Jordan's return, the ratings shot up to easily surpass those of the 1993–94 season.

Yet NBA commissioner David Stern was not about to credit Jordan.

"Increased ratings are a blip," Stern said. "I think the ratings were unnaturally bumped up because of the extraordinary interest in Michael's return, but the TV ratings were going to be up [anyway]."

Still, Jordan felt the league needed him more than he needed the league.

"I have the freedom to make the choices I want to," Jordan emphasized. "I walked away from the game because that's what I chose. Then I chose to walk back."

But the NBA didn't care for the footwear Jordan had chosen to walk in.

Yes, it was the shoes.

NBA rules state that teams can wear any color shoes they want in the playoffs as long as every player wore the same color shoes. And since the 1989 playoffs, when the Bulls made their first major run toward a championship, it had been their tradition to wear black sneakers, an idea originally suggested by Brad Sellers. Kind of a good-guys-wear-black theme.

And it had always been good luck.

For these playoffs, the Bulls were still wearing black, but Jordan had picked out a new sneaker made of black-and-white patent leather.

Too much white, the league said.

It was reminiscent of David Letterman's famous line when Jordan had appeared on his show about five years earlier. Jordan was explaining about his shoes, which he said had no white in them. "Just like the NBA," quipped Letterman.

But this time no one was laughing, least of all Jordan's teammates. It seemed to put Jordan farther apart from the team: one guy going his own way. The league would fine Jordan $5,000 for wearing a different color shoe than his teammates. It would be just the beginning of the NBA versus Michael Jordan, circa 1995.

At the Orlando practice the day after Game 1, Nick Anderson had drawn a large media contingent after having outscored and outplayed Jordan the night before.

Anderson was trying to offer some perspective.

"Age, it catches up with you," Anderson was saying, sort of in defense of Jordan. "When Michael was a twenty-eight-, twenty-nine-year-old player, he was like a space shuttle taking off. Now he's like he's still trying to rev up, trying to get ready. Before he retired, he had quickness and explosiveness. Not that it's not there now, but it's not as sharp as when he was number 23. He still does some of the things, but not like number 23 did. Number 23, he could just blow right by you. Number 45, he revs up, but he doesn't really take off.

"He looks tired," said Anderson, not realizing the firestorm he had just set off. "Shots he normally makes, he somehow doesn't make now. And I didn't see him once go to the basket with his right hand. I don't know if he's injured or what, but I'm not seeing number 23."

He soon would.

GOOD OL' NUMBER 23

Jordan came out blazing in Game 2 against the Magic.

He hit his first shot, a 3-pointer, and then a jumper, the Bulls bolting out to a 10–4 lead.

"I'm sitting with Steve Kerr on the bench," recalled Pete Myers, "and he says, 'Look at M.J.' I say, 'Yeah, he's really got it going tonight, he's really getting off fast.' Steve said, 'No, no, look at his number.'"

It was 23 again, the number that hung from the rafters, retired in Chicago Stadium, the number Jordan said he was pleased his father had seen him play his last game wearing, the number Nick Anderson said he identified with the old Michael Jordan.

Nobody on the Bulls knew of Jordan's plans, not Jackson or Krause or Reinsdorf. Only equipment man John Ligmanowski, who had been carrying the number 23 jersey around since Jordan returned. After the Game 1 loss, Ligmanowski told Jordan he had both jerseys with him. Anderson's comments Monday were fuel enough. Jordan would show them all.

In one petty action, the paradox of Jordan's character was on display as vividly as ever.

He was a strong-minded individual who would chart his own course, yet he was willing to sacrifice the poignancy of his dedication to the memory of his late father by switching back to that number 23 he said he wore last for his father.

It was just a number, and there was no specific rule, anyway, insisted Jordan, although as one NBA official put it, "There's no rule that says you can't urinate on the floor. But you can't." Sure, hubris was a flaw, but this was just basketball, after all, and Jordan was not here to teach lessons, despite what the commercials might suggest. He was doing it his way. And the object, after all, was to win. C'mon society,

Jordan was saying, if you need me to show you how to live, get a life.

"I think he was responding," said Jackson, "like, 'Okay, check this out.'"

The NBA checked it out and didn't like what it saw. Neither did the Magic, who had been denied permission a few months before when Shaquille O'Neal asked to change his jersey number back to the number 33 he wore in college. O'Neal would get a little playful revenge, though, changing into the number 33 to wear to postgame press conferences.

Although there's no rule officially noting number changes in midseason, NBA policy had been clear for years: No changes in midseason because of licensing agreements and computer programs and statistical records set up for the season. Even the Bulls had stumbled over the policy in the past, when Stacey King, in one of his many slumps, tried to change his number but was told a player could do that only at the start of a new season. Jordan had laughed about it at the time, mocking King and telling other players the team would run out of numbers if King wanted to change every time he played poorly.

But now the Bulls would be at Jordan's mercy.

"He's real adamant about wearing that number," said Jackson. "It's important to him."

So much so that Jordan suggested to team officials he couldn't be responsible for his play if he had to switch back to number 45.

"What can we do?" Reinsdorf told the staff. "Let him do what he wants."

Jordan had considered Nick Anderson's remarks, and he agreed to an extent. He felt he was the same Michael Jordan that had left the game almost two years before, and that Michael Jordan wore number 23. Relax, everyone, Jordan thought. James Jordan would understand. He always supported Michael. Why did everyone think Michael was tarnishing the gesture he'd made to his father by saying he would never again wear number 23?

It was his number, and he would wear it. It was really quite simple to Jordan. He was coming back and wearing his Bulls uniform, his Nike sneakers, his North Carolina powder blue shorts, his wristband—everything the same as before. So why not number 23 on his back? So determined was Jordan now to retain and reclaim the number that he even asked the Bulls to take the retired number 23 jersey down from the rafters in the new United Center until he was done with it again.

As for the Bulls, they would take the heat for now, as well as the fines, which the league said would mount daily for every game of defiance, finally adding on $100,000 after the season for Jordan's attitude.

Not surprisingly, Jordan's behavior would once again create a national debate. David Falk told the *Sun-Times* that Jordan "has the standing to be a brat. But he doesn't have the personality or values to be a brat."

The *New York Times* thought he did with a column headlined, "Be like No. 23, the NBA's Biggest Brat."

TV host Pat O'Brien tracked down Jordan's mother, who said, "It was good to see 23 again. He surprises you in so many ways."

Hundreds of calls flooded the Bulls' switchboard claiming Jordan had only worn number 45 in a marketing stunt to sell jerseys, and now was switching back to number 23 once the sales of number 45 jerseys slowed.

Asked about that particular theory, Jackson said parents should forget buying either number 23 or number 45. "Buy 'em books," Jackson scolded.

Jackson told Jordan that since he had hit .202 wearing 45 and now was shooting about the same, maybe it was a good idea to change.

Pippen said Jordan was lousy as number 45, didn't even look good. "Like Kilroy," Pippen said of the character in a Jordan Nike commercial.

"Tell them to dig deep in the draw and get a number 23," Pippen suggested to angry parents, prompting one parent to send a fax to the Bulls' offices, with a middle finger highlighting the page with the words, "Hey, Scottie, reach down deeper for this."

"The bigger issue was the shoes," said Steve Kerr. "He should be fined because they were so embarrassing looking."

As for the game, yes, there was still a game. Jordan was the old number 23.

Jordan hit seventeen of thirty shots for 38 points, the Bulls breaking the game open to even the series 1–1, fueled by Jordan's eleven-of-thirteen second-half shooting. His final basket of the game was a two-handed over-the-shoulder SO THERE slam dunk after he blocked a Dennis Scott shot. Final score, Chicago 104–94.

"After you guys embarrassed him for forty-eight hours, he came out and had a pretty good night," said Magic coach Brian Hill to the media.

"Maybe my quote did make him change it," lamented Anderson, whose five-year-old son, dressed in a number 45 Bulls jersey, dribbled a basketball playfully as Anderson dressed after the game. "I didn't think you could wear your retirement jersey. He'll get fined. But does he care? Maybe he was thinking about me. But he made the shots. Give him credit for that."

"I was a firm believer in letting sleeping dogs lie," Hill said about Anderson's choice of analogies. "But it's not the number on the shirt. It's the basketball player inside it.

"I really didn't realize until the third quarter," said Hill. "I looked up [at the scoreboard] to see how many fouls he had, then I looked at his shirt and said, 'Oh shit, he's wearing number 23 tonight.'"

But there wouldn't be much more for Jordan to celebrate the rest of the way, for despite the great jersey switch, number 23 would continue to look mostly like number 45. Jordan would shoot a meager 47 percent in the last four games and make crucial, game-costing turnovers in Games 3 and 6. After his eight turnovers in Game 1, he would commit four in Game 3 and six more in Game 6 to average more than four per game in the playoffs.

As would be the case throughout his exciting comeback, Jordan would not be able to repeat the successes as he once did. It would take time, if ever, to regain that ability, to learn to overcome the adversity that now was becoming as common as ever. Whether he could was a question that would remain unanswered.

Yet there was no question that the diversion that Jordan supplied the NBA in 1994–95 was the most entertaining one sports has seen in years. And, after all, that is what sports is supposed to be, a diversion, a recreation, an examination of character and morality within the context of games. Jordan would provide the enticing backdrop for it all.

Back in Chicago, about an hour before game time of Game 3, Jordan, who still was not discussing his number change, whether he would continue to wear number 23 in defiance of league orders to the contrary, or even his golf schedule in his renewed anger at the media, walked through the locker room. No other Bull was there, but about two dozen reporters milled around searching for some scrap of information.

As Jordan headed into the off-limits trainers' room, he said to the group, "How do you like my jersey?"

In Jordan's locker hung a Bulls jersey with no number on it.

He flashed that endorsement smile and then closed the door behind him.

But the smile would vanish quickly.

Steve Kerr knew the Bulls had lost the series to the Magic by the end of the first quarter of Game 3.

"They were tight in Games 1 and 2, but we let them off the hook by losing Game 1," said Kerr. "Then when we got that lead to start Game 3 and couldn't hold it, well, I think we would have broken their spirit if we'd won the first two games. Those first two games we played the way we wanted, kept the score down in the 90s, slowed the pace. Then they found their rhythm."

The Bulls had become the Pistons and the Magic had become the Bulls.

It used to be that in the playoffs against Detroit, the Bulls would say that if they could get the game over 100 points, they could win. A high-scoring, more open game had nullified Detroit's holding and grabbing tactics, and now the Magic was doing the same against the Bulls' three centers, who were trying to grab and hold O'Neal; the Bulls' only flagrant foul of the series would be committed by Perdue, grabbing O'Neal in a bear hug.

And on it went, the Magic just trying to play. The Pacers' Reggie Miller would complain in the next series that it was hard to get up for the Magic because they were so nice, always helping him up and saying things like "nice shot." Miller said he preferred Knicks like Anthony Mason and Charles Oakley, who would step on you when you were down and kick you when the referee wasn't looking, like WWF wrestling.

"You can't hate those Orlando guys," said Miller.

The Bulls could if they had had the energy, but suddenly they looked very old against the Magic.

Ol' number 23 was back again, Jordan with a nineteen-footer, then a drive and two free throws, an eighteen-footer, a sixteen-footer, and a fourteen-footer after two B. J. Armstrong 3-pointers. Less than five minutes into Game 3, the Bulls were leading 20–10 on their way to shooting 63 percent in the first quarter, and they were going to show these kids something. The Chicago fans were going crazy.

But the Magic took the Bulls' best shot. They got within 37–32 after one quarter, a red flag for the Bulls' coaching staff, who urged the team to slow down, that the Magic were running and that was to Orlando's advantage. By halftime, the Magic had pulled ahead and then led by 10 midway through the third quarter when Jackson pulled Jordan. The Bulls then took a 1-point lead after three quarters.

Jackson knew he had a huge problem on his hands: Jordan. In his quest to show he was number 23, he was off on his own again, taking thirty-one shots on the way to a 40-point game. But it made Kukoc invisible, the bench no factor.

Jackson felt he needed Jordan as his closer, yet Jordan was wiping himself out during the game in his quest to prove his critics wrong.

In the past, before Jordan's return, the Bulls had their greatest success against the Magic because they moved the ball so
well without him and Orlando didn't respond well. Against a
team like the Knicks, Jordan was invaluable because his fierce-
ness made the other Bulls brave. But Orlando didn't hit anyone
hard, didn't rotate well or follow the cutters. They were more
vulnerable to Tex Winter's triangle than to Jordan's attack.

Former Bulls assistant Bach felt he'd seen it coming in the
Bulls' series with Charlotte. He thought Jordan was expending
energy quicker than usual, that Pippen had backed off when
faced with a lesser role, that Armstrong was lost and Kukoc
confused.

"You watch them and it looks like they grew without him,
but now they were stepping out of the way for him," said Bach,
a huge Jordan fan. "They got used to playing without him, and
it looked like as a team they played better when he was off the
floor."

It was a heretical notion, impossible for the layman to
understand, that a team could be better without one of the
great players of all time, who, even if he had lost a step, still
had more talent and ability than anyone on his team, perhaps
even in the entire league.

And Jordan was still a joy to watch. As veteran *Los Angeles
Times* columnist Mark Heisler gushed during one game, "The
most interesting thing about the Bulls is when Jordan scores.
The second most interesting thing is when he misses."

But a team is a delicate blend, and the Bulls had been without Jordan for almost two seasons. Jackson believed that in the
long run, if not now, the Bulls could win another championship
with Jordan. They couldn't without him. But as for now, he was
having doubts as to whether Jordan was helping or hurting. It
was too hard to overlook Jordan's distance from his teammates,
the controversy that was following Jordan everywhere, the way
everyone had been thrown out of the roles they'd become
accustomed to during the last year and a half.

"With Michael out there, sometimes the ball didn't move,"
said Jackson. "He knew our offense as well as anybody, and he
was seeing when he first came how everyone fit in, checking

out how everyone played when he was on top of the circle, on the wing, in the pinch post. But as the playoffs went on, I wasn't seeing that from him. We weren't seeing the same kind of action. Sometimes we reacted better with our second unit playing with Scottie Pippen. The function of the offense is not whether you're selfish or unselfish. It's moving the ball. Everything stops if the ball stops."

The ball was stopping too often in Jordan's hands.

Once again, Game 3 came down to the last few minutes with the Bulls having a chance to win. The game was tied with under two minutes left after Pippen had made one free throw. Hardaway made two of three free throws when he was fouled behind the 3-point line, and then Jordan, driving down the left side with a chance to tie the game with ninety seconds left, lost the ball to a swipe by Grant, and the Magic converted five more free throws down the stretch. The Bulls would not score again.

Jordan didn't score a basket in the last six and a half minutes of the game, as Anderson would hit a pair of 3-pointers over him. The Bulls simply wilted, aired out, if you will, in the face of the strength of the young Magic.

Worst of all, it was Grant who led the way.

He added 18 points and 14 rebounds, bringing his three-game average to 22.3 points and 12 rebounds, this from a player who was discouraged from shooting when he was with the Bulls, who blasted the Bulls every chance he got after leaving.

"Sweet, very sweet," Grant said smiling afterward.

After the Bulls practiced Saturday between Games 3 and 4, Jackson gathered the team for the usual postpractice words of encouragement.

One member of the Bulls' entourage noticed something peculiar about Jordan. He still wasn't talking to his teammates much, he never looked at Jackson or anyone, just stood there cleaning his nails, picking at them, looking down. Someone had mentioned the media was outside, would Jordan be coming out? "Fuck 'em," he'd said. Jordan sets the tone at practice, and this one had been lazy, lethargic.

So many problems. Jordan couldn't feel confident about

Longley and Buechler, he didn't understand Armstrong's inces-
sant pouting at such an important time, he didn't know why
Blount was on the playoff roster instead of Simpkins, and why
Kukoc would be brilliant one game, invisible the next.

The playoffs were moving forward, but it seemed Jordan
was growing uncertain about the speeding diesel he'd boarded.

"There was a distance about him, sort of a sadness," said
one Bulls player about that practice session before Game 4. "It
was like he was standing there thinking, 'What have I gotten
myself into?'"

Jordan had decided to see what everybody else could do
for Game 4.

After averaging 39 points on 30.5 shots in the previous two
games, Jordan took twenty-one shots. He hit just nine. But
Pippen got fifteen shots and scored 24 points, Kukoc got thirteen shots and Armstrong scored a playoff high 18 points. Even
Will Perdue got seven shots and scored 11 points.

"What happens when he's scoring well," explained Jud
Buechler, "is that it hurts down at the end when a guy like Toni
hasn't touched the ball. Then the other team doubles Michael
and Michael dishes to Toni for a shot and Toni's confidence
isn't there because he hasn't touched the ball for a quarter."

The key shot in Game 4 was a Kukoc 3-pointer with just
over a minute left that clinched the Bulls' 106–95 victory.

"I think we are better when he does that," said Kukoc, in
what *Sun-Times* columnist Jay Mariotti called the most pointed
commentary of Kukoc's career in Chicago. "He can always take
over when he wants. But the Bulls need more than one or two
players. My opinion is if all the guys get to touch the ball early
and to be involved in the offense, it's much easier for Michael
after that to step in. The other players have to be able to feel the
game, but they can't if they aren't involved. We have to keep
playing this way. This team has a lot of players to help out. We
were more than just Michael and Scottie. We were a team."

The Bulls won. That was the good part for Chicago. But
Jordan wasn't the hero. That was the bad part for Chicago.

Chicago is not the most sophisticated basketball city. Oh,
sure, it is in the west-side and south-side projects, out in some

of the neighborhoods, but not with most of the fans who attend games now. When Michael Jordan became Air Jordan, Bulls games became a civic event. Famous, important rich people came, not necessarily because they cared so much about basketball but because it was a place to be seen, an event, a happening. And Jordan was the star.

Chicago wanted Jordan to score 50. And have the Bulls win. And given a choice between the two, the 50 points would probably win out, especially with those who flocked to the new arena, paying an average cost of about $40 per ticket or hundreds of thousands of dollars for skyboxes. And during the playoffs, those were going for an average of ten times higher. But no amount of money was too much to see Jordan. This time, no one was going to miss the show.

So when the Bulls won Game 4 by running the offense and getting more players involved, there was some disappointment, not with the win but with the method.

"This is all very nice for basketball fans, this Team Michael stuff, this spreading the ball around and playing within Himself, this shooting in single coverage after a return pass, screening and honoring the Triangle," wrote highly regarded *Tribune* columnist Bernie Lincicome. "Anyone with a Red Holzman playbook is no doubt applauding. But record TV ratings, street gossip, and elevator chatter between strangers does not depend on Michael Jordan being, oh, Doc Rivers."

CAN YOU READ BETWEEN THE LIES?

Be like Mike? Maybe it was no longer every player's goal on the basketball court, but Jordan still was the main man in the NBA to be admired and copied.

And it seemed to the Magic players that if Jordan didn't have to address the bothersome, repetitious, and often inane media questions, they wouldn't either.

So after the Game 4 loss to the Bulls, most of the Magic's main stars—O'Neal, Grant, and Anderson—followed the Bulls' example and left without speaking. Anfernee Hardaway, proving himself a little classier that most of the players on either side, remained, along with a few Bulls like Kerr, Wennington, and Perdue, the only players still taking questions. O'Neal did wish everyone a happy Mother's Day.

Magic executives said the concept of a media boycott was something Grant had brought from Chicago, telling players how the Bulls would stay in the trainers' room and then duck out without talking, while management would always back them because Krause hated the media so much. But the Magic would have none of that.

Quietly holding out the possibility of fines of $20,000 to $25,000 per game, NBA executive Brian McIntyre chased down Krause after the game and said the commissioner was not very happy, that the NBA liked to promote its players and wanted its players to be cooperative, and that if the Bulls continued this childish nonsense, there could be another $25,000 per game coming their way in fines.

"I'd be surprised if you don't see an increased spirit of cooperation by the next game," said McIntyre as he left the arena.

The Bulls again hid from questions Monday after Game 4. Jackson, not usually overly cooperative with the national media, was almost presidential in comparison to his players, who were scattering all around him. "Nobody has an obligation to talk to the press," said Jackson. "The president, now there's a guy that has an obligation."

The Magic, though, looked at it somewhat differently. One of the most community-friendly organizations in the NBA, Orlando pushes its players out routinely for all sorts of activities and events. Management was horrified. And they let it be known that while the pockets of benevolent owner Rich DeVos of the Amway fortune can be deep, all of that would stop if the players acted like babies.

"We're not that kind of organization," said John Gabriel, the Magic's personnel director, who masterminded the building of the potential dynasty. "And we won't become one. We feel we have an obligation to be courteous to the media and to promote our product. Part of the maturing process and growth in basketball includes taking care of the media.

"It's the trend of the nineties," Gabriel told *Los Angeles Times* columnist Mark Heisler about the I'm-bigger-than-the-league act. "And [Jordan's silence] doesn't help you when you're trying to convince younger players that talking to the media is the right thing to do."

A chastened Grant apologized for his actions and then got in another laugh at the Bulls' expense.

"I didn't talk because I was pretty upset we lost," Grant said. "When I'm upset I'd rather cool off before saying something I might regret. But that's not us. We don't want to be like Mike."

MICHAEL SPEAKS

Game day before the fifth game in Orlando began with Jordan, under league pressure, reluctantly deciding to speak to the media.

"Only because I had to," Jordan emphasized. "I have been breaking a rule. I'm not here to break rules."

Then about that uniform number change? someone wondered.

"There's no rule saying I couldn't change my jersey," Jordan continued to insist. "I think everyone is misinterpreting that. I think the league understands that."

Actually, NBA commissioner David Stern had shown up that day to make sure all the parties were being good boys and putting on the good face that the NBA likes. But Stern, ever the smooth politician, was not about to walk into any more Jordan controversies.

"There are enough distractions with shoes and uniforms and conspiracy theories," Stern said.

But Jordan was having none of this bad-guy stuff. There clearly was an edge to his voice, and he felt he'd again been railroaded by the media and the league.

Even his former Bulls coach, Doug Collins, a TNT broadcaster before taking over the Pistons for the 1995–96 season, told *USA Today* that Jordan's antimedia behavior and disappointingly inconsistent play throughout the playoffs could well lead Jordan to retiring again if the Bulls lost to the Magic.

Jordan tried to quell that theory. "That's his opinion," Jordan said. "I have admired Doug for a long time. I came back for this season and next season and from that point on we have to evaluate. Everybody is going to have his own opinions about what I'm doing."

And NBC, which televised the NBA games and was reaping big ratings from Jordan's return, didn't like the media's opinions about Jordan. NBC Sports president Dick Ebersol charged, "The media is nitpicking Jordan to death. It's killing me to see them raise up our sports heroes and movie stars, then tear them down. This guy wants to psych himself up by changing to his old jersey number, and it's treated like a crime against humanity."

But Jordan didn't need NBC to defend him.

He was working on it, as he also began to formulate his "screw everyone" plan for the game. He was going out to take charge and let the chips fall where they may, according to friends.

"I didn't take a number I'm not used to," said Jordan. "So what's the big hype? It's basically they didn't let O'Neal change, which he has the right to if he wants to challenge the rule, which, as you know, there is no rule.

"I kind of forgot about the rule you have to notify the league," said Jordan. "But everyone's making it seem like I'm setting a precedent. Others have done it. I didn't make the league aware, so the $25,000 fine was appropriate."

Apparently that wasn't enough for the NBA, which added on another $100,000 after the season for other games Jordan played wearing number 23.

"Number 23 is me," explained Jordan, "so why try to be something else? I know my father never saw me in 45. Number 23 is something I feel comfortable with and that's why I went to it. If it's a mental confidence, it's a mental confidence. It has been and I'm going to stick with it. I'm sure marketing has something to do with it. But whatever I have to say I'm basically going to say on the basketball court."

But that was the problem; it wasn't so easy to say it on the basketball court anymore. And no one was more stunned than Jordan.

"Coming back, I've tended to make more mistakes than what I've been accustomed to," added Jordan of his Err Jordan phase against Orlando, when he'd become uncharacteristically unsure of himself. "That's because I want it too much and sometimes I try to do a little too much. That's the mental anguish I've had. I get frustrated. It's not I can't do it. It's a matter of doing it when everyone's looking for little mistakes. When you make one, it's magnified, so knowing that rushes you and makes you do things you're not accustomed to doing."

It was a rare airing for Jordan, in that he acknowledged less failure than uncertainty. Jordan had failed before. As with most legends, the mystique of Jordan hitting every game-winning shot was mostly the stuff of myth (and NBA Entertainment film clips). Jordan, in some way, was like golfer Greg Norman, known for blowing so many tournaments. Supporters pointed out Norman only had those chances to lose because he was good enough to put himself in position to win. Likewise, Jordan had always had the last shot, and, often, he'd be so worn out from bringing the team close enough to win that he missed those winning shots much more often than he converted them.

But Jordan never believed he couldn't, nor made excuses for why he didn't.

Now, curiously, his ability to concentrate and block out distractions and rise up in the face of challenges was coming back more slowly than his jump shot. And that's not how the script was supposed to read.

He'd dominated when he came back for that Scottie Pippen charity game, and he was beating up Pippen in practice. It didn't make sense to Jordan. He thought he was trying just as hard as ever, felt he was in good shape and rested after just playing baseball for a year, which Jordan regarded as only slightly more physically taxing than golf.

Back in 1986, when Jordan put up that playoff record 63 points against the Celtics, Boston players, while respectful publicly, were angry that Jordan, who had missed much of the season with a broken foot and was now returning on fresh legs after everyone else had dragged through an entire season, would go off on a one-on-one orgy. Jordan felt he was now in position to do the same thing, that the season would be catching up with everyone but him. But it was the exact opposite. He was wearing out at the end of games, unable to concentrate and focus, and guys like Nick Anderson and Anfernee Hardaway, even Grant, were making big plays, hitting big shots, and Jordan was making the dumb mistakes, committing the turnovers, taking the bad shots, unable to finish.

Jordan was devastated.

Before the start of Game 5, Scottie Pippen sat in the cramped visitors' locker room studying the tapes of the previous games. He'd watch formations and shots, watch the triangle form, then break apart, the Magic running out for quick baskets, Bulls players too often frozen in their spots.

"I know sometimes I need to be more like M.J.," Pippen was saying, acknowledging that sometimes he doesn't take over offensively enough, "but M.J. also needs to be more like me. He needs to be the player he is with more my mentality."

It was clear, going into the fifth game of the series, their ninth playoff game and twenty-sixth game with Jordan, that neither side—Jordan or Everyone Else—had made the adjustments to one another yet. Jordan felt increasing pressure to prove that he was the player he was before, and Bulls players increasingly strained to complement him.

They had been thrilled at his return, excited about playing in his reflected glory, seeing the fans energized again, opponents wary. But now they were getting close to the end, and they weren't any further than they had been last season without Jordan. Then, they had proved themselves as players. Now, they were being reviled for not helping Jordan do enough. After all, Jordan was averaging almost 30 per game. So it must be their fault. The old "Jordanaires" label was starting to get stitched back on, a group of players Jordan helped win and prevented from losing. But the uneasy truce was starting to come apart.

In the second half of Game 5, as the Magic rolled past the Bulls in a welter of 3-point field goals by Dennis Scott and Hardaway, and Horace Grant hitting jumpers and put-backs, Jeff Turner walked over to Grant during a time-out and wondered, "Is there something wrong between Scottie and Michael?"

"What do you mean?" asked Grant.

"Scottie doesn't seem to want to pass him the ball," Turner noticed.

Grant smiled. He'd seen that situation before: Pippen slipping away out of the offense as Jordan fired shot after shot, eight in the third quarter as Pippen would get five shots the entire second half, a 12-point Bulls second-quarter lead being erased as the Magic blitzed the Bulls 35–20 in the third quarter to effectively wrap up the game, a 103–95 Magic win, sending the teams back to Chicago for Game 6, the Magic ahead three games to two.

That Grant scored 10 points in that pivotal third quarter and had 6 rebounds was perhaps no coincidence. He was, throughout the series, "a man on a mission," as Pippen put it, a mission that became even more intense every minute.

It seemed there were shots coming from everywhere, and not necessarily on the basketball court. Grant had gotten divorced before coming to Orlando, but his ex-wife in the Chicago area retained custody of their son, Horace Jr. Grant was growing sentimental about his six-year-old son as the playoffs opened, so he asked his wife to send the boy down for a few days so he could see what his father did, take in the excitement of the playoffs. Finally, after various foul-ups in the arrangements, Grant suspicious of the reasons, Horace Jr. made it down after the series opened.

He arrived dressed from head to toe in Michael Jordan apparel, complete with number 23 clothes, hat, and jacket. Grant, angry at what he felt was an attempt by his former wife to embarrass him by using his son, had told Pippen about it.

Pippen already knew. Grant's ex-wife had told Juanita Jordan what she had done, and Michael had passed on the story and everyone had a big laugh about it.

Everyone except Grant. "I didn't think it was funny," Grant said.

There were a lot of unsmiling Bulls heading back to Chicago for Game 6, especially Bill Wennington, the jump-shooting center with the bulldog look and Labrador disposition.

Not only were the Bulls heading home on the brink of playoff elimination, but Wennington had been given the chance of a lifetime, and it eluded him.

Five times in the last seven minutes of Game 5, he had point-blank, open jumpers. And missed them all. Thirteen-footer with the Bulls behind by nine with 6:40 left. Miss. Eighteen-footer with the Bulls down by eight with 4:29 left. Miss. Sixteen-footer with the Bulls trailing by eight with two minutes left. Miss. Seven-footer with the Bulls down by 10 with 1:20 left. Miss. Thirteen-footer. . .

"I remember walking off the court," recalled Wennington of his uncharacteristic two of eleven shooting, uncharacteristic not because of the poor percentage but because of the number of shots. "And I'm thinking, 'You suck!'

"It was pretty quiet on the bus," recalled Wennington, who averaged just 5.1 shot attempts per game in the playoffs. "I had the stat sheet rolled up, and all I could see was my line: fourteen minutes, two for eleven, 4 points. I stared at that for like forty-five minutes. When we got on the plane, guys started coming over saying, 'It happens.' 'Don't worry about it.' Trying to cheer me up. Phil slapped me on the knee and shrugged. Steve and Jud patted me on the back, M.J. gave me a little nudge. I guess B.J. was the one who made me laugh. He came over and said, 'Bill, I'm proud of you because of the quantity of shots you got up. You kept shooting.' It's something he and I talked about all year. I kind of cracked a smile, and it brought me out of it a little bit.

"Overall," said Wennington, "I have an attitude that you

don't worry about things you can't change. You worry about what you can do something about. I was upset I didn't shoot well because it's something I had control over. But I've been around long enough to know that sometimes it happens. You just hope it doesn't happen to you. But I've been through it before. And worse things can happen."

Say, like, being told by your parents they don't like you anymore and don't want you to live with them. That's what happened to Bill Wennington when he was a carefree sixteen-year-old high school student in Montreal, Canada, where he grew up. He went on a trip and was told not to come home.

"My parents had gotten divorced when I was eleven," Wennington recalled. "My mother left and I was living with my dad. That summer I was visiting my mom in Long Island. She had remarried and they took me out and told me. They said my father and stepmother didn't want me back home. My immediate reaction was, 'I want to go home.' But within about five seconds things were running through my mind, and it was like, 'Why do I want to go home? Everything I did was wrong.' They didn't want me back. So I said I didn't want to go home and I stayed."

That decision probably enabled Wennington to become an NBA player. Wennington had been the typical big kid who played basketball because he was big, too big and awkward for hockey. But Montreal wasn't exactly a haven for future NBA stars, so Wennington just stood around in the middle, blocked some shots, and bought everyone beer afterward because he looked much older and was able to buy alcohol even though he was underage.

"It made me popular," he admits.

It wasn't until he enrolled at Long Island Lutheran High School and started playing basketball that he began dreaming of what he could be, and yet realizing how far he had to go, a six-ten 240-pounder who was being outrun and beaten up by players a foot shorter. His coach, Bob McKillop, who Wennington says was the strongest male influence in his life and the most important male figure he ever had around him, took the big, lazy Wennington under his care, trying to break him to see if there was anything worth working with. Wennington ran sprints until he vomited, until he was ready to quit. But he wouldn't.

"He broke me, then he broke me down, then he taught me all over again," says Wennington. "He made me want it."

It was a stunning change for Wennington, who never had much discipline. He was one of four children, all adopted, some troubled.

"My brother, Nicholas, he had troubles," Wennington recalls. "He was always very hyper. We didn't know about him when we got him, which was when he was about two and a half. I remember him literally curled up for six months after we got him. Finally, he opened up a little bit. It was a year before his hands opened up. He was literally black and blue when we got him. We found out later he'd already been in two homes. It was difficult. He was a deviant from society. He didn't go to school, he was stealing, fighting all the time. He was in boarding home, detention homes, he went to jail. It made life difficult for my dad. It was a trying time for him."

Wennington's sister, Beth, was a diabetic who suffered kidney problems. As a result, she sought the answers Bill never did. She wanted to know who her biological parents were, perhaps to find out why she suffered the problems she did.

Bill never had such desires, knowing only that his parents were eighteen when they gave him up, his father in the military and neither ready for parenthood. He had been given the name Robert when he was born to them, but it was changed to Bill by his adoptive father, whose name was also Bill.

"I never felt I needed to know who my parents were," said Wennington. "There are a lot of theories for adopted kids, but I didn't feel I was brought up lacking anything. I didn't feel I needed to find someone else to love me. A lot of people say they're not whole unless they find their real parents. My sister was the only one who really seemed to have the need, but she didn't have any luck.

"There was that big Baby Richard case in Illinois [where the biological father won the right to get his child back after the child had been with his adoptive parents for about four years]," noted Wennington. "I thought it was wrong. The child doesn't know who the biological parents are. The child just knows the face and hand and body of who loves it. If someone came up to me now and said they were my real father, it wouldn't mean anything to me. He'd just be a guy. After three, four years you get a feeling of family and I think you're just hurting the child. If someone tried to take my boy [born in 1991] from me, they might as well write me off."

Bill Sr. would eventually write off his son.

"My dad didn't want to grow old by himself, so he picked her over me," Wennington says now of his father and step-mother, somewhat matter-of-factly. "I can understand."

Not that he liked the feeling of rejection and failure at the time.

"I was feeling a lot of self-pity," Wennington admitted.

Under McKillop, Wennington developed into a seven-footer with a reliable shot, went to St. John's, where he was a third or fourth option on a team that had future NBA players Chris Mullin, Mark Jackson, and Walter Berry, and found himself a first-round pick of the Dallas Mavericks in 1985.

He drifted off in trade to Sacramento in 1990 when the Mavericks changed coaches, then went to play in Europe for two years after his best NBA offer was about $300,000 from the Knicks. He earned about $800,000 in Europe, where he was befriended by future Bulls teammate Pete Myers. Wennington recovered his skills and confidence playing in Italy after years of sitting on the bench in Dallas, and then took a shot at making the Bulls in 1994 as a minimum-salaried free agent.

"I had two offers, one from Portland, but they just signed Chris Dudley, so I knew I wasn't going to make their team, and Chicago, which was starting Bill Cartwright slowly," recalled Wennington. "So I thought I'd get two months in. And it worked out."

Wennington played well off the bench and got a four-year guaranteed offer from the Bucks. But with players departing the Bulls in droves, the Bulls offered Wennington $1 million per year for three years. He re-upped in Chicago.

And never had any regrets.

"Life is what you make of it," says Wennington, who counseled himself a little after that Game 5 loss. "With all the hardships I went through as a kid, being rejected and forced to move to New York, now I look back and I've got a beautiful wife, a fantastic son, and I know a lot of people who don't have that. You look around and see so many people not in good health, and here you are playing a game for money. I love playing the game. I'm not saying I would play for free. That would be stupid. But I'm able to play and make good money and I love what I do. There's a lot of happiness, I've met a lot of great people, so to dwell on the negative things, no matter what they are, is a waste."

Toward the end of *The Shawshank Redemption* there is a scene where the prisoner, played by Tim Robbins, crawls through a drainage pipe filled with sludge and excrement to reach freedom, a path called a "river of shit" in the film.

Will Perdue had seen the movie and waited for that scene to be mixed in among the game films Jackson was splicing during the playoffs.

"I think he was trying to ask us how much were we willing to go through, would we crawl through that five hundred yards of shit to get to our goal," said Perdue, "a championship.

"We never did get to see that last scene."

Game 6 of the Eastern Conference Semifinals showed, in some sense, what Jordan was and what he had become.

To open the game, in addition to having Pippen remain closer to Grant, the Bulls put Jordan on point guard Anfernee Hardaway. It was a common tactic the Bulls had employed over their championship years: Put the best player on the other team's ball handler to disrupt the opponent's offense. And it has worked, even on All-Star players like Mark Price, Kevin Johnson, Mookie Blaylock, even Magic Johnson.

But sensing the challenge, Hardaway attacked Jordan right away, posting him up for a basket and hitting a pair of 3-pointers as the Magic ran out to a 25–16 lead. By the end of the first quarter, the Bulls had reclaimed the lead, and by the middle of the

fourth quarter, Jordan had chased Hardaway from the game, the
Magic pulling Hardaway for Brian Shaw as Hardaway committed a series of what appeared to be game-costing gaffes.

Grant had effectively been neutralized, although the strategy would be costly. With Pippen staying closer, Hardaway
and Anderson were able to hit four 3-pointers each, including a
crucial one by Anderson with two minutes left, giving Orlando
hope when all appeared lost for them.

Earlier, in the third quarter, Grant appeared lost for the
game. He dislocated a finger and went to the locker room,
where he accused the Bulls of sabotaging him.

It's common in the NBA for the home-team doctor to treat
injuries to players on both sides, and the Bulls' doctor, John
Hefferon, a respected surgeon, went to attend to Grant. The
Magic were clinging to a 4-point lead, and Jordan, bothered by a
slight flu, was taking himself out for a rest. To Grant and the
Magic trainer, Hefferon's examination seemed painfully slow.

"You're trying to keep me in here," Grant accused. "Tape
me up."

Hefferon, of course, would not risk his impeccable reputation, but the tension was palpable.

With just over three minutes left, the Bulls were leading by
8 after an Armstrong 3-point field goal. The Bulls had the ball,
and a seventh game seemed certain. But the Bulls, remarkably,
would not score again.

With 1:20 remaining and the Bulls ahead by 1, Jordan shot
an air ball. Anderson then hit an eighteen-footer to put the
Magic ahead. And then came perhaps the most ironic play of
the series.

Jordan tried to take on the Magic defense, but by now they
were sending three players at him.

Jordan got up in the air but couldn't get his shot off. He
passed to Luc Longley, the same Longley whom Jordan had
chastised Pippen for passing to during fast-break drills, the
Longley whom Jordan was harshest toward on the team. The
same Longley who had frustrated his teammates to no end
with his penchant for layups instead of slam dunks.

Longley wheeled toward the basket, might have been fouled, although a player like Longley would have to be brutalized at that point to get a call, and missed a short push shot. And how much could the referees do for the Bulls? Chicago had an 8-point lead with three minutes left, and both Jordan and Pippen were in double figures in free throw attempts for the game, the only players at the free throw line so often.

"I hesitate to blame the officials," said the gentlemanly Longley. "We never should have been in that situation."

Neither should have Longley, who had taken his last shot midway through the third quarter.

On the Bulls' next possession, Jordan would throw the ball away. And that was it.

And the Magic, the team of the future, would pull away for the 108–102 victory.

Jordan, once again, looked nothing like the player he had been in the past.

It should have been the Bulls' game, although the loss would put an end to the NBA conspiracy theories for now. There would be no seventh-game ratings bonanza featuring Jordan and O'Neal. These conspiratorialists could no longer speculate about NBC's Ebersol yelling into the phone at David Stern, "But you promised. . . . "

The Bulls' loss put an end to all that nonsense.

As the final seconds ticked off and all hope for the Bulls had clearly expired, former Bull Horace Grant was hoisted atop the shoulders of his teammates.

O'Neal called Grant the MVP of the series, as did Jordan, admitting the Bulls were perhaps "a Horace Grant away from winning" another title. Magic reserve guard Brian Shaw said, "Maybe the difference in this series is Horace playing for us as opposed to them. The things they're lacking he's given us."

Like rebounding, tough play. And Grant wasn't past pointing that out yet.

"The Bulls don't have a power forward to keep me off the boards," said Grant. "Scottie Pippen's playing out of position and it hurts them."

Richie Adubato, the former Mavericks coach and Orlando assistant, had gushed about Grant.

"Horace is the best defensive player I've been around," Adubato said. "He recognizes things he shouldn't recognize. Pick and roll other side, guy gets beat, he sees that and comes up right away. I don't know who taught him how to play. But he's one of the most fundamentally sound players I've ever seen."

When an Orlando writer asked Grant who taught him to play, Grant quickly responded: "Johnny Bach."

The Bulls' plan had been to let Grant shoot, figuring they had to double-team O'Neal or Hardaway. And Anderson and Dennis Scott, who had moved into the starting lineup for Game 3, were both good 3-point shooters.

Jackson didn't care for the Magic's game anyway, dumping the ball into the center, waiting for the double team, and then tossing it out for a shot. Even his former teammate on the ball-movement team-oriented Knicks, U.S. senator Bill Bradley, had called him during the playoffs and said, "Phil, what have they done to our game?"

Jackson felt Grant always got nervous in pressure situations and would point to incidents when Grant ran away from the ball, like in that sixth game against the Suns in the 1993 Finals when he passed so quickly back to John Paxson for the game-winning shot. Jackson had also liked to show overhead shots of the Bulls coming out of huddles with Grant often in the wrong spot. Jackson had felt he could challenge Grant. He would dare Grant to shoot every time he had the ball.

Grant again would have the last laugh.

"I'm happy no one is guarding me," Grant had said during the series. "I'm having a ball out there. That's Phil's philosophy, 'Let Horace beat you.' But I'm not going to say anything to get Phil mad or anyone mad so they can guard me. Phil is a stubborn guy, so we'll see what happens."

What happened was this: In Games 4 and 5, Grant added on 21 and 24 points, respectively, with remarkable nineteen for twenty-four shooting. Jackson was pressured by the media after

Game 5 about why he continued to leave Grant unguarded. It would result in the harshest criticism of Jackson in the Chicago media since he had become coach, although Jackson remained relatively unruffled.

Jackson would make a change on Grant just before the start of Game 6, although he had said after Game 5 that he didn't plan any changes. He came to Pippen at the shootaround and said he should stay closer to Grant all game, not let him get his shot off.

"He didn't want me to have a chance to beat them that last game," said Grant.

After the series, when a friend asked him how he was doing, Jackson smiled and said, "I am starting to get over being outcoached by Brian Hill."

But Jackson had no hard feelings. After the series was over, his wife would say she most regretted how well Grant had performed after leaving the team.

But Jackson smiled.

"I was happy for Horace," he conceded. "He showed that he'd grown into a solid player. He proved his value. And no matter what he says, he grew up in this organization and we can take pride, even if he's somewhere else, that we had a part in that. Like with a child. He may be gone, but you're proud of what he's done."

Krause wasn't quite as magnanimous. As he hurtled through the hallway to the Bulls locker room, Magic general manager Pat Williams, once the Bulls' general manager, reached out his hand to shake. Krause gave Williams a shoulder block, grunted, and hurried past.

Krause was still simmering when he reached the Bulls locker room.

It was his habit to make a postseason speech.

"I didn't have to make a speech like this for three years," Krause said, "and I don't want to make any speech like this next year."

Same one as last year, Kerr and Wennington agreed, Krause not being much with words.

Meanwhile, Scottie Pippen was telling reporters he felt he'd played his last game as a Bull.

"If I had to pick between one or the other, I'd probably say this is my last game," Pippen said. "I laid it on the line. I think everyone knows I tried my best. But this doesn't change my contract situation [three years remaining at less than $3 million per year]. My future is here for now."

But he had told Grant he now wanted to go to the Clippers, and since Grant had signed a contract with an escape clause, how about Grant jumping to the Clippers with him? Grant laughed and said he'd think about it.

But Grant knew Pippen perhaps better than Pippen even knew Pippen.

After the game, the two went out to dinner, Grant's grin like a fixture on his face.

"Let's go have a couple of beers," Grant said to Pippen as the two left the United Center. "Remember, Scottie, you don't have to practice anymore."

Jordan happened to stop at the same restaurant, but he wouldn't talk to Grant, even though Jordan's driver and body-guards stopped by Grant's table to congratulate the former Bull.

After the two former teammates parted, Grant said to a friend, "He really wants to stay with the Bulls. I know he's dying to. But because they don't want to give him a new deal, he wants to leave to show them."

By midsummer, Pippen had come to that realization him-self and decided he'd have to be the one to back off a little.

Chicago would have an unbearably hot summer, with stun-ning numbers of resulting casualties. So Pippen contacted his agent, Jimmy Sexton, and the two went into some of the hard-est hit communities in Chicago's inner city to distribute portable fans.

And with it came something of a realization for Pippen.

He was mobbed wherever he went, congratulated for his stance against management, for his play, for his commitment. "These people like me," Pippen thought. "They don't think about all the controversies. They don't hold it against me."

There would be several problems in Pippen's personal life following Jordan's return, though none connected to Jordan.

There was a paternity suit that was settled, a breakup of a four-year relationship with Yvette, and then an assault charge by Yvette that was later dismissed. Pippen was hurt by the events, but the slate was somewhat clean now.

Grant was gone, and so was Pippen's girlfriend. The U.S. Olympic team had selected Pippen for the 1996 Olympic games, while excluding so-called bad boys like Larry Johnson, Alonzo Mourning, and Derrick Coleman. And there was that hot summer day in late July with the adoring, supportive fans.

At that moment—and his friends hoped it would last—Pippen resolved to work out his problems with the Bulls and to spend the next season not only trying to win but to cleanse his image for America. And see what would happen with a season of Good Scottie.

For Phil Jackson, Game 6 had been a microcosm of the season. No trust of Kukoc on defense, no trust guys would be in the right spots for Jordan, no trust of his teammates by Jordan, no trust by Armstrong of the system.

"That game was like the season," Jackson said. "We were not able to finish. We had leads and could not maintain the energy, we could not make defensive stops at critical times. We couldn't make critical baskets. We weren't able to control the tempo. We don't get a call when Luc gets hammered. But that's part of what the season was about. We didn't have the intestinal fortitude to dig things out.

"I told [the players] I was remiss in not having more time-outs at the end to stem the momentum. I had called an extra time-out to get Michael through a period where he was fatigued and dehydrated," Jackson said. "He was under the weather and felt badly about not being able to slow down their momentum."

Jackson said he was pleased Jordan had come back. It was a worthwhile experience for the team, even if it didn't turn out as everyone had hoped, and Jackson, too, had learned some lessons.

"Looking back at everything, if I had it all to do over again—and I expect I will—I would have locked them all together in a room for a day and let them get this all hashed out," said Jackson of the pattern of isolation and alienation between Jordan and his teammates that Jackson said he felt powerless to overcome.

"Michael's sometimes abusive and confrontational ways, their looking up to him and backing away, [I wanted] to let them find the best way to come at this thing on their own," Jackson said. "He did always have that leadership quality to make others match his level of competitiveness. But the ball didn't move a lot of the time, guys commiserated about their problems. It wasn't the happiest group. We even asked him after that last game whether he could still function in this kind of setting, in the way we play. He said he could.

"We had the illusion we could win," Jackson said, "but we learned a lesson from it. You can't do things shorthanded. In the locker room after the game, I thanked Scottie for being the leader he was for us all season and told them all we'd see them individually next week before they left town."

Then it was left to Jordan.

Initially angry and disappointed, Jordan said he wasn't going to talk to the media. But when he cooled down, he said he wouldn't go into the interview room but the media could come stand around his cubicle.

It would be an event. Jordan laughed with the reporters whom he sneered at days before, was humble and humbled, proud and sure. This was the very best of Jordan on display, the Jordan in the TV commercials and with the sick kids, the Jordan with the charming smile, the soft, endearing eyes, the little boy asking for acceptance, the Michael that had come to the NBA before the money and the acclaim, before the sharks got hold of him and persuaded him it was he who made the league instead of the other way around, the kid who just loved the game.

Veteran reporters sat enraptured, as Jordan spun his head around to meet their eyes, smiling, frowning over his mistakes, contrite about his controversies, chastened by the defeat, but hopeful and positive.

"We were not the same team we were eighteen months ago," Jordan acknowledged. "But the fun part was trying to live up to those expectations. We'll have some growth from our young players. Dickey Simpkins is in a promising situation. But if it doesn't work, we'll have to use drastic measures in terms of bringing in a more mature player at that position.

"I'm very glad I came back," said Jordan. "I'm disappointed because I felt we had a good opportunity to steal a championship, if you want to call it that. But I'm happy to be back in the game. I still love the game and I still have challenges to play the game.

"The season was fun," Jordan said. "It's been an eye-opening experience, of revisiting some of those things that have been fun for me for years. In certain situations, I was able to be my old self. In other situations, I was able to learn. That's part of the game and that's part of me. I will never feel I've conquered the game to the point where I don't make mistakes. If that's ever the case, it will be boring for me. I can learn from this like everyone else and I'm looking forward to next year.

"I think everyone will say 'Michael Jordan has to go through the regular season to adjust and maintain his skills back where they need to be.' Maybe I do," said Jordan. "I'm not afraid to go back to the regular season and see where that leads me. I thought I could come in and jell with this team in a short period of time, and it didn't happen. I'm disappointed I wasn't able to blend in with this team like I was able to with other teams. That was part of the problem down the stretch [in games]. Normally, you have to go through disappointments in learning each other to be a success. Now I'm looking to see if I can do it in an eighty-two-game schedule. I'm not afraid to go back and go through the basics and see where that will get me down the stretch. I need training camp."

And perhaps a sip from the Fountain of Youth.

Jordan admitted that for the first time since perhaps his sophomore year of high school he was unsure about himself, his ability to perform under pressure, to succeed.

"I was sure mentally," Jordan said. "But I was unsure physically, if you could say that. I knew what I wanted to do. I'd been in those circumstances before, but my reaction time was not the same. I knew I could play better, so I will want to go through the course of a season to gear myself up mentally and physically for these types of games."

But can he, at thirty-three?

Jordan would be ready to answer that in the 1995–96 season, he insisted.

"I'm looking forward to starting over and getting to know everybody in a season," said Jordan. "What I did was try to get to know this team in seventeen games, and maybe that was part of this team's downfall, just trying to rush getting to know each other, and we had a lot of different problems down the stretch between the two entities.

"My biggest challenge now is to get this team back to where it once was," said Jordan. "Whatever adjustments they make over the summer, hopefully it's going to be in that frame of thinking. But we're not that far away. We haven't gone from the top to not making the playoffs."

Jordan went on to say the Bulls' priorities should be to pay Pippen, not trade him, and give Jackson a new contract, as well.

"If money is an issue, he [Pippen] can make more than me," Jordan said. "Winning is all that matters to me. Money comes and goes, but history books you don't forget. If I was worried about money, I wouldn't be back. I'm not making extra money by coming back. I'm not worried about getting my net worth. I wish I could go to the NBA and negotiate my contract because I think certain marquee players have an impact on the league and bring money in which drives the NBA, in a sense. How do we get those financial situations for the marquee players? That's where the collective bargaining agreement comes in.

That's something that's going to be discussed all summer long. Will I be involved? I probably will. But I don't think Jerry Reinsdorf is even in position to compensate me. That's one of the leverages you lose [with a long-term contract] and I'm willing to accept it because I came back to the game of basketball, which I love."

Jordan even praised Grant, saying that Grant was always more negative about their relationship than he was.

"I always considered Horace a hard worker," said Jordan. "I always respected him for that. He felt the need to go to Orlando for his well-being. I'm not against that. Athletes have a short time, so I wish him well. I always understood Horace.

"Now I have a whole summer to say 'what if.' What if I wasn't sick and could make jump shots down the stretch [in Game 6]? What if I had been here a whole season? What if I were here last year? Would Horace have left? A lot of things are what-ifs. Things happen for a reason. It wasn't meant to be. We still have a lot of growth for this team, and maybe some changes. We'll get back to where we were."

And Jordan insisted that no matter what, he would be back to see to it.

"Those little nicks and picks don't bother me as much," Jordan insisted. "A lot of people anticipate that will run me out of the game. That's not going to happen. I love the game and I'll do whatever I have to to play the game. Going against the grain, changing my jersey number, what I did was for the players. I was saying, 'Don't let marketing keep you from doing something.' Comments I made about the young players was because of my love for the game.

"We could have won a fourth [title] last year," added Jordan. "But I don't know if I would have been as energized as I am today. Now I have the same hunger and willingness to put forth the effort to get better and hopefully help this team get back where it was. It's a whole new beginning now. We have very few of the pieces from before, but we can build back to that. I didn't think about the lack of experience on this team."

As for baseball, Jordan said: "I wouldn't call what happened a lack of success in my game. I needed to rejuvenate my love for this game of basketball. And I did. Call it a fantasy camp, or whatever. It was a break and I needed a break. I met a lot of good people, and even though I was not as good as I wanted to be, I enjoyed it and it meant a lot to me. Mentally, it gave me a good outlook to come back and play the game of basketball. I don't have any regrets."

And with that, Jordan finally left, after almost an hour greeting wave after wave of reporters on deadline. The security guards fidgeted, but Jordan held them off until one said his mother wanted to leave.

So that was it.

It sounded like a farewell speech, except Jordan said it was an acceptance speech, of what had occurred, of what he was. Almost all of it was carried live by the cable-TV station that carries Bulls games, and a city sat spellbound.

And then Jordan said he'd see everyone next season and they should enjoy the summer.

As he set out for his car parked inside the United Center, he crossed through the back press room, walking briskly as his entourage of security and friends stepped behind him. A few reporters remained.

As Jordan was about to walk out of the room, he stopped and retraced his steps back to the podium, where the microphone was still live.

Jordan leaned over into the microphone and smiled.

"They ought to blow this place up," he said.

CAN WE TRADE MICHAEL JORDAN?

Donald Sterling was still looking for his star.

The Clippers' owner had tried desperately to obtain Scottie Pippen just before the NBA trading deadline in February 1995, but Pippen had balked and the deal fell through.

Now Sterling was interested in dealing with the Bulls again—but he had other ideas about how to get his star.

This time, Donald Sterling wanted to deal for Michael Jordan.

Sterling had seen the impact Jordan had had on the league and the nation and only imagined what it would be like to have a star of that magnitude on his club. He'd fantasize about it, asking friends upon Jordan's return whether they thought there was any chance the Bulls would make a deal.

"What about Pippen?" he'd be asked. "What about Jordan?" he would respond.

Jerry Reinsdorf smiled to himself.

He knew what that would mean.

He could trade Jordan to the Clippers, but then Jordan would certainly retire. The Bulls could have virtually all the Clippers' first-round picks for the rest of the decade, plus a player or two. Reinsdorf knew it could mean a harvest of talent for the Bulls at a time when the Bulls were, in effect, being held hostage by Jordan.

The Bulls now believed Jordan would play a few more seasons, but no one could be sure. His mood changes now were frequent, and he was demanding more benefits for his stardom: the bodyguards, the private planes and limousines, influence in personnel decisions, particularly regarding Pippen.

Jordan didn't care much for Pippen as a person, felt that Pippen was irresponsible and eccentric. Jordan had told *New York Post* writer Peter Vecsey the summer before, while he was still playing baseball for Birmingham, that Pippen had proven himself a liability under pressure again with that walkout with 1.8 seconds left.

"For the first half of the season he did great carrying the team, but the second half not so great," said Jordan. "Sitting at the end of Game 3 was the worst thing he could have done. I don't think he'll ever live it down. He should have known better. I covered their [Horace Grant and Pippen] asses when they got tight at the end of games, and I had to overcome fourth-quarter deficits all by myself. It bothered my father a lot. It bothered me, to hear them bitchin' about not getting enough credit, or not getting enough shots, or squawking about the supposed preferential treatment I was getting."

Jordan was also becoming something of a modern-day Samuel Gompers of the NBA. Jordan had never much cared about the rank and file in NBA labor, had never even spoken to the team's player representatives about labor issues, and watched as the Bulls went without a player representative in 1992–93 after Craig Hodges was let go. A few years back, when the union backed a so-called prepension plan to support players who had retired but could not yet access their pensions, Jordan, goaded by his agent, David Falk, tried to rally players against it. Jordan said the money should be left in the salary cap (the prepension plan would require a $1 million subtraction from the salary cap each season) so it could be distributed to today's players. Translation: The stars, who usually skim off most of the salary cap, with commissions to their agents, didn't want to give up that $1 million. It was much the same tack Jordan would take in the summer of 1995 as he sought to overturn a tentative agreement that would poten-

tially limit large contract payments to stars, among other pro-
visions. But the Bulls also wondered if Jordan would walk
away again in anger if he lost his union fight (which he did)
and his image took another hit. Pacers coach Larry Brown, a
Jordan admirer, even asked North Carolina coach Dean Smith
to tell Jordan that he would look greedy if he continued the
union decertification effort even after winning changes from
the proposed deal of June 1995.

More than anything, though, Jordan was stunned by the
mediocre players the Bulls had assembled in his absence. Once,
during the playoffs, Jordan had driven inside and gone for the
basket as his teammates stood open on the wings. Jackson
instructed him to fan the ball out.

"You don't see what I'm looking at," Jordan shot back.

So Jordan needed Pippen back for the 1995–96 season.
When Jordan met with Jackson and Krause after the season, he
said he planned to return for a full season but his decision
would be influenced by what the Bulls did with Pippen. Jordan
said he wouldn't be part of a rebuilding, which was what the
Bulls would be in without Pippen. And he knew he had the
ultimate leverage: If Pippen was traded, the Bulls could forget
about him, Jordan said.

"Trading Scottie Pippen would mean a commitment to
rebuilding," he told the Bulls. "If that's what you want to do
now to cut down the time that you'll be a mediocre team, fine,
do that. But I don't want to be part of that."

Jordan was clear. He said Pippen had three more years
remaining on his contract, so just as Jackson had considered
extending his contract as long as Jordan was around, Jordan
would consider playing with the Bulls as long as Pippen was
around, which, under Pippen's current deal, would be through
the 1997–98 season.

Jordan felt he and Pippen could coexist better now that
Pippen had gone through a season without him, a season in
which Pippen almost self-destructed under the glare of the
spotlight. Jordan could smile to himself because he said Pippen
now knew not only what it meant to be like Mike but also how

much Jordan did for him by absorbing the pressures of expectations and media scrutiny.

Jordan would be sure Pippen would want to stay with the Bulls now, even if Pippen was unsure of it himself. And Jordan couldn't stand not having a chance to win every year, which he didn't think was possible without Pippen by his side. Jordan could never just play for the love of the game, because for him, that love was inexorably linked with success.

If the Bulls traded Pippen, he warned in June 1995 just before the draft, "I'm gone."

Then Jordan left for the summer to play golf, try to break the NBA Players Association, and head for Hollywood to work on a live/animated movie that would come out in 1996.

The Bulls weren't sure what to make of Jordan, since they knew him to be so insincere about so many things. He had said he played the game for the love of it, yet he wouldn't play it without Scottie Pippen? He wasn't in the game for the money, yet he was fronting a large group of players in the labor negotiations because they felt the players were getting a bad financial deal?

Still, was taking the chance worth it? Could the Bulls afford to make it appear they drove Jordan back out of the game?

Reinsdorf knew the proper move was still to deal Pippen. Otherwise, the Bulls could be left going through a decade-long rebuilding once Jordan retired again and Pippen's value diminished to the point where they couldn't trade him. It was the type of mistake made by the Boston Celtics when they held on to Kevin McHale and Robert Parish, didn't win a title after 1986, and stumbled into what appears will be years of failure.

But Reinsdorf, although his motives often seem profit oriented, thirsts for success for his teams. Many close to him advised him to deal Pippen. But he asked himself: Do we have a better chance to win next season with Scottie Pippen or with what we get for Scottie Pippen? Of course, the answer for the short term was Pippen.

"I made the decision," he said. "As long as Michael is here we have to try to win and worry about what happens later."

It could be costly, too, for if he retained Pippen, there would be the pressure of writing out a large contract extension for Pippen, as well as what Jordan would inevitably demand. But Reinsdorf cared more about athletic success than his critics cared to admit.

"I'd rather break even and win," Reinsdorf often said, "than not win and make money."

Of course the worst prospect was *losing* money.

So was there a chance of making a deal with the Clippers, a deal that could amount to an ultimate instant rebuilding, the chance to win a title without Jordan, to be proclaimed a genius of sport?

"Nah," Reinsdorf said with a smile, "I'd have to send them the statue, too."

THE MICHAEL JORDAN TIME LINE

February 17, 1963   Born Brooklyn, NY. His family moves to North Carolina before the end of the year.

June 1981   Graduates Emsley A. Laney High School in Wilmington, NC, where he was raised. At Laney, Jordan didn't make the varsity basketball team as a sophomore, a motivating force in his life, he said.

March 1982   Hits "The Shot," the jumper that beat Georgetown in the NCAA finals.

June 1984   Selected number three in the NBA draft behind Hakeem Olajuwon, number one to Houston, and Sam Bowie, number two to Portland.

August 1984   Leads the U.S. team to the gold medal in the Olympics.

October 1984   Plays his first NBA game. Scores 16 points in Bulls win.

May 1985   Named NBA Rookie of the Year.

October 1985   Suffers a broken foot and misses sixty-four games, the only serious injury of his basketball career.

April 1986   Sets an NBA playoff scoring record with 63 points against the Boston Celtics.

April 1987   Wins his first of seven straight NBA scoring titles by averaging 37.1 points per game. Earlier in the month his 23 consecutive points against the Atlanta Hawks sets an NBA record.

February 1988   Named Most Valuable Player in NBA All-Star game as he scores 40 points and wins his second straight slam dunk contest.

May 1988	Named NBA Most Valuable Player for 1987–88 season and Defensive Player of the Year while leading the league in steals for the first of three times.
May 1989	Hits "The Shot II" to knock the heavily favored Cleveland Cavaliers out of the playoffs in the opening playoff round and the Bulls get to the Conference Finals for the first time in fourteen years.
March 1990	Scores career-high 69 points against the Cleveland Cavaliers.
May 1991	Named NBA Most Valuable Player.
June 1991	Member of NBA championship team as Bulls defeat Los Angeles Lakers in five games after sweeping the defending champion Detroit Pistons to get to the franchise's first NBA Finals. MVP of Finals.
October 1991	Skips trip to White House with team for a high-stakes gambling weekend that becomes public when one participant is later murdered and another is arrested in connection with a money-laundering case.
May 1992	Named NBA Most Valuable Player for third time as team wins franchise record of sixty-seven games, fourth best single-season record in league history.
June 1992	Member of NBA championship team as Bulls defeat Portland Trailblazers in six games. MVP of Finals. Sets Finals record for points in a half with 35.
October 1992	Testifies in federal court case of James "Slim" Bouler and admits money he lost was for gambling, not a loan as he'd long stated. Bouler is convicted in a money-laundering case.
January 1993	Scores 20,000th point second fastest in NBA history to Wilt Chamberlain.
May 1993	Trip to Atlantic City to gamble before a playoff game creates a national sensation along with publication of a book by a former golfing partner who claimed Jordan lost $1.3 million in gambling wagers to him.
June 1993	Member of NBA championship team as Bulls defeat Phoenix Suns in six games. MVP of Finals even though he refuses to talk to the media much of the

series. Breaks Finals record by averaging 41 points per game.

July 1993   His father, James Jordan, is murdered in North Carolina.

October 1993   Announces his retirement from NBA. His career scoring average of 32.3 ranks highest in NBA history. Jordan also holds the record for highest scoring average in All-Star games history, 22.1, and in playoff history, 34.7.

February 1994   Signs a free agent contract to play baseball for the Chicago White Sox and plays for the Birmingham Barons in Double A and hits .202.

October 1994   Plays for the Scottsdale Scorpions of the fall Instructional League in Arizona and bats .252.

November 1994   His number 23 jersey is retired in a nationally televised ceremony from the new United Center in Chicago.

March 1995   Retires from baseball and returns to the NBA and scores 19 points as the Bulls lose in overtime to the Indiana Pacers. Nine days later he scores 55 points against the Knicks.

April 1995   Scores 48 points, including 10 in overtime, to lead the Bulls to victory in the first game of the 1995 playoffs.

May 1995   Scores 24 points as the Bulls are eliminated in Game 6 of the Eastern Conference Semifinals by the Orlando Magic.

June 1995   Tells the Bulls he may consider not returning for the 1995–96 season if they trade Scottie Pippen and becomes the leader of dissident players trying to decertify the NBA Players Association as the bargaining unit for NBA players.

August 1995   Goes to Hollywood for the month to star and play himself in as yet untitled movie with animated figures like Bugs Bunny due out in 1996.

JORDAN'S COMEBACK STATS

March 19   Pacers at Indianapolis. Pacers 103–96. Jordan: 7 of 28, 19 points, 6 rebounds, 6 assists

March 22   Celtics at Boston. Chicago 124–107. Jordan: 9 of 17, 27 points, 3 rebounds, 3 assists

March 24   Magic at Chicago. Orlando 106–99. Jordan: 7 of 23, 21 points, 4 rebounds, 8 assists

March 25   Hawks at Atlanta. Chicago 99–98. Jordan: 14 of 26, 32 points, 4 rebounds, 2 assists

March 28   Knicks at New York. Chicago 100–82. Jordan: 21 of 37, 55 points, 4 rebounds, 2 assists

March 30   Celtics at Chicago. Chicago 100–82. Jordan: 8 of 17, 23 points, 11 rebounds, 6 assists

April 1   76ers at Chicago. Chicago 91–84. Jordan: 5 of 19, 12 points, 5 rebounds, 6 assists

April 5   Nets at New Jersey. Chicago 109–101. Jordan: 13 of 31, 37 points, 11 rebounds, 2 assists

April 7   Cavaliers at Chicago. Chicago 97–88. Jordan: 9 of 27, 28 points, 8 rebounds, 9 assists

April 9   Cavaliers at Cleveland. Cleveland 79–78. Jordan: 9 of 26, 21 points, 9 rebounds, 5 assists

April 11   Pacers at Chicago. Chicago 96–89. Jordan: 8 of 27, 25 points, 11 rebounds, 6 assists

April 12   Pistons at Detroit. Chicago 124–113. Jordan: 12 of 23, 29 points, 9 rebounds, 9 assists

April 16   Knicks at Chicago. Chicago 111–90. Jordan: 8 of 10, 28 points, 6 rebounds, 4 assists

April 1   Heat at Miami. Chicago 98–93. Jordan: 9 of 21, 31 points, 5 rebounds, 4 assists

April 20   Pistons at Chicago. Chicago 120–105. Jordan: 8 of 16, 17 points, 8 rebounds, 7 assists

April 22   Hornets at Chicago. Chicago 116–100. Jordan: 8 of 16, 19 points, 2 rebounds, 4 assists

April 23   Bucks at Milwaukee. Milwaukee 104–100. Jordan: 11 of 29, 33 points, 11 rebounds, 7 assists

•Jordan shot .411 and averaged 26.9 points, 6.9 rebounds, and 5.3 assists.

•Bulls were 13–4.

PLAYOFFS
BULLS VERSUS CHARLOTTE HORNETS

April 28   Bulls at Charlotte. Chicago 108–100 (OT). Jordan: 18
                  of 32, 48 points, 9 rebounds, 8 assists
April 30   Bulls at Charlotte. Hornets 106–89. Jordan: 13 of 25,
                  32 points, 7 rebounds, 7 assists
May 2   Hornets at Chicago. Chicago 103–80. Jordan: 9 of 19,
                  25 points, 6 rebounds, 3 assists
May 4   Hornets at Chicago. Chicago 85–84. Jordan: 8 of 21,
                  24 points, 4 rebounds, 5 assists

•Jordan shot .495 and averaged 32.3 points, 6.5 rebounds, 5.8 assists.

BULLS VERSUS ORLANDO MAGIC

May 7   Bulls at Orlando. Orlando 94–91. Jordan: 8 of 22, 19
                  points, 5 rebounds, 3 assists
May 10   Bulls at Orlando. Chicago 104–94. Jordan: 17 of 30,
                  38 points, 7 rebounds, 3 assists
May 12   Magic at Chicago. Orlando 110–101. Jordan: 15 of 31,
                  40 points, 7 rebounds, 4 assists
May 14   Magic at Chicago. Chicago 106–95. Jordan: 9 of 21,
                  26 points, 7 rebounds, 3 assists
May 16   Bulls at Orlando. Orlando 103–95. Jordan: 15 of 28,
                  39 points, 4 rebounds, 2 assists
May 18   Magic at Chicago. Orlando 108–102. Jordan: 8 of 19,
                  24 points, 9 rebounds, 7 assists

•Jordan shot .477 and averaged 31 points, 6.5 rebounds, and 3.7 assists.
•For entire playoffs: Jordan shot .483 and averaged 31.5 points, 6.5 rebounds, and 4.5 assists.
•Jordan also had 17 turnovers in four games against Charlotte for a 4.3 average and 24 in six games against Orlando for a 4.0 average. He committed 41 turnovers in ten games for a 4.1-turnovers-per-game average.

CHICAGO BULLS ROSTER AFTER JORDAN'S RETURN

No.	Player	Pos.	Hgt.	Wgt.	Birthdate	College	Yrs. Pro
7	Toni Kukoc	F-G	6-11	230	9-18-68	Croatia	2
8	Dickey Simpkins	F	6-10	248	4-06-72	Providence '94	R*
9	Ron Harper	G	6-6	198	1-20-64	Miami-Ohio '86	8
10	B. J. Armstrong	G	6-2	185	9-09-67	Iowa '89	6
13	Luc Longley	C	7-2	265	1-19-69	New Mexico '91	4
20	Pete Myers	G-F	6-6	180	9-15-63	Arkansas–Little Rock '86	7
25	Steve Kerr	G	6-3	180	9-27-65	Arizona '88	7
30	Jud Buechler	F-G	6-6	220	6-19-68	Arizona '90	5
32	Will Perdue	C	7-0	260	8-29-65	Vanderbilt '88	7
33	Scottie Pippen	F-G	6-7	225	9-25-65	Central Arkansas '87	8
34	Bill Wennington	C	7-0	260	4-26-63	St. John's '85	8
42	Larry Krystkowiak	F	6-9	240	9-23-64	Montana '86	8*
44	Corie Blount	F	6-10	242	1-04-69	Cincinnati '93	2
45	Michael Jordan	G	6-6	210	2-17-63	North Carolina '84	10

HEAD COACH: Phil Jackson   ASSISTANT COACHES: Jim Cleamons, Jimmy Rodgers, Tex Winter   TRAINER: Chip Schaefer

*Inactive for playoffs